Social Security Programs

Recent Titles in
Contributions in Political Science

SOCIAL SECURITY PROGRAMS

A Cross-Cultural Comparative Perspective

Edited by John Dixon
and Robert P. Scheurell

Prepared under the auspices of the Policy Studies Organization
Stuart S. Nagel, Publications Coordinator

Contributions in Political Science, Number 359

GREENWOOD PRESS
Westport, Connecticut • London

Library of Congress Cataloging-in-Publication Data

Social security programs : a cross-cultural comparative perspective /
    edited by John Dixon and Robert P. Scheurell.
        p.   cm.—(Contributions in political science, ISSN 0147–1066
; no. 359)
        "Prepared under the auspices of the Policy Studies Organization."
        Includes bibliographical references and index.
        ISBN 0–313–29654–5 (alk. paper)
        1. Social security—Case studies. I. Dixon, John E.
    II. Scheurell, Robert P. III. Policy Studies Organization.
    IV. Series.
    HD7091.S624 1995
    368.4—dc20   95–7438

British Library Cataloguing in Publication Data is available.

Library of Congress Catalog Card Number: 95–7438
ISBN: 0–313–29654–5
ISSN: 0147–1066

First published in 1995

Greenwood Press, 88 Post Road West, Westport, CT 06881
An imprint of Greenwood Publishing Group, Inc.

Printed in the United States of America

The paper used in this book complies with the
Permanent Paper Standard issued by the National
Information Standards Organization (Z39.48–1984).

10 9 8 7 6 5 4 3 2 1

Copyright Acknowledgment

The editors and publisher gratefully acknowledge permission to use the following:

Anne Corden, "Financial Support for Long-Term Institutional Care in Britain," © Crown Copyright 1990. Published by permission of the Controller of
Her Majesty's Stationery Office. No part of this publication may be repro-
duced in any form without the permission of the Department of Social
Security.

For
Tina, Piers, and Aliki
and
Sally, Lynn, and Laura

Contents

Acknowledgments

We would like to thank all of our contributors for their enthusiastic support throughout the protracted preparation of this volume.

We would also like to express our appreciation to several reviewers for their insightful comments on manuscripts included here.

Publication of this book would not be possible without the support received from the Policy Studies Organization (United States), Lingnan College (Hong Kong), the School of Social Welfare at the University of Wisconsin-Milwaukee (United States), and the Faculty of Management at the University of Canberra (Australia).

To Professor Stuart Nagel, the Publications Coordinator for the Policy Studies Organization, go our sincere thanks for his advocacy of and support for the volume.

Our wives, Tina and Sally, fully deserve our thanks for putting up with our idiosyncrasies throughout the preparation of this manuscript.

For any errors of fact and for all opinions and interpretations, the authors and the editors accept responsibility.

John Dixon and Robert P. Scheurell

I.

INTRODUCTION

Social Security and the Ghosts That Haunt It

John Dixon

Social security covers a wide variety of public measures that provide cash or in-kind benefits in the face of two broad contingencies. The first is when an individual's earning power

- ceases permanently (due to old age, invalidity, permanent and total incapacity, or death);
- is interrupted (by short-term injury or sickness, maternity, or loss of employment);
- never develops (due to a physical or intellectual handicap, an emotional disturbance, or an inability of gain first employment);
- is unable to avoid poverty (due to inadequate work remuneration or inadequately developed personal or vocational skills); or,
- is exercised only at unacceptable social cost (such as single parenthood, individual support of elderly parents, or support of disabled or handicapped children or siblings).

The second contingency is the raising of children. Five major social security models can be identified: social insurance, social assistance, social allowances, provident funds, and employer liability (Dixon 1994a). The overwhelming majority of countries have constructed their social security systems by adopting one or more of these, exclusively European, models (Dixon 1986; Guhan 1994; Gruat 1990; Iyer 1993).

It must be recognized that the concept of social security has many blurred boundaries. Fiscal welfare (that is, the use of tax allowances or credits or use of taxable income deduction, to reduce the tax liabilities of particular target groups to achieve social security objectives) and non-statutory occupational welfare (that is, benefits voluntarily paid by employers to their employees and their dependents) may impinge on what constitutes social security in specific countries. The provision of statutory benefits to public employees—civil servants and military personnel—is treated as a social security measure in some countries (Dixon & Scheurell 1994). Moreover, cash payments dispensed by non-statutory agencies constitute a form of social security in some countries. Adding further complexity is the lack of consensus on what in-kind benefits should be treated as part of social security. In continental Europe and Latin America, medical care is considered an inseparable component of social security, whereas in most English-speaking countries it is not. Under the auspices of social security, some countries provide food rations, clothing, orthopedic appliances, pharmaceuticals, recreational activities, sheltered workshops, occupational training, and social work services. It must also be recognized that in many countries, especially those in the Third World, informal social protection mechanisms exist at the village, tribal, or family level which interface with formal social security measures (Zacher 1988).

SOCIAL SECURITY: THE GHOST OF THE PAST

Social security can usefully be thought of as the product of centuries of effort to provide people with a means of support in the face of individual, social, or economic distress (Dixon 1986, 1989a). The social norms, especially those surrounding the causes and consequences of poverty, that infiltrate and mold a society's perceptions of social security are the result of an accumulation of preferences generated by a people as they shape their specific society. The institution of social security has, ipso facto, both a past and a future. The way a society views social security and its underlying dominant values is, of course, a crucial factor in the evolution of a social security system within that society. The dominant values, in essence, mold the broad contours of the building blocks that the social security technocrats sculpt and adorn to construct their systems.

The social security milieu in Europe, the birthplace of social security, for almost three hundred years (from the 1600s to 1880s) insisted upon the categorization of the poor into those who were deserving of relief and those who were not and demanded adherence to the work ethic and to the principles of individual responsibility. Equally important, it required that poverty relief be paid for from a compulsory tax rather than from charitable donations that fulfilled a religious obligation and promised a reward beyond the grave. Indeed, the sleep of the burgeoning middle class was, no doubt, made considerably easier by the comforting thought that poverty was both inevitable and morally culpable. The proposition that poverty was the self-inflicted lot of the poor made it clear that what the poor needed more than other people's money was "re-moralization" by proselytizing moralists; after all it would be sinful to subvert God's will by mitigating poverty. That the good intentions of the Poor Law taxpayers—the losers —were forever under threat by the moral turpitude of the poor —the gainers—with their perfidious expectations must have been solid grounds for minimizing any income redistribution. The containment and, indeed, the repression of pauperism was thus both morally right and highly desirable, to all but the poor.

This European Poor Law experience, by focusing on the morality of the poor, has substantiated and propagated the belief that poverty was the fault of the poor. This was achieved over time by the convenient use of anecdotal evidence. Thus "need" per se did not generate a "right" to social security, it merely justified "public charity." The corollary is, of course, that social security, ipso facto, always remained a form of "public charity." Under this set of values, social security programs designed to assist the poor were selectivist, with an emphasis on deterrence. Ideally, everybody ought to have been independent, healthy, and well-adjusted and thus ought to have been able to participate in an economic system through work or some other productive activity. It was acknowledged that some people failed to achieve a minimum acceptable standard of living, and thereby created a real or potential public menace by becoming a focus for political dissent, by creating a health hazard, or by representing a moral or aesthetic defect of the existing social order. Under the influences of these values, public relief became a mechanism that kept society's failures without work above an acceptable level of basic subsistence.

The European Poor Law tradition has cast an inordinately long inter-temporal shadow over social security. Public relief, at the time of its birth and throughout its childhood, was a strategy designed only to ameliorate absolute poverty, constrained by an adherence to an ethic that held as sacrosanct the proposition that hard work, self-denial, and self-discipline would provide serenity, if not happiness, in this life and ensure moral and even spiritual progress towards the next. This ethic remains a ghost that still haunts social security, to be exorcised only by the attachment of categorical tests, contribution or employment tests, income and/or asset tests and, where appropriate, work tests to social security programs, and by an administrative preoccupation with the search for real and imagined malingerers in every social security nook and cranny under the guise of not wasting public monies, which is not surprising when work is seen as the panacea for man's intransigent welfare maladies. All this is now rationalized by the need for government to achieve from any social security initiative adopted greater target efficiency, greater cost effectiveness, greater economy and, of course, minimal vertical income redistribution. The belief that a selectivist approach to social security has deterrence as its objective, because it excludes would-be recipients, and stigma as its outcome, irrespective of the administrative processes used, has now raised to the realms of mythology. Australia and New Zealand have carried this burden long after deterrence had been replaced by poverty amelioration (and to a lesser extent, vertical income redistribution) as the governing focus (Saunders 1991; Dixon 1977, 1983; Uttley 1989). Yet deterrence as a governing value still survives in the United States and Western Europe (Dixon & Scheurell 1987, 1989) and in many developing countries in Africa (Dixon 1987a; Midgley 1984), the Middle East (Dixon 1987b, 1987c), Latin America (Dixon & Scheurell 1990), and Asia (such as in India, Sri Lanka, and China) (Dixon 1981, 1992, Dixon & Kim 1985, Dixon & Chow 1992), where social assistance acts as a last-resort welfare safety net for those falling through (because of maximum benefit payment periods) or who entirely miss (because of the eligibility criteria) the dominant poverty prevention net.

SOCIAL SECURITY: THE GHOST OF THE FUTURE

From the end of the nineteenth century, social security shifted its focus from poverty amelioration to poverty prevention and social compensation. Essentially, the social security policy debate focused on how to keep people, increasingly those in the growing middle class, out of poverty rather than how to help people in (or about to enter) poverty. With this shift in emphasis came a shift in perspective and a shift in paradigms. The product was the emergence of employer liability measures, social insurance, national provident funds, and social allowances, all of which have as their focus either poverty prevention or social compensation.

Employer Liability Measures

The gradual introduction throughout Europe of statutory employer liability measures in the mid-nineteenth century was the product of the juxtaposition of increasing humanitarian concern with the employer-biased common law approach to employer liability and the growing cost of industrial injuries as a result of the European industrial revolution. This culminated in the emergence of workman's compensation toward the end of that century, embodying the legal principle of "occupational risk" or liability without fault (ILO 1936: 26–28). This moved social security into a legalistic domain, dominated by lawyers and the judiciary, who brought to social security a quite different conceptual framework. It also cast the employer into the role of one of the tripartite social security financiers. Employer contributions to social security became legitimate production cost rather than donations to charity. This, in turn, fostered the proposition that recipients of employer-financed social security benefits were not receiving charity, but rather employment-related benefits as a matter of right. Indeed, this re-conceptualization of social security has created a global social security elite: employment injury victims (Spielmeyer 1965: 41; Higuchi 1970: 111). By the end of the twentieth century employers throughout the world became a vehicle for financing other social security contingencies. This is merely a reflection of how many societies favorably viewed this redistribution process and outcome. The ghost created is, of course, the burgeoning social security cost burden being carried by employers, which, arguably, has to be exorcised by recasting the roles of the other tripartite social security financiers, and/or by the adoption of tactics (such as risk pooling through public or private insurance carriers, or government subsidies or tax advantages to employers) that could ultimately transform this social security strategy into either a social insurance strategy or even a social assistance strategy. This is a ghost that already haunts China (Dixon 1992).

Social Insurance

The private insurance model, with its commercial preoccupation with actuarial soundness, provided a means by which social security could be re-conceptualized as an economic activity obeying market forces, rather than as a non-market, charitable activity. In the language of social security, insurance concepts replaced Poor Law concepts: "needs" became "contingencies;" "deserving beneficiaries" became "the insured;" "poor levies" or "poor taxes" became "contributions." In short, social security moved from being largely a welfare concept to being largely an insurance concept. This re-conceptualization of social security has made poverty prevention the preeminent social security objective, has moved the focus of social security from the poor to the potentially poor, has legitimated horizontal rather than vertical income redistribution as a social security objective, and has removed stigma from the receipt of social security benefits. Encouraged by proselytizing technical experts from international agencies, long nurtured in the nuances of social insurance, and who perceive it as the ne plus ultra of social security, developing countries in the 1950s and 1960s began replicating the European social insurance model, without much thought being given to its appropriateness to local socioeconomic conditions, in the naive belief that, as in the developed countries, it was appropriate to the needs of an industrializing and modernizing country. An extreme illustration is the wide adoption of French social insurance legislation throughout Francophone Africa. The ghost created is, of course, the arguably unrealistic community expectations (in the light of demographic and economic considerations) about appropriate levels of income replacement, which can be exorcised by recasting those expectations, perhaps at considerable political cost, and by adopting target efficiency tactics (such as the payment of flat-rate benefits, with or without a means test, or the means testing of benefits based on past earnings, past employment period, or past contributions) or even privatization (Estrin 1992; Campbell 1992; Borzutzky 1990). This is a ghost that actively haunts Europe and North America.

National Provident Funds

The idea of compulsory savings as a means of preventing poverty has its roots in nineteenth century European industrial welfare paternalism, which began as a reaction of humanitarian employers to the shocking working conditions prevailing during the Industrial Revolution. Occupational provident funds were established by individual employers seeking to provide a means by which their provident employees could be protected against invalidity, old age, and death. This idea moved to the British colonies, where it soon came under the patronage of colonial authorities. Expatriate employers were commonly among the first to establish occupational provident funds for their employees, to help attract and retain expatriate employees. By the middle years of the twentieth century these occupational provident funds were peppered throughout the British empire (Pilch & Wood 1960: 18–19). They provided a useful social and institutional heritage upon which newly emerging countries could build their first social security systems (Dixon 1989a, 1989b, 1994). This has a curious corollary: since contributors are able to identify their social security deposits, they are inclined to claim proprietary rights over them. This brings into focus the libertarian principle that since individuals should be considered the best judges of their well-being, they should be able to use, perhaps within limits, "their" social security deposits to improve their immediate "quality of life." This principle has been accepted by all national provident funds. Provident funds are, unquestionably, the enfant terrible of social security (Dixon 1989c). Because they are effective mobilizers of domestic savings, they are faced with the dilemma of balancing the need to pay a reasonable real rate of interest on members' deposits and the need of their sponsoring governments for cheap developmental finance. To a significant degree, the poverty prevention objective being sought by national provident funds has become subservient to social and economic objectives. This is, of course, the ghost that haunts this form of social security, which can be exorcised only by the political recognition of the primacy of their social security goal of poverty prevention and the adoption of tactics to ensure its achievement (such as government-guaranteed benefit levels or contributions subsidized by government), which may well encourage the conversion of this strategy into a social insurance strategy or even a social assistance strategy.

Social Allowances

The emergence, with affluence, of state welfare paternalism is a twentieth century phenomenon driven by a desire by government either to maintain social control, harmony, and stability, which has a certain empathy with the residual welfare paradigm, or to promote social progress, by creating a milieu in which the individual is able to develop to the greatest extent, which is firmly within the Titmussian institutional-redistributive paradigm. The intellectual antecedents of this tradition can be found in romanticism, humanism, and functionalism. The way a society views state welfare paternalism influences its perception of social security. Clearly, it ipso facto justifies the quintessential quiddity of social security: the compulsory financing of social security benefits by society. Yet what a society views as acceptable forms and degrees of state paternalism has a profound impact on its perceptions of acceptable social security, especially values surrounding poverty, poverty alleviation, and both vertical and horizontal income redistribution. This tradition has incubated the only novel form of social security to emerge in the twentieth century: notably social allowances, which have as their focus social compensation rather than either poverty prevention or poverty alleviation. Their emergence in particular societies may have been the product of economic and political pragmatism (see, for example, Heckscher 1984; Wilson 1979; Kewley 1972; Mendelsohn 1954), but they are the embodiment of all that is important to those infatuated with the social progress mode of this tradition, the expression of the common responsibility of all people for all people and acknowledgement the dignity of the individual, in stark contrast to demeaning social assistance. For most of the second half of the twentieth century, social allowances have been, for most of the developed world, and some of the developing world, the desideratum of social security. They are, of course, the progeny of affluence. Social compensation is a luxury that most developing countries cannot afford. The ghost that has come to haunt this form of social security is the cost burden falling upon the taxpayer, both corporate and individual, which can only be exorcised by the adoption of tactics (such a means testing or the introduction of employer and/or employee contributions) that might eventually transform this social security strategy into either a social assistance strategy or social insurance. Scandinavian countries are grappling with this ghost.

The development of social security over the last century largely buried all but the very remnants of the Poor Law ghost, along with legitimacy of social security's poverty alleviation role, but it has given birth to new ghosts that have come to haunt social security, the exorcising of which requires the recasting of social security strategies and tactics so as to achieve greater target efficiency, greater cost-effectiveness, greater economy, and less vertical but perhaps more horizontal income redistribution. Ironically, this has begun to put poverty alleviation back onto the center stage of social security policy deliberations, under the guise of achieving greater target efficiency, thus greater cost-effectiveness and greater economy and less vertical redistribution of income.

SOCIAL SECURITY: THE GLOBAL PERSPECTIVE

Social security has long been dominated by the social insurance model (Dixon 1986). Most industrial market countries focused their attention in the early to mid years of the twentieth century on constructing a poverty prevention safety net that would protect and enhance the welfare of the middle class, as have, more recently, developing countries, where that net's limited coverage ensures that it focuses on keeping the frequently small, urban wage-earners in the formal sector out of poverty, which makes it irrelevant to the needs of those in poverty (Midgley 1994). Governments were generally not looking to social security to ameliorate poverty or to redistribute income vertically (Dixon 1994a). Gradually, however, it became clear even to the staunchest social insurance (poverty prevention) advocate that social insurance alone was not capable of addressing extant poverty. The result has been the development of a social security melange in most developed countries, and, indeed, in a few developing countries: social insurance (perhaps in conjunction with employer liability) for the employed, some social allowances for every family, and modest social assistance for the indigent. Social assistance, for so long the social security outcast, has thus acquired the role of providing a last-resort safety net, modestly protecting those who fall through, or who entirely miss, the dominant poverty prevention net. Yet in those countries where it has long had predominance, notably Australia and New Zealand (Dixon 1977, 1983; Uttley 1989), it is an effective vehicle for the focusing of assistance on groups in poverty.

SOCIAL SECURITY: INTERNATIONAL PERSPECTIVES

The purpose of this volume is to explore diverse perspectives on social security in an international setting.

Historical Perspectives

Skidmore, Ichien, and Ramesh place the national social security systems of the United States, Japan, and South Korea, respectively, in their historical context and draw out the lessons of history.

National Overviews

Hirtz and the von Benda-Beckmanns explore the interrelationships between formal social security and family and social networks in providing social protection to rural populations in the Philippines and Indonesia, respectively.

Chow, Ruzica, and Kaseke examine the social security policies and practices in China, Yugoslavia, and Zimbabwe, respectively.

Program Analyses

Corden and Tracy focus their attention on the elderly in Britain and Malaysia, respectively.

Westerhall examines the disabled in Sweden, while Leite provides a critical review of the special relationship the industrial accident protection programs have traditionally had in social security systems.

REFERENCES

Benda-Beckmann, F. von, Benda-Beckmann, K. von, Casino, E., Woodman, G. R. & Zacher, H. (eds.) 1988. *Between Kinship and the State: Law and Social Security in Developing Countries* (Dordrecht: Foris).

Borzutzky, S. 1990. "Chile" in Dixon, J. & Scheurell, R. (eds.) *Social Welfare in Latin America* (London: Routledge).

Campbell, G. R. 1992." Argentine Privatization and Other Reforms" *Social Security Bulletin* 55(3): 80.

Dixon, J. 1977. *Australia's Policy Towards the Aged: 1890– 1972* (Canberra Series in Administrative Studies, 3) (Canberra: Canberra College of Advanced Education).

Dixon, J. 1981. *The Chinese Welfare System: 1949–1979* (New York: Praeger).

Dixon, J. 1983. "Australia's Income Security Systems: Its Origins, its Features and its Dilemma" *International Social Security Review* 36 (1): 19–44.

Dixon, J. 1986. *Social Security Traditions and Their Global Applications* (Canberra: International Fellowship for Social and Economic Development).

Dixon, J. (ed.). 1987a. *Social Welfare in Africa* (London: Routledge).

Dixon, J. (ed.). 1987b. *Social Welfare in the Middle East* (London: Routledge).

Dixon, J. 1987c. "Social Security in the Middle East" in Dixon, J. (ed.) *Social Welfare in the Middle East* (London: Routledge).

Dixon, J. 1989a. "Social Security Traditions and Their Global Context" in Mohan, B. (ed.) *Dimensions of International & Comparative Social Welfare* (Canberra: International Fellowship for Social and Economic Development).

Dixon, J. 1989b. "A Comparative Perspective on Provident Funds: Their Present and Future Explored" *Journal of International and Comparative Social Welfare* 5(2):1–28.

Dixon, J. 1989c. *National Provident Funds: The Enfant Terrible of Social Security* (Canberra: International Fellowship for Social and Economic Development).

Dixon, J. 1992. "China" in Dixon, J. & Macarov, D. (eds.) *Social Welfare in Socialist Countries* (London: Routledge).

Dixon, J. 1994a. "Social Security in the Nineties—Challenges and Prospects: Reflections on the Connection between Social Security and Poverty" in *Asia Regional Conference on Social Security (September 14–16, 1993), Conference Proceeding* (Hong Kong: Hong Kong Council of Social Services).

Dixon, J. 1994b. "National Provident Funds: The Challenge of Harmonising Social Security, Social and Economic Objectives" *Policy Studies Review* 12 (1/2): 197–213.

Dixon, J. & Chow, N.W.S. 1992. "Social Security in the Asia-Pacific Region" *Journal of International and Comparative Social Welfare* 8(1&2): 1–29.

Dixon, J. & Kim, H. S. (eds.) 1985. *Social Welfare in Asia* (London: Croom Helm).

Dixon, J. & Macarov, D. (eds.) 1992. *Social Welfare in Socialist Countries* (London: Routledge).

Dixon, J. & Scheurell, R. P. 1987. "Social Security in Australia and the United States: A Comparison of Value Premises and Practices" *Journal of International and Comparative Social Welfare* 3 (1&2): 1–18.

Dixon, J. & Scheurell, R. P. (eds.) 1989. *Social Welfare in Developed Market Countries* (London: Routledge).

Dixon, J. & Scheurell, R. P. (eds.) 1990. *Social Welfare in Latin America* (London: Routledge).

Dixon, J. & Scheurell, R. P. (eds.) 1994. "Symposium: Social Welfare for Veterans of Military Service" *Journal of International and Comparative Social Welfare* 10 (1 & 2): 1–73.

Estrin, A. 1992. "Peru's Privatization Option for Pension and Health Systems" *Social Security Bulletin* 55(3): 79–80.

Gruat, J.-V. 1990. "Social Security Schemes in Africa: Current Trends and Problems" *International Labor Review* 129 (4): 405–21.

Guhan, S. 1994. "Social Security Options for Developing Countries" *International Labor Review* 133 (1): 35–53.

Heckscher, G. 1984. *The Welfare State and Beyond: Success and Problems in Scandinavia* (Minneapolis: University of Minnesota).

Higuchi, T. 1970. "The Special Treatment of Employment Injury in Social Security" *International Labor Review* 102(2): 109–26.

International Labor Organization (ILO). 1936. *Studies and Reports* (Series M, 16) (Geneva: ILO).

Iyer, S. M. 1993. "Pension Reform in Developing Countries" *International Labor Review* 132 (2): 187–207.

Kewley, T. H. 1972. *Social Security in Australia, 1900–1972* (Sydney: Sydney University Press).

Mendelsohn, R. 1954. *Social Security in the British Commonwealth: Great Britain, Canada, Australia and New Zealand* (London: Athlone Press).

Midgley, J. 1984. *Social Security, Inequality and the Third World* (New York: John Wiley and Sons).

Midgley, J. 1994. "Social Security and Third World Poverty" *Policy Studies Review* 12 (1/2): 133–143.

Pilch, M. & Wood, V. 1960. *Pension Schemes* (London: Hutchinson).

Saunders, P. 1991. "Selectivity and Targeting in Income Support: the Australian Experience" *Journal of Social Policy* 20 (July): 299–326.

Spielmeyer, G. 1965. "General Report" in *Ascertaining Entitlement to Compensation for Industrial Injury* (Bruxelles: International Institute of Administrative Sciences).

Uttley, S. 1989. "New Zealand" in Dixon, J. & Scheurell, R. P. (eds.) *Social Welfare in Developed Market Countries* (London: Routledge).

Wilson, D. 1979. *The Welfare State in Sweden* (London: Heinemann).

Zacher, H. F. 1988. "Traditional Solidarity and Modern Social Security: Harmony or Conflict?" in Benda-Beckmann, F. von et al. (eds.) *Between Kinship and the State: Law and Social Security in Developing Countries* (Dordrecht: Foris).

II.

HISTORICAL PERSPECTIVES

2

Social Security in the United States

Max J. Skidmore

The term "social security," in its broadest sense, encompasses all social welfare measures. In the United States, it can mean the specific programs authorized by the Social Security Act (such as unemployment insurance, Medicaid, Supplemental Security Income, and so forth), but for most Americans, the term means the contributory social insurance programs of old-age, survivors', and disability benefits, and possibly the health-care coverage generally known as "Medicare." This chapter uses the latter, popular, narrower definition.

BACKGROUND

The Social Security Act of 1935 was a latecomer to the roster of modern social security systems, and provisions for health coverage did not come until 1965. Its roots, however, reach back at least to the 1909 White House Conference on Care of Dependent Children. After the 1909 conference, new associations brought social workers, such as Jane Addams and Grace and Edith Abbott, together with such influential figures as Eleanor Roosevelt, Newton D. Baker, Louis Brandeis, and the economist John R. Commons. One of the most militant organizations was Florence Kelley's National Consumers' League. Another, the Women's Trade Union League, fought the exploitation of industrial workers. The American Association for Labor Legislation, headed by John B. Andrews (and jointly with his wife, Irene Osgood, following their marriage in 1910), grew from some 200 members in 1906 to more than 3,000 in 1919. It helped bring about rudimentary laws for workman's compensation in many states (Chambers 1963).

There are numerous reasons for the tardy acceptance of social security programs in the United States. Traditional American individualism combined with a history of resistance to governmental action to encourage the attitude that such programs at best were unnecessary, and at worst were alien and "un-American." As early as 1798, Thomas Paine in *Agrarian Justice* had outlined a scheme that was strikingly similar in principle to social security, but in America, the ideas continued to sound radical well into the twentieth century (Skidmore 1970).

The first actual step toward social insurance in the United States was a mothers' pension plan, established in Denver under the leadership of Gertrude Vaile. In 1914, Vaile wrote in Paul Kellogg's magazine of social reform, *The Survey*, of the great difficulties that faced social reformers. Many early laws only authorized localities to set up programs if they chose (Pumphrey & Pumphrey 1961: 319).

There was even brief support for governmental health insurance. In 1912, the American Association for Labor Legislation created a Committee on Social Insurance, and in 1913 sponsored a national conference on social security. The result was a draft of a model bill, including health insurance.

In 1915, the American Medical Association (AMA) also displayed interest, and formed its own Social Insurance Committee. Three of its members, Alexander Lambert, I. M. Rubinow, and S. S. Goldwater, all physicians, were members of the committee formed earlier by the American Association for Labor Legislation. By 1918, however, many insurance and pharmaceutical companies had begun to work against the idea, and opposition had developed within the AMA (Anderson 1951: 106–13). The concern resulted from apprehension regarding governmental involvement in medical practice and from fear that there could be control of fees. By 1920, the AMA's opposition had become so strenuous that governmental health insurance ceased for decades to be a serious political issue in the United States.

The theoretical justification for the Social Security Act emerged in 1913 in Rubinow's classic *Social Insurance*, which established him as America's pioneer authority on the subject. The prevailing mood, however, was apathetic, or even hostile. President Harding in 1921 did call a Conference on Unemployment, but it accomplished little. In 1925, University of Chicago economist and future United States Senator Paul H. Douglas aroused scant interest with his study, *Wages and the Family*. The few proposals for social insurance brought reactions of horror. A Massachusetts study, for example, branded old-age pensions "a counsel of despair" and said that "if such a scheme be defensible or excusable in this country, then the whole economic and social system is a failure" (Hicks 1960: 73).

Nevertheless, there was some support. The American Association for Labor Legislation and the Fraternal Order of Eagles jointly drafted a model pension bill for states. Douglas has written that even before the Depression there were "certain undercurrents of public opinion which were beginning to change on the subject of old age pensions." Eight states had adopted enabling acts permitting counties to establish them, and Wisconsin in 1925 and Minnesota in 1929 provided for state aid to any county that did so. California and Wyoming, in 1929, were the first states to adopt mandatory acts (although the Territory of Alaska had done so in 1915), and New York and Massachusetts followed in 1930. By the middle of 1934, 28 states plus Alaska and Hawaii had passed old-age pension acts, all but five of them mandatory (Douglas 1936: 5–7; Epstein 1936).

Every victory was hard won because of anti-governmental attitudes and general hostility to social legislation. The Chief of the Children's Bureau (then in the U.S. Department of Labor), Julia C. Lathrop, expressed astonishment at "the popular distaste for governmental activity." The head lobbyist for the Women's Trade Union League, Ethel Smith, echoed Lathrop's sentiments in a 1925 report (Chambers 1963: 33, 40).

The complacent public policy reflected public attitudes that disregarded clear danger signals. Rubinow (1926) keenly observed that, despite rising wages, there was also a rising case load occasioned by increasing unemployment. Others, especially settlement workers, also had become aware that something was wrong. In the winter of 1928, residents at the Chicago Commons began to report growing unemployment; similar reports began to come from other settlements (Chambers 1963), but there were no national statistics to sound the alarm.

In 1927, in the midst of these developments, Abraham Epstein, research director for the Pennsylvania Old Age Pension Commission, took the initiative by forming the American Association for Old Age Security. In 1928 he complained of a lack of zeal and understanding among welfare workers, and Harper's Magazine rejected one of his manuscripts, sensing in it a "Bolshevik air." By 1931, however, the conditions of the Great Depression had made his organization influential. In recognition of expanded needs, it became, in 1933, the American Association for Social Security.

Epstein had become one of America's most prominent advocates of social insurance, along with Douglas and Rubinow. In the early 1930s, each of these three pioneers produced a book that gave considerable impetus to the movement for social security: Douglas's *The Problem of Unemployment* (1931), Epstein's *Insecurity: A Challenge to America* (1933), and Rubinow's *Quest for Security* (1934).

THE SOCIAL SECURITY ACT

The presidency of Franklin D. Roosevelt brought to an end the official disdain for social insurance. Harry Hopkins, the Federal Emergency Relief Administrator, and Secretary of Labor Frances Perkins (the first woman to hold a Cabinet post), became influential supporters. Perkins had been with Jane Addams at Hull-House, had studied economics with Simon Patten, had been executive secretary of the Consumer's League in New York, and had long been within the "inner circle" of the social work profession (Schlesinger 1959). She had also travelled to the United Kingdom in 1931 at the request of Roosevelt, who was then Governor of New York, to study the British system of unemployment insurance (Bernstein 1960). Hopkins had worked at Christadora House, a settlement in New York, and had been President of the American Association of Social Workers (Pumphrey & Pumphrey 1961).

On June 29, 1934, Roosevelt issued an Executive Order creating the Committee on Economic Security. Its members were the Attorney General, the Federal Emergency Relief Administrator, and the Secretaries of Agriculture, the Treasury, and Labor (as chair). The Committee's January 15, 1935, report outlined what was to become the Social Security system.

The House Committee on Ways and Means offered a substitute for the original Economic Security Bill, and thereafter it was known as the Social Security Bill (Douglas 1936). The final vote in the House was 372 in favor (288 Democrats, 77 Republicans, six Progressives, and one Farmer-Labor), and 33 opposed (13 Democrats, 18 Republicans, and two Farmer-Labor). In the Senate, the final vote was 77 in favor (60 Democrats, 15 Republicans, one Progressive, and one Farmer-Labor), and 6 opposed (one Democrat and five Republicans). The Republicans, however, just prior to the final vote, had voted 12 to eight to eliminate Old-Age Insurance, that is, "Social Security" (*Congressional Record*, 1935: 9,648–50; 6,069–70).

The idea of incorporating some of the principles of private insurance (such as "premiums," or "contributions" rather than "taxes," the inclusion of certain provisions for individual equity, and the like) into a social insurance system did not originate in the United States. In fact, although Social Security's supporters described it as "peculiarly American," the system's framers drew directly upon European precedent dating from 1883 in Germany. Yet despite experience elsewhere, the structure of Social Security in the United States appears to have been dictated much more by American affection for private enterprise than by precedent.

It was the general applicability of old-age benefits that gave Social Security its special characteristics, and doubtless was responsible for its enormous popularity through the years. There is no question that many persons who could qualify for "welfare" avoid applying because of the stigma and humiliation that means tests (that is, the financial disclosure required to demonstrate poverty) impose (see, for example, Derthick 1990: 212n4). No such stigma or humiliation is connected with Social Security (including Medicare), because it is deemed to have been earned, and the citizen considers himself or herself to have a right to the benefits (Skidmore 1970).

To avoid contributions to old-age benefits from general revenues, the tax rates finally voted were higher than those recommended by the Committee on Economic Security (1937: 212–13). Both worker and employer were to pay at the rate of one percent of wages up to US $3,000 annually, beginning January 1, 1937. Benefits were not to begin until 1942.

The original Act also provided for a rebate to those who paid taxes, but did not qualify for benefits. The 1939 amendments changed the benefit formula, dropped the rebate provisions before they applied, and began benefits in 1940.

Throughout the years the emphasis upon individual equity lessened steadily. Even in the early program, low-income and short-term workers received benefits in excess of those that would have been provided by strict equity. The revisions in 1939 provided both major additions and definite changes in the system's principles. Survivors' and dependents' benefits emerged, giving not only a new benefit, but also introducing an emphasis upon the family. From then on, married workers, especially those with children, received much greater coverage for their contributions than did others. The benefit advantage for low-income and short-term workers also increased.

In 1950, Congress extended compulsory coverage to the self-employed, except for farmers and certain professionals, and to farm and domestic workers. It extended coverage on an optional basis to non-federal governmental employees and to those employed by non-profit organizations. It raised the taxable wage base to US $3,600 beginning in 1951, increased benefits, and raised the tax to 1.5 percent. In 1952, benefits increased once again, as they did also in 1954. Compulsory coverage expanded that year to include self-employed farmers, those farm workers who had not been covered by the 1950 amendments, and various professionals, while voluntary coverage became available to ministers and members of religious orders. The 1954 amendments raised the wage base to US $4,200 as of 1955.

Congress added disability coverage in 1956 and enabled women to retire early, at age 62, with reduced benefits. Self-employed lawyers, optometrists, veterinarians, and dentists also came under coverage. The 1958 amendments increased benefits again, raised the wage base to US $4,800, added benefits for eligible dependents of disability beneficiaries, and provided for a tax of 2.5 percent as of 1959. Disability benefits had been denied originally to those under 50, but the 1960 revisions eliminated that restriction. In 1961, men became eligible for early retirement at 62 with reduced benefits, and the tax increased to 3.125 percent beginning in 1962.

The 1950 amendments began a period of increasing benefits or adding to the system in each election year, demonstrating Social Security's great popularity. In 1962, however, there were no amendments. Although each house of Congress had passed a bill providing for benefit increases, the Senate added hospital benefits for the aged, or "Medicare." The Senate conferees refused to eliminate Medicare, while the House conferees refused to accept it. The bill therefore died, resulting in an election year with no Social Security improvements (Skidmore 1970).

It was 1965 that brought the huge Medicare addition. Although most social insurance systems throughout the industrialized world long had provided for health benefits considerably more extensive than the limited Medicare program, it required a protracted battle before they were accepted in the United States. The AMA had become the most bitter foe of such benefits, and succeeded in delaying them for years by branding them "socialized medicine." The 1965 amendments also increased the tax to 4.2 percent, and the wage base to US $6,600 beginning in 1966. Moreover, they extended compulsory coverage to medical practitioners (doctors of osteopathy had been covered previously).

New legislation brought benefit increases in 1968, 1971, and 1972. The wage base increased to US $7,800 in 1968, and US $9,000 in 1971. As of 1973, the tax rate increased to 5.85 percent, and the wage base to US $13,200. The 1972 amendments also introduced automatic adjustments relating benefits to the Consumer Price Index, beginning in January of 1975. Shortly after these amendments, however, the system for the first time faced a period of retrenchment. In 1973, in response to fears of a cash shortage, legislation delayed the onset of automatic adjustments from January to June of 1975. A cash-flow shortage nevertheless developed by 1977. Congress then added a tax increase to 6.13 percent in 1979 and raised the rate increases and wage bases already scheduled for subsequent years. Then, serious retrenchment became a reality.

The 1980 elections brought to the presidency a long-time foe of Social Security, Ronald Reagan, who nevertheless had promised repeatedly in the 1980 campaign to preserve and protect the program. Despite the promises, his administration had been in office hardly four months when it proposed sweeping cutbacks in benefits for future retirees, the elimination of the minimum benefit (even for those already receiving it), and other restrictions. Public outcry forced Congress to reject most of the proposal, but it did eliminate college benefits (to college student children of deceased workers), and the minimum benefit (though it was restored to those already receiving it).

In 1983, in response to continuing concern for fiscal soundness, Congress changed the policies that through the years had evolved to produce what was largely a pay-as-you-go system. The new approach provided for huge trust funds to finance the retirement of the "baby boom" generation. The changes included compulsory coverage for federal civilian employees and those employed by non-profit organizations, provisions prohibiting state and local governments from opting out of the system, a delayed cost-of-living adjustment, accelerated tax increases, taxation of some previously tax-free benefits, and a gradual increase of the retirement age from 65 to 67.

A GLANCE AT AMERICAN OPPOSITION TO SOCIAL SECURITY

In 1936, various minor parties called for measures to relieve poverty, and Democrats boasted of the Social Security Act. In contrast, the Republican platform charged that the Act was too complex to be administered, that its tax burden would be too great, and that its benefits would go to too few persons (Porter & Johnson 1956). There were criticisms from liberals as well.

The public, however, received Social Security with enthusiasm. This popularity ensured that both Democrats and Republicans would officially accept the fundamental principle of governmental responsibility for the welfare of the people. Republicans did criticize the Act, but not its basic justification. Governor Landon, their 1936 presidential candidate, said of social insurance in a radio address on May 7: "I'm for it. Every big industrial nation has had to move in that direction." But he did say that the Act was "complicated legislation that the Administration rushed through in characteristic fashion" (*New York Times*, May 8, 1936).

The first organized attack was the "pay envelope" campaign. Throughout the country employers included slips in pay envelopes charging that the new program was merely a tax increase. As a rule, the notices mentioned neither benefits, nor the requirement that the employer match the worker's contribution toward old-age insurance. The Chairman of the Securities and Exchange Commission, Joseph P. Kennedy, said the campaign was designed to "create the impression that giving old age insurance at half-price to the worker [was] an unfair tax on the worker" (*New York Times*, November 1, 1936). Roosevelt charged on October 31 in an address in Madison Square Garden that those employers were deceitful and were attempting to coerce their workers into voting against him (Roosevelt, 1957). On the second of November, the New York *Herald Tribune* called his speech "bitter and defiant." The Lynds found in Muncie, Indiana that "Landon and higher wages" was the basis of the pay-envelope attack there (Lynd & Lynd 1937).

The Hearst newspapers spearheaded much of the opposition. An editorial in the Washington *Herald* of May 28, 1936 was typical. It said that Landon was careful to imply that social security "must be along AMERICAN lines, and not . . . be a detail in a general scheme such as this Administration has put forth, to reduce millions of Americans to the condition of STATE PARASITES." It said that while Roosevelt's extreme methods had discredited all progressive ideas, Landon "indicates that no social security legislation based on COLLECTIVIST DELUSIONS or that is plainly UNCONSTITUTIONAL will receive his assent."

Such attacks caused the President, in a major speech in Syracuse, to defend the Social Security Act against allegations that it was "radical and alien" (Washington *Herald*, September 29, 1936). At the same time, Governor Landon sought to bring his state of Kansas under all portions of the Act, and called for a special session of the legislature for the following July to allow it to participate.

The sweeping Roosevelt victory of 1936 and the clear popularity of Social Security taught politicians the folly of direct attacks. For a while some private groups and individual spokesmen continued severe criticisms. Henry Ford's statement was typical: "Under some social security systems abroad," he said, "a man cannot quit his job, or apply for another, or leave town and go to another even to get a better job because that would break the 'economic plan.' Such a restriction of liberty will be almost a necessity in this country too if the present Social Security Act works to its natural conclusions" (New York *Herald Tribune*, November 2, 1936). The U.S. Chamber of Commerce spoke more moderately, but said of Social Security that "interference by government in attempts to reduce the whole complex problem to one of legislative formulae can only postpone the final solution by making it more difficult for business to assume its own obligations in the matter" (*New York Times*, August 30, 1936).

Throughout the 1950s, 1960s, and 1970s, most of the few overt attacks came from the far right. Political analysts and the public generally dismissed such groups and their spokesmen as insignificant. Gradually, however, one such spokesman emerged to gain prominence, and Social Security's opponents began to coalesce as his supporters. That spokesman was former film actor Ronald Reagan, who prepared the way for the attacks on the system during the 1964 campaign by presidential candidate Senator Barry Goldwater.

As early as 1954, Reagan began developing what he referred to simply as "The Speech," when he hosted television's "G.E. Theater" and assisted the General Electric Company's public relations efforts by speaking at hundreds of conventions, banquets, and other forums throughout the country (Ritter 1972). He stressed such things as the threat from communism, both without and within, the dangers of big government and centralization, the evils of governmental paternalism and high taxes, and the "failure" of Social Security.

In 1961, Reagan escalated his attacks on social insurance. Speaking to the Phoenix Chamber of Commerce on March 30 (Reagan 1961a), and again giving "The Speech" to the Orange County, California, Press Club on July 28, he referred to the proposals for "Medicare," and said: "Traditionally, one of the easiest first steps in imposing statism on a people has been government paid medicine. It is the easiest to present as a humanitarian project" (Reagan 1961b: 678). He proceeded to attack the existing Social Security system as bankrupt and as an intrusion upon liberty. These claims became staples of "The Speech."

During the same talk, he suggested the sources for the massive restructuring of the tax system that occurred 20 years later under his presidency. The changes brought increasing government reliance upon the regressive Social Security tax as opposed to income taxes. Progressive taxation, Reagan said, came "directly from Karl Marx who designed it as the prime essential of a socialist state" (Reagan 1961b: 679), and he followed with: "There can be no moral justification of the progressive tax" (Reagan 1961b: 680).

"The Speech" served to thrust Reagan into national prominence on October 27, 1964, when he gave a nationwide television address supporting

Senator Barry Goldwater's presidential candidacy. Goldwater lost overwhelmingly to Lyndon B. Johnson. Nevertheless, Reagan's effective presentation made himself a major force within the Republican Party, which pointed him toward the governorship of California, and ultimately—after he succeeded in reassuring a somewhat nervous public that he bore no hostility to Social Security—to election twice as President of the United States.

Reagan's principles remained consistent from his beginnings as a corporate spokesman to his flowering as a candidate. The only true change came in his increasing awareness of the demands of politics. He developed skill in balancing the demands of the right, and the need for general appeal. He accomplished this by stressing certain themes only in private, or less well publicized, talks while publicly proclaiming his "eagerness to solve the problems of age, health, poverty, and housing 'without compulsion and without fiscal irresponsibility' " (Ritter 1972: 112–13). His radio broadcasts, which received little coverage, were considerably less inhibited than his television presentations. The texts of these talks are extremely difficult to obtain, but some are available in the Reagan Collection at the Hoover Institution at Stanford University, and Ronnie Dugger has succeeded in unearthing a number of others (Dugger 1983).

Dugger in 1983 concluded that

the man in the White House is a dedicated foe of Social Security. He regards it as welfare, which he detests. In 1964 he agreed with Goldwater that Social Security should be made voluntary. In 1975 Reagan in effect proposed to abolish the whole system, in 1978 he declared that Social Security "is in effect bankrupt." From the White House he has led a war on the Social Security system. (Dugger 1983: 43)

Supporting this conclusion is Laurence Barrett's revelation that the President's aides knew that the massive cuts proposed in 1981 were more than double any that might be needed to ensure solvency for the system, but they proceeded nonetheless (Barrett 1983). Moreover, the architect of much of the Reagan Administration's economic policy, his Budget Director, David Stockman, has conceded that the phrase "future savings to be identified," in the first budget proposal, was simply "a euphemism for 'We're going to go after Social Security' " (Stockman 1987: 175).

Barrett noted that Reagan's doubts "gave him trouble in both the 1976 and 1980 campaigns, so he muted them. In 1980 he promised repeatedly both to protect the long-term integrity of the system and to maintain benefits for those already receiving them" (Barrett 1983: 155). "When he became a national candidate in 1976 and 1980," Barrett continued, Reagan "had to adjust his public rhetoric to some extent" (Barrett 1983: 59).

The Reagan scorn for Social Security seemed to increase as the years progressed. In 1972, in a New York speech delivered to the National Association of Manufacturers on December 8, he became explicit. "Take for example," he said, "the biggest sacred cow in all of the United States: Social Security. I have to say that if you couldn't come up with a better idea than that, you wouldn't still be in business" (Reagan 1973: 200–1). His opinion remained the same as of 1975.

In that year, he broadcast a series of three radio programs on Social Security. The printed transcripts in the Reagan Collection at the Hoover Institution are not dated, except with "(1975)," in pencil, but Dugger has identified the dates as September 24, 25, and 29 (Dugger 1983: 47). Reagan ended the first, saying that "social security reduces your chances of ever being able to enjoy a comfortable retirement income" (Reagan 1975). In the second, he called Social Security "a sure loser" and claimed that "If there were no Social Security . . . wages would be 15 percent higher and interest rates 28 percent lower" (Reagan 1975). On the third day he called for elimination of Social Security taxes, with the employer's share to be added to the worker's wage, and a choice provided the worker between investment in a government-insured private pension plan, or a series of new "U.S. Retirement Bonds with annuity pay off" (Dugger 1983: 49–50).

Reagan's attack was typical of Social Security's opposition, which generally portrays the program as nothing other than a pension. It adopted the common argument that the worker could receive greater support for retirement if he or she were to invest privately the money that now goes to Social Security. Even if the argument were correct, and even assuming that the employers' amounts would remain available and that workers would invest all funds, and invest wisely, it would be misleading. The other benefits from Social Security would vanish, such as benefits for survivors and dependents, protection in the event of disability, and Medicare.

Reagan opposed government health benefits, if anything, even more strongly than he did "Social Security." He began his political career by preparing a phonograph record in 1961 for the American Medical Association's "Operation Coffeecup." The recording, "Ronald Reagan Speaks Out Against Socialized Medicine," was the heart of a campaign designed to stimulate letters to Congress opposing the proposal that later became "Medicare." The AMA designed the campaign to be as secret as possible, and not until 1989 was Reagan's text published publicly (Skidmore 1989).

Because of the prestige of his office, his willingness to be pragmatic, and his general affability, the public appeared to forget that up to within a year of his becoming President, Reagan represented the far-right fringe of American politics. What Ritter, Barrett, and others have documented should be clear to anyone familiar with the Reagan career: he softened his rhetoric in discussing social programs before the general public, but he retained his views. In 1981, when Reagan, as President, "took one more whack at the Social Security system," the "fact that he was willing to act out another of his long-held instincts despite the political price was significant" (Barrett 1983: 63). That price was his acceptance that there could be no additional overt attacks on Social Security. The long pattern of opposition that began in the 1930s and culminated in the Reagan Administration, thus shifted its emphasis from overt calls for the system's elimination to support for more subtle restrictions, and for manipulation of the system to serve other purposes, especially the avoidance of progressive taxes, and the maintenance of a low level of income taxation.

Republican political analyst Kevin Phillips has provided extensive documentation of such manipulation of the system to redistribute income upward.

The . . . redistributive spur was Washington's decision to let Social Security tax rates climb upward from 6.05 percent in 1978 to 6.70 percent in 1982–83, 7.05 percent in 1985 and 7.51 percent in 1988–89—a schedule originally voted in 1977 under Carter—while income tax rates were coming down. By 1987, however, Maine Democratic senator George Mitchell complained that "as a result, there has been a shift of about $80 billion in annual revenue collections from the progressive income tax to the regressive payroll tax. The Social Security tax increase in 1977 cannot be attributed to the current administration, but the response in the 1980s, to make up for a tax increase disproportionately burdening lower-income households, can be laid to the policies of this administration." Mitchell was hardly overstating the new reliance on Social Security. Between 1980 and 1988, . . . the portion of total annual federal tax receipts represented by Social Security rose from 31 percent to 36 percent while income tax contributions dropped from 47 percent to under 45 percent. (Phillips, 1990: 80)

Although the situation was not widely recognized during the Reagan years, eventually it did at least cause public comment. As Phillips (1990: 80n) notes:

In December 1989 reaction against shifting the federal tax burden onto Social Security levies would break out into open political warfare with the proposal by

New York Democratic senator Daniel Patrick Moynihan to roll back Social Security rates. Moynihan charged that "no other democratic country takes as large a portion of its revenue from working people at the lower ends of the spectrum and as little from persons who have property or high incomes."

As of the end of 1990, however, Moynihan's proposal had done nothing more than to cause controversy and to call attention to the nature of the policies involved.

SOCIAL SECURITY TODAY

Support appears to include all age groups, as Barry Sussman reported the findings of a Washington *Post*–ABC News Poll, in an article, "Social Security and the Young: They Are Just as Eager as the Elderly to Protect It" (*The Washington Post National Weekly Edition*, May 27, 1985). Unpublished data that colleagues and the author collected in 1987 from an in-depth study of the attitudes of a representative sample of Missourians strongly document the existence of considerable support, although they also suggest concern for the future. Cook and Barrett in 1988 reported finding similar enthusiasm for Social Security in their 1986 national study (Cook & Barrett 1988). Their findings, too, reflect both apprehension for the system's future, and a desire to protect it that cuts across all ages.

The apprehension results largely from years of criticism, especially from Reagan. He long charged that the system was bankrupt (Reagan 1962, 1977). Dugger (1983: 44) wrote that "by Reagan's outcries that the system was in danger of bankruptcy, he and his agents did profound damage." Dugger documented the Reagan Administration's publicity campaign against Social Security, and noted that "in the Republican-controlled Senate, as the subcommittee on Social Security opened its hearings that first summer of the Reagan administration, an aide to the panel's chairman (Senator William Armstrong [Republican-Colorado]), told the *Wall Street Journal* about a deliberate plan to fill the air with the word 'crisis.' It will be well-orchestrated—lots of horror stories, the aide said. . . . There was no crisis; the whole outcry would have been ludicrous if [the] facts had been made clear. Instead . . . Reagan deliberately created the panic. . . . He is using his presidency to undermine Social Security with specious alarms and arguments that conceal his ideological purpose" (Dugger 1983: 56, 58).

Although the Administration learned to avoid attacking the program directly, it encouraged the idea of means tests that would cause it to be limited, at best, to the poor, that is, to be converted into a "welfare" measure that would make it politically vulnerable. For example, Drew Lewis, former Reagan Administration Secretary of Transportation, on a December 11, 1988 broadcast of NBC's "Meet the Press," advocated that benefits be virtually eliminated for those earning in excess of US $90,000 annually, and that cuts, based on income, be applied to those earning less.

Inspired by the Reagan Administration and its deficits, the word quickly spread among many neo-conservative circles outside of government that Social Security is a "middle-class" program and that society no longer can afford such luxuries for the middle class. Moreover, they raised questions of inter-generational equity by arguing that the elderly as a group now are relatively affluent and thus receive more than their "fair share." Paul Light has pointed out the flawed nature of an argument that the policy system "can compare one generation in its third quarter of life to another in the first or second, and make reasoned choices on that basis" (Light 1988: 3).

Criticism from these groups nonetheless had an effect, possibly because they did not have to restrain their rhetoric as politicians did. One of these effects was the establishment of an organization, Americans for Generational Equity, devoted to asserting the insolvency of the Social Security system, imposing means tests upon Social Security and Medicare, and establishing "inter-generational equity" as the foundation of public policy (Longman 1987). Such attitudes toward the Social Security system became grist for the popular mill, as reflected by an article appearing in supplements to Sunday newspapers around the country in mid-1990. It was written by a staff writer for Knight-Ridder newspapers; its various titles, "Scammed," "Insecurity," "A Nation of Suckers," clearly reflected its contents (*The Kansas City Star Magazine*, June 3, 1990). Similar artilcles abound. In one year alone examples appeared in the *New York Times* (February 28, 1993), *Newsweek* (May 31, 1993), *Parade* (February 21, 1993), and the *Christian Science Monitor* (February 16, 1993).

Even some liberal spokesmen came to accept the opponents' rhetoric and to adopt some of their premises. They forgot that without Social Security, the elderly again would be thrust as a group into their previous poverty, also that the programs protect all classes and all age groups, including not only survivors and the disabled, but also young workers who no longer are burdened by supporting elderly parents. Thus, they too questioned why Social Security and the "entitlements" should be exempted from the cuts necessary to deal with the deficit. The opponents' strategy had been at least somewhat effective. Although the Reagan Administration, and the Bush Administration that followed, were forced to exempt Social Security from cuts, Reagan had created such a grave situation—and his aides used the deficit so adroitly—that even some of the system's most ardent supporters came to question why the "middle class should not shoulder its share of the burden of deficit reduction." In 1990, the Chairman of the House Ways and Means Committee, Dan Rostenkowski (Democrat-Illinois), suggested a deficit-reduction package that would involve not only tax increases, but also spending freezes that would include Social Security cost-of-living increases. Senator Daniel Patrick Moynihan (Democrat-New York) attacked this freeze as a benefit reduction.

Of course, with the unified budget that included all trust funds, Social Security affected the overall budget "balance" (that is, the relation between income and expenditure), as did the other trust funds for other programs. Thus, the reported budget deficit, though huge, was considerably less than the true deficit because of masking by the enormous surplus balances in the trust funds. When Senator Moynihan proposed in late 1989 that Social Security taxes be cut to pare back trust funds so that the system again would be on a "pay-as-you-go" basis, his purpose was to reveal the true size of the deficit and to prevent the government from borrowing Social Security funds to use for other purposes. Although Moynihan's proposal made no progress, in October of 1990 much of the goal was achieved: A new budget agreement separated Social Security from the budget, thus removing the incentive to cut benefits in order to make the deficit appear to shrink.

The Social Security system in the United States is strong. It retains the firm support of the people, although their confidence has been shaken by decades of attacks, both overt and covert. Such attacks, coupled with governmental policy changes that originated mostly within the eight years of the Reagan Administration, caused Social Security again to be a major political issue. Not since the program's beginning in 1935, or the battle in the early 1960s for Medicare, had there been anything resembling the controversy. There are already some indications that yet another controversy is on the political horizon, one that could be the greatest of all. The inadequacies of the health-care delivery system in the United States are extraordinary among industrialized countries, and are coming to be recognized. Despite vested interests and entrenched opposition to governmental action, there ultimately will have to be some form of comprehensive health care for Americans, as there is in virtually every other developed country. Whether such a program will be a part of the Social Security system (as Medicare now is) or established separately, it will be a part of social security in America, broadly defined.

The enormous escalation of the national debt that the Reagan tax cuts and military spending increases generated does create some fear that the

Social Security trust funds will never receive payment for the amounts that the government has borrowed. If this were to happen, benefits could be reduced or eliminated, and the system could be weakened, or even destroyed. More likely, however, is that there will ultimately be a restoration of the tax base, or perhaps a "peace dividend," to provide adequate support for the government without interfering with the trust funds, and that Social Security will remain secure as one of the world's greatest social programs. It is also likely that it will continue to be financed by regressive measures, and that it will continue to be subject to subtle attacks that will restrict its development relative to the systems in other industrial countries.

REFERENCES

Anderson, O. W. 1951. "Compulsory Medical Care Insurance, 1910–1950" *Annals* (American Academy of Political and Social Science) 273: 106–13.

Barrett, L. I. 1983. *Gambling with History: Ronald Reagan in the White House* (Garden City, NY: Doubleday).

Bernstein, I. 1960. *The Lean Years, A History of the American Worker, 1920–1933* (Boston: Houghton Mifflin).

Chambers, C. A. 1963. *Seedtime of Reform* (Minneapolis: University of Minnesota Press).

Committee on Economic Security. 1937. *Social Security in America, The Background of the Social Security Act as Summarized from Staff Reports to the Committee on Economic Security* (Washington: U.S. Government Printing Office).

Congressional Record. 1935. (74th Congress, 1st Session).

Cook, F. L. & Barrett, E. J. 1988. "Public Support for Social Security" *Journal of Aging Studies* 2(4): 339–56.

Derthick, M. 1990. *Agency Under Stress* (Washington: Brookings Institution).

Douglas, P. H. 1925. *Wages and the Family* (Chicago: University of Chicago Press).

Douglas, P. H. 1931. *The Problem of Unemployment* (New York: Macmillan).

Douglas, P. H. 1936. *Social Security in the United States* (New York: McGraw-Hill).

Dugger, R. 1983. *On Reagan: The Man and His Presidency* (New York: McGraw-Hill).

Epstein, A. 1933. *Insecurity: A Challenge to America* (New York: Harrison Smith and Robert Haas).

Hicks, J. D. 1960. *Republican Ascendancy* (New York: Harper and Row).

Light, P. C. 1988. "The Future Politics of Social Security." Paper presented at the Annual Scientific Meeting of the Gerontological Society of America.

Longman, P. 1987. *Born to Pay* (Boston: Houghton Mifflin).

Lynd, R. & Lynd, H. 1937. *Middletown in Transition* (New York: Harcourt Brace and World).

Phillips, K. 1990. *The Politics of Rich and Poor* (New York: Random House).

Porter, K. & Johnson, D. 1956. *National Party Platforms, 1840–1956* (Urbana, Ill.: University of Illinois Press).

Pumphrey, R. E. & Pumphrey, M. W. 1961. *The Heritage of American Social Work* (New York: Columbia University Press).

Reagan, R. 1961a. "Encroaching Control." An address at the Phoenix Chamber of Commerce, March 30 (Stanford: The Reagan Collection, the Hoover Institution, Stanford University).

Reagan, R. 1961b. "Encroaching Control: Keep Government Poor and Remain Free" *Vital Speeches* 37: 22 (September 1).

Reagan, R. 1962. "Transcribed From Ronald Reagan's Television Appearance— Nov. 4, 1962" (Stanford: The Reagan Collection, The Hoover Institution, Stanford University).

Reagan, R. 1973. "Free Enterprise" *Vital Speeches* 39 (January 15).

Reagan, R. 1975. "*Viewpoint* with Ronald Reagan (Reprint of a Radio Program entitled 'Strengthening Social Security—1,2,3')" (Stanford: The Reagan Collection, The Hoover Institution, Stanford University).

Reagan, R. 1977. "Reprint of a Radio Program Entitled 'Social Security'" *RR Radio Commentary Disc 77–24B* (Stanford: The Reagan Collection, The Hoover Institution, Stanford University).

Ritter, K. W. 1972. "Ronald Reagan and 'The Speech': The Rhetoric of Public Relations Politics" *Western Speech* 32 (1) 1968; reprinted in Skidmore, M. J. (ed.) *Word Politics: Essays on Language and Politics* (Palo Alto, CA: James E. Freel & Associates).

Roosevelt, F. D. 1957. *Selected Speeches, Messages, Press Conferences, and Letters* (Rauch, B. ed.) (New York: Holt, Rinehart & Winston).

Rubinow, I. M. 1913. *Social Insurance* (New York: Henry Holt).

Rubinow, I. M. 1926. "The Status of Social Insurance" *Survey* 58(4) (May 15): 242–44.

Rubinow, I. M. 1934. *The Quest for Security* (New York: Holt, Rinehart & Winston).

Schlesinger, A. M. Jr. 1959. *The Age of Roosevelt: The Coming of the New Deal* (Boston: Houghton Mifflin).

Skidmore, M. J. 1970. *Medicare and the American Rhetoric of Reconciliation* (Tuscaloosa, AL: University of Alabama Press).

Skidmore, M. J. 1989. "Ronald Reagan and 'Operation Coffeecup': A Hidden Episode in American Political History" *Journal of American Culture* 12(3): 89–96.

Stockman, D. A. 1987. *The Triumph of Politics: The Inside Story of the Reagan Revolution* (New York: Avon Books).

3

Japanese Social Security:
Its Past, Present, and Future

Mitsuya Ichien

Japan started industrialization much later than most Western countries, with a large population remaining in rural areas for a long time. In such circumstances, the introduction of a social security system would probably benefit a small group of modern industrial workers rather than the rural majority. The objective of this chapter is to examine how different social security schemes with different benefit levels for different groups of people developed, how the problems of unequal social security schemes were solved, and future prospects for the unification or coordination of stratified schemes.

PRE-WAR DEVELOPMENT OF PUBLIC ASSISTANCE
AND SOCIAL INSURANCE

The term "social security" was born in Japan in the making of the present constitution in 1946, immediately after the Second World War. However, the two main components of social security, namely public assistance and social insurance, started much earlier.

Soon after the Meiji Restoration in 1868, the poor law, the "Jukkyuk-isoku" was enforced in 1874, which provided for the state to pay the cost of necessary rice to the disabled, the old, the sick, and children who could not expect any help from other people. Though the level of relief and the number relieved were not sufficient in comparison to the need, it is significant that the state poor law was enacted at this time against a background of vast poverty and social unrest. The law was replaced in 1929 by the "Kyugo-Ho," which extended the number to be relieved with a clearer definition of responsibility on the part of the state.

After the Second World War, the Daily Life Security Law ("Seikatu-Hogo-Ho") of 1946 replaced several pre-war laws for the relief of different categories of the poor, with the principle of equal justice and non-discrimination, and the law was further amended in 1950 to confirm the people's right to claim the benefit. It was through these post-war reforms that the people's right to relief was clearly defined and that the means-tested system became the safety net of the total social security system in securing people's right to maintain a minimum standard of living (Sakayori 1974; Tada 1977; Soeda 1985).

Along with the history of public assistance for the poor, the state provisions to protect the newly born industrial workers also developed as Japanese industrialization proceeded. As was the case in many European countries, the experience of mutual aid associations paved the way for the state health insurance. The first Japanese social insurance law, the "Kenkohoken-Ho" (the Health Insurance Law) was enacted in 1922 to maintain "industrial peace" at the time of a growing labor movement and an upsurge of socialist thought.

Compared with the European mutual associations, the Japanese counterparts lacked the sense of independence and active participation on the part of employees. One of the earliest examples was the Mutual Aid Association of Kanegafuchi Spinning Company established in 1905. The association collected three percent of the wages from each worker in order to provide benefits in times of sickness, injury, death, and so forth. It was the employer that took the initiative and controlled the management of these funds, with the idea of paternalism in the employer–employee relationship similar to the father–child relationship.

By the time the Health Insurance Law was enacted in 1922, these company-based mutual aid associations had developed, but they were all started by the employers and mostly subsidized by them. Although the employees paid the contributions, they did not have the right to participate in the running and management of these associations.

In introducing the Health Insurance Law, one of the issues was the relationship between the new state health care scheme and the mutual aid associations of the private and public sectors. Employers who had developed their own schemes for their employees wanted their schemes to be independent of the state administration. The government, however, included them as part of the statutory health insurance, and health insurance came to be administered by these approved health insurance societies organized on a company basis. The government intention was to expand gradually these company-based health insurance societies to cover a much wider section of working population. However, it was necessary for the government to undertake the management of health insurance for workers of many smaller businesses that could not organize health insurance societies by themselves. Thus the administration of Health Insurance came to be pursued by the government as well as by the health insurance societies, and the former served for the workers of smaller businesses, and the latter for those in larger companies.

Besides the company-based mutual associations, there developed associations for the employees of public corporations, such as the Japanese National Railways, as well as the statutory schemes for navy and army personnel and government officials. These occupations were excluded from the health insurance scheme on the ground that their financial position was secure and their organizational basis was firm. Thus in the sphere of health care for employees, there were different forms of protection depending upon one's occupation and employment (Kondo 1963).

In Japan, the role of the state in industrialization was much greater than in European countries. The state took the initiative in implanting strategically important industries and supported them until they could financially operate without a government subsidy. The newly introduced industries could attract only a small proportion of the population, and industrialization developed with a large population remaining in rural areas, resulting in a formation of the stratified industrial structure.

In these circumstances, the economic positions of the different sectors of the economy varied from state corporations to small cottage industries, with the working conditions of the employees also varying. The structure of social protection against sickness was thus composed of different schemes, ranging from the state scheme for government officials and military personnel, the mutual aid associations of public corporations, the society-administered health insurance for large companies, government-administered health insurance for small businesses, to the National Health Insurance ("Kokumin-Kenko-Hoken," the community-based health insurance that started in 1938 to cover the rural population). This stratified structure of the social insurance system, together with the interference of labor management, has been regarded as a characteristic defect of the Japanese social insurance system.

This stratified structure also characterizes the pension system. Protection for retired employees developed from the most secure employment to a more vulnerable one, creating the stratified structure of a pension system with different contribution and benefit conditions. The state schemes for navy and army personnel came soon after the Meiji Restoration, followed by the scheme for the government officials and the mutual aid associations in public corporations. The first compulsory pension insurance to cover private sector employees was the Seamen's Insurance of 1939. In 1941 the Workman's Pension Insurance Law was enacted to extend the pension insurance coverage to manual workers, which was replaced in 1943 by the Employees' Pension Insurance Law ("Kosei-Nenkin-Hoken-Ho") to cover almost all the employees in the private sector.

THE DEVELOPMENT OF SOCIAL SECURITY IMMEDIATELY AFTER THE SECOND WORLD WAR

The Japanese economy was completely devastated by the Second World War, as were the living conditions of the people. At the same time there was a feeling of release and hope for a new democratic society among people who had been oppressed by the long totalitarian regime during the war. In democratizing the political and economic framework of the country, the Allied Forces and the Occupation played an important role.

The word "Shakai-Hosho," meaning social security, appeared for the first time in Article 25 of the constitution established in 1946. The General Headquarters (GHQ) of the Allied Forces wanted a similar article in the constitution, but it was the Japanese House of Representatives that put life into it. The English word "social security" was first translated as "Shakai-no-Annei," meaning peace or order of society, which was later replaced by the expression "Seikatsu-no-Hosho," or security of living. Finally, through discussion in the House of Representatives, the word "Shakai-Hosho" was born as a single term rather than a set of descriptive words, and the first clause of the constitutional article prescribing the people's right to a minimum standard of living was included. Inclusion of the article on social security in the new constitution shows the fact that the Japanese people were prepared to accept the ideal and the concept of social security, though the word was a mere translation of the English word that appeared in the GHQ's draft of the constitution (Kondo 1974). Article 25 of the constitution of 1946 reads as follows:

All people shall have the right to maintain the minimum standards of wholesome and cultured living.

In all spheres of life, the State shall use its endeavours for the promotion and extension of social welfare and security, and of public health.

GHQ attached importance to social security as part of the overall occupation policy and exerted influence to strengthen the Japanese social security system, especially readily effective public assistance. As for means-tested assistance, Japan has a few programs for different categories of the poor, such as soldiers and war victims, in addition to the general assistance of the "Kyugo-Ho." However, GHQ laid the principle of demilitarization and non-discrimination as the basis of social security, and these pre-war laws were repealed and replaced by the Urgent Relief Measure for the Destitute in 1945 and by the Daily Life Security Law in 1946.

In forming the budget for the fiscal year 1946–1947, GHQ insisted on raising the expenditure for the relief of the poor to three billion Yen, while the government planned for only 200 million Yen. This shows the difference in the ideas of needed relief between GHQ and the Japanese government. The latter prepared the budget by adding all the assistance-related budget items, while the former attained the estimate by multiplying the minimum cost of living by about one-tenth of the population (Soeda 1985). This budget of three billion Yen for the Daily Life Security Law symbolizes the birth of a new public assistance program for the relief of ordinary citizens.

In effect, the cost of public assistance within the total social security system became enormous, but is was not necessarily the intention of GHQ to place special importance to public assistance. GHQ urged the government to appoint a council on social security to draw up a plan for overall social security. The Advisory Council on Social Security was appointed in 1949, which reported *Recommendation on Social Security System* to the Prime Minister in the next year.

The 1950 Recommendation defined social security as composed of four programs, namely social insurance, public assistance, public health, and social welfare, attaching the most important role to social insurance (Secretariat of Advisory Council on Social Security 1961). This was partly because Japan had developed social insurance to a limited extent before the war and partly because members of the Council, especially scholars who had studied the Beveridge Report, supported the idea of insurance-oriented social security rather than assistance-oriented social security. As can be seen in Table 3.1, the share of social insurance increased from 76.2 to 85.4 percent from 1950 to 1960, while that of public assistance decreased from 13.9 to 8.3 percent over the same period.

DEVELOPMENT OF SOCIAL INSURANCE

The 1950 Recommendation covered health insurance, pension insurance, unemployment insurance, and industrial injuries compensation in-

Table 3.1
Cost of Social Security and Its Distribution since 1950

	1950	1955	1960	1965	1970	1975	1980	1985
Distribution among different schemes:								
Public assistance	13.9	11.9	8.3	8.5	7.6	5.6	4.53	3.82
Social welfare	2.9	2.9	2.0	4.0	4.6	9.1	8.1	4.9
Social insurance	76.2	79.8	85.4	75.6	78.3	77.7	79.6	75.2
Public health	7.0	5.7	4.2	12.0	9.4	7.5	7.8	5.8
Health service for the aged	–	–	–	–	–	–	–	10.2
TOTAL	100.00	100.00	100.00	100.00	100.00	100.00	100.00	100.00
As percentage of National Income								
Medical care	1.8	2.8	2.2	3.4	3.4	4.6	5.4	5.6
Pension	1.7	2.8	2.7	1.3	1.4	3.1	5.3	6.7
Other*	–	–	–	1.3	1.0	1.7	1.7	1.8
TOTAL	3.5	5.6	4.9	6.0	5.8	9.4	12.3	14.0

Note: *"Others" includes such benefits and services as social welfare, children's allowance, unemployment benefit. These are included in "Pension" before 1965.
Sources: Secretariat of Advisory Council on Social Security 1961 and Social Development Research Institute 1990: 324.

surance. For health insurance, the Recommendation proposed two programs, one for the employees administered by prefectural governments and health insurance societies and the other for the self-employed and farmers administered by cities, towns, and villages. For pension insurance, the Recommendation proposed an insurance program for employees and a non-contributory program for the self-employed and farmers (Secretariat of Advisory Council on Social Security 1961).

The recommendation to unify different insurance schemes was completely neglected by the government. The Private School Teachers and Employees' Mutual Aid Association and the Agricultural, Forestry and Fishery Institutions' Mutual Aid Association were established in 1953 and 1958, respectively. The members of these associations seceded from the Employees' Pension Insurance in order to obtain a better pension with higher salaries. In this sense, stratification of the Japanese insurance system was intensified in the 1950s.

On the other hand, the proposal of the 1950 Recommendation to extend insurance coverage to the entire population was eventually attained with a delay of about ten years. In 1958, the new National Health Insurance Law was enacted to enforce every city, town, and village to organize and administer the National Health Insurance. Everybody who had not been covered by an occupational scheme became insured under the National Health Insurance. This program is called "Kai-Hoken," meaning nation-wide health insurance coverage, and it was accomplished by April 1961.

Likewise, the National Pension Law was passed in 1959. This is basically a contributory pension insurance with flat-rate benefit for flat-rate contribution, and every citizen aged between 20 and 60 who is not covered by the occupational schemes is expected to join the scheme. The National Pension scheme also pays non-contributory pensions for those elderly people who could not join the contributory system, the payment of which started in 1959. Payment of a contribution to the National Pension started in April 1961, and this is called "Kai-Nenkin," meaning nation-wide pension coverage.

In contrast to the insurance schemes for unemployment and industrial injuries, which were implemented in 1947 to include almost all the employees under one structure, "Kai-Hoken" and "Kai-Nenkin" were attained by adding another scheme for farmers, the self-employed, and many employees in small businesses who had not been included under occupational schemes. If the idea of social security is to attain equality among people by protecting above all the most vulnerable, then stratified social insurance with its considerable differences in benefit levels and financial positions could hardly be supported.

On the other hand, if the idea of autonomy or participation on the part of the members is stressed, the decentralized or pluralistic system may be supported rather than the single unified system. The idea becomes especially important in the field of health care, where preventive measures can be encouraged to avoid unnecessary expenditures. In this case, it becomes an important issue to attain an equal level of protection throughout the entire scheme, while attaching autonomy to an individual organization.

In Table 3.2 the three main health insurance schemes are compared in the fiscal years 1961–1962 and 1972–1973. In the 11-year period, the difference of per capita expenditures narrowed to a great extent while the financial dependency rates on public subsidies grew. In the case of the National Health Insurance, the cost met by the public subsidies, mainly state contribution, amounted to almost two-thirds of the cost in 1972.

Table 3.2
Cost of Health Insurance and Cost Met by Public Subsidies

		1961–62	1972–73
Government Administered H.I.			
Total cost	(billion Yen)	114.7	761.2
Per capita cost	(Yen)	6,173.0	29,273.0
Cost met by public subsidies (%)		0.6	13.0
Society Administered H.I.			
Total cost	(billion Yen)	92.1	630.2
Per capita cost	(Yen)	7,231.0	28,320.0
Cost met by public subsidies (%)		–	2.0
National Health Insurance			
Total cost	(billion Yen)	100.6	865.2
Per capita cost	(Yen)	2,179.0	19,789.0
Cost met by public subsidies (%)		52.0	65.0

Source: National Federation of Health Insurance Societies, *Social Security Yearbook* (Tokyo:Tokyo-Keizai) 1963, 1964, 1974, 1975.

The Advisory Council on Social Security made a recommendation calling for "comprehensive coordination" among social insurance schemes in 1962, in view of the difficulty of establishing a unified framework of social insurance. The coordination was expected to be pursued by pooling a part of financial resources of different insurance schemes and by deliberately using these funds to aid poorer schemes. However, this pooling of resources proposed by the Advisory Council did not take place during the period of high economic growth. There was no system to transfer resources from better-off schemes to worse-off ones. This does not mean, however, that the poorest scheme could not improve the standard of benefits. On the contrary, benefit levels of different schemes became much closer, the superior schemes enhancing the benefit level, and the inferior schemes trying to narrow the gap. In a sense, "comprehensive coordination" was attained not by pooling the resources but by attracting ample state subsidies as shown in Table 3.2.

If the country's economy is well matured and the living conditions of the people are well enhanced, it can be a reasonable and practical policy objective to establish a unified social insurance system with generous benefit for all. However, if the economy is still in a process of rapid growth and society is going through great change, a rigid uniform social insurance system may not cope with people's rising expectations, though it can be regarded as ideal from the egalitarian point of view. In Japan, where rapid industrialization took place, keeping a large population in rural areas until recently, it is understandable that nation-wide coverage was accomplished by adding an inferior scheme to the existing schemes to cover the rest of the population.[1]

Professor Bunji Kondo, who had been an active member of the Advisory Council on Social Security since its birth, once wrote in defending the 1962 Recommendation:

The critics might be reasonable enough so long as one takes the view that the principle of non-discrimination of Beveridge style should be the basis of social security and that any attempt to classify people into social groups means retreat of the principle of social security. However, we should note that if we stick blindly to the principle of equity, the minimum level of standard guaranteed by the social security system gradually comes down, and that it is extremely difficult to improve the standard level under these circumstances. (Kondo 1971: 8)

An an example, he pointed out that in the United Kingdom the selectivity principle was gaining recognition. This parallels the following notion by Abel-Smith:

By trying to do everything all at once, the government did nothing really well. The jam was spread thinly over every service, and has been ever since. Moreover, there was a lack of thinking about priorities. . . . In some respects therefore the principle of universality was stretched unnecessarily far. In other respects (because benefits were never high enough to prevent means-tested supplements), it never got properly off the ground. (Abel-Smith 1983: 13)

The Japanese social insurance has also been criticized for its close link to labor management, which is due mainly to the stratified insurance structure and the company-based insurance organization. If the realistic approach to accept the diverse schemes is supported in the developing economy, these defects of the Japanese social insurance can also be overlooked.

TOWARD UNIFICATION

The year 1973 was called "the first year of the Welfare Era." The government's *Basic Economic and Social Plan 1973–77* issued in February

1973 had the subtitle, "Toward a Vigorous Welfare Society" and expressed the government's strong intention "to expand social security, to improve housing and the living environment" (Steslicke 1982). In January of 1973, medical care became completely free for the elderly (70 years and over). Before then many elderly people had to pay 30 percent of the medical care cost as the cost-sharing of health insurance. In January, the 30 percent came to be borne by the central and local government as a result of amending the Welfare Law for the Elderly. This is why the cost of "others" in Table 3.1 rises sharply from 1970 to 1975.

The Health Insurance Law and related insurance laws were amended in 1973 to raise the benefit level of the dependent family member from 50 to 70 percent of the medical cost, the benefit level of the insured themselves having been already 100 percent with a nominal cost-sharing. At the same time a high-cost medical care benefit was introduced and an upper limit of 30,000 (now 60,000) Yen a month was set to the patient's cost-sharing. These reforms helped narrow the gap of benefit levels among different schemes, by pushing up the bottom benefit level for all health insurance schemes (Ichien & Chester 1983).

As for pension insurance, the formula was revised to raise the model pension for an average employee to 60 percent of the average earnings.[2] With this revision of the pension formula, an automatic indexation system was also introduced so that the pensions can be raised in line with consumer prices.

In Table 3.2, the trend of the social security benefit cost as a percentage of the national income is shown. The figure jumped from 5.8 percent in 1970 to 9.4 percent in 1975, showing the effects of these social security reforms, though we should not overlook the effect of exceptionally low economic growth in that period. If we look at the trends of different programs in the table, the cost of medical care rises from 3.4 percent in 1970 to 4.6 percent in 1975, while that of pension more than doubled in the same period to 3.1 percent. As Japanese pension schemes are in a process of rapid maturity, the percentage share of the pension cost to national income is growing much faster than that of medical care.

In effect, structural improvement of social security was accomplished in 1973. Since then, the cost of social security has been expanding automatically without any institutional improvements. This cost expansion will be the feature of the Japanese social security system for the coming decade or two.

The level of social security was improved in the 1960s, but the economic expansion was so great that the society could easily bear the cost. The government could find extra money to implement new policy by keeping the present scheme as it was. However, after the oil crisis of 1973, the economic climate changed and the government had to cope with the rising demands with less income. To lessen its expenditures the government had to revaluate all activities, including social security. Less government expenses and privatization became key words in the early 1980s.

The state subsidy played an important role in helping the financially weak health insurance schemes, thus achieving a similar effect to "comprehensive coordination" recommended by the Advisory Council on Social Security in 1962. But in the late 1970s and in the early 1980s, the financial ground for the government to hand out an ample subsidy to the National Health Insurance was collapsed, and a new method of comprehensive coordination had to be sought out unless the level of benefits was reduced. This could be done only by utilizing resources from the financially better-off schemes and placing these financial resources with the National Health Insurance program.

The financial coordination among different insurance schemes was first introduced by the Health Service Law for the Aged, which was put into effect in 1983. The average personal cost of health insurance grows as one's age increases and the cost of medical care after the age of 65 is a little more than half the lifetime medical care cost in 1988, supposing that a person lives an average life of nearly 80 years.

Many retired elderly people are insured members of the National Health Insurance program. However, if they do not have enough income and are dependents of their children, they can be covered as dependents of the children's health insurance. In this case, the cost of medical care of the elderly people could be borne evenly among different schemes. But now, as more and more retired people came to live independently on their own pensions, the National Health Insurance came to be a prime insurance scheme for retired people.

The Health Service Law for the Aged introduced the system that every health insurance scheme bear the medical care cost of the elderly evenly, by making a separate account for those 70 years of age and over. In other words, financial coordination was finally realized in the Japanese health insurance system with regard to medical care of the elderly (Ichien & Chester 1983).

Similar coordination or unification was accomplished in the old age pension system by the reforms of 1985. If financing of the pension system is on a pay-as-you-go basis, while the size of the occupational pension scheme is small, and if the size of the pension scheme becomes smaller due to the reduction of the number of employees in the industry, it becomes impossible for the insured employees to raise enough contributions for their retired pensioners. In the case of the Mutual Aid Association of the Japanese Railways (the Japanese National Railways before privatization), there are more pensioners than employees.

In 1985 the pension reform bill was passed to unify the basic components of the different occupational pension schemes and the flat-rate National Pension. By these reforms the different pension schemes with different pensioners–contributors ratios came to contribute evenly to the unified basic pension system, occupational schemes managing only the earnings-related part of the pension (Japan Foundation for Research and Development of Pension Schemes 1986). This unification of the basic pension, together with the financial coordination of medical care for the aged, could be regarded as partial unification of the social insurance system.

The Japanese population is aging very rapidly. The rate of the elderly (65 years and over) in total population increased from 7.1 percent in 1970 to 9.1 percent in 1980 and 11.5 percent in 1989. With this growth of the elderly population, the cost of social security has increased even faster, with the share of the social security cost devoted to the elderly being 25.6 percent in 1973, 43.7 percent in 1980, and 57.2 percent in 1988 (Social Development Research Institute 1990).

In the year 2000, the elderly population will be 16.3 percent of the total population, and in 2010 it will be over 20 percent. During that period, the total cost of a pension will grow much faster than the rate of growth of the retired population as more pensioners will get higher benefits with longer contribution records. It will become necessary in the near future to review and rationalize the framework of the pension structure once again so that the basic part of the pension system can be strengthened in the light of Japan's changing economy (Noguchi 1992).

In the field of medical care, it is apparent that the cost for the aged will continue to grow and that the role of financial coordination will become much larger. In addition, there will be a growing importance of the care of the elderly, or welfare services for the elderly. Indeed, the greatest issue of social security in the 1990s may well be the care of the elderly. Until recently, the Japanese families played a major role in the care of their frail parents, but the families' ability to care for their parents is rapidly decreasing as more families became nuclear families. Services for the elderly will be provided on the basis of the local community rather than on the basis of "occupational community," which has long served as the main instrument of Japanese social insurance. In this sense, the Japanese social security system seems now in the process of moving from an occupational and a company-based system to a system with stronger elements of a unified nation-wide scheme and community service targeting the growing elderly population.

NOTES

1. Those working in a primary industry in the total working population shrank from 48.3 percent in 1950 to 8.8 percent in 1985 (41.0 in 1955, 30.0 in 1960, 23.5 in 1965, 17.4 in 1970, 12.7 in 1975, and 10.4 percent in 1980).

2. For the purpose of calculating contributions and pensions, Japan uses an earning with upper ceiling, excluding bonuses. When the average pension is about 60 percent of the average earning, then that earning is the one used for pension purposes. In other words, the average pension level equals about 45 percent of the average of earnings, including bonuses and so forth.

REFERENCES

Abel-Smith, B. 1983. "Assessing the Balance Sheet" in Glennerster, H. (ed.) *The Future of the Welfare State* (London: Heinemann).

Ichien, M. & Chester, T. E. 1983. "Health Care in Japan—Its development, structure and problems" *The Three Banks Review* 137 (March): 17–26.

Japan Foundation for Research and Development of Pension Schemes. 1986. *National System of Old-Age, Disability and Survivors' Benefits in Japan* (Tokyo: Japan Foundation for Research and Development of Pension Schemes).

Kondo, B. 1963. *Social Insurance* (Tokyo: Iwanami).

Kondo, B. 1971. "Reminiscence" in Secretariat of Advisory Council on Social Security (ed.) *Twenty Years of the Advisory Council on Social Security* (Tokyo: Shakaihoken-Hoki-Kenkyukai).

Kondo, B. 1974. *History of Social Security in Japan* (Tokyo: Kosei-shuppansha).

Noguchi, Y. 1992. "The Changing Japanese Economy and the Need for Fundamental Shift in the Tax System" *American Economic Review* 82 (May): 226–30.

Sakayori, T. 1974. *Social Security* (Tokyo: Iwanami).

Secretariat of Advisory Council on Social Security (ed.). 1961. *Ten Years of the Advisory Council on Social Security* (Tokyo: Shakaihoken-Hoki-Kenkyukai).

Social Development Research Institute. 1990. "The Cost of Social Security in fiscal year 1988" *The Quarterly of Social Security Research* (Japan) 26(3): 320–31.

Soeda, Y. 1985. "Formation of Daily Life Security Law in Postwar Japan" in Tokyo
        University Social Science Institute (ed.) *Welfare State (6) Japanese Soci-
        ety and Social Welfare* (Tokyo: Tokyo University Press).
Steslicke, W. E. 1982. "National Health Policy in Japan: From the Age of Flow to
        the Age of Stocks" *Bulletin of the Institute of Public Health* 31(1): 1–35.
Tada, H. 1977. "The Economic Crisis of Showa Era and Laws Related to Social
        Welfare" in Uda, K. et al. (eds.) *History of Social Welfare* (Tokyo: Yuhi-
        kaku).

4

Politics of Illiberal Capitalism:
The State, Industrialization,
and Social Security in South Korea

M Ramesh

Since the mid-1970s, South Korea has rapidly established an elaborate social security system covering health, old age, invalidity, and poverty. While the programs are less comprehensive than those available in the advanced welfare states, they are more comprehensive than those in most industrializing nations, and certainly more than in the other Asian Newly Industrializing Countries (NICs) (Hong Kong, Singapore, and Taiwan). This is contrary to the widespread perception of Korea as a nation committed to economic development at the expense of other social objectives. An interesting question, then, is why did a nation so ardently committed to economic development channel resources into social security?

Explanations for the origin and development of social security programs are plentiful, but they can be categorized according to their focus on either technological or political factors. A common theme in the technological explanations is the role played by industrialization in creating a need for social security, which is eventually met by society (Cutright 1965; Jackman 1975; Rimlinger 1971; Wilensky 1975; for a Marxist variant of the argument see Gough 1979). While the significance of industrialization in providing the basic prerequisites for the emergence of a modern social security system is undeniable, it would be wrong, as many observers have noted, to ascribe historical inevitability to the process. After all, the other Asian NICs, which are equally or even more industrialized, have not developed similar programs. This fact alone indicated that the adoption of social security cannot be explained solely in terms of functional necessity (Ashford 1986). However, the importance of industrialization and the associated social processes in creating the "need" for social security in Korea cannot be denied and will be acknowledged in this chapter. Yet, it will be argued, the need was addressed only because it served the state's objectives.

The political explanations themselves can be classified according to their emphasis on society—or state-related factors. Among the society-centered explanations, the currently popular "labor mobilization" approach explains the origin and level of social security in terms of the role played by working class movements and their political representatives in forcing recalcitrant governments to adopt policies that advance the interests of labor (Esping-Andersen 1990; Myles 1989; Korpi 1983). The public choice theory, another societal explanation, explains the development of social security in terms of efforts at vote-maximization by politicians and benefits-maximization by voters (see, for example Verbon 1988; Van Velthoven & Van Winden 1985). The relevance of these approaches to the emergence of Korean social security, however, is limited insofar as they presume the existence of liberal democracy and state sanctions allowing for trade unions. It must be remembered that democracy in Korea was severely restricted, and trade unions were banned from engaging in political activities or bargaining freely with the employers throughout the time period in which social security programs were established.

The second set of political explanations, those focusing on the state itself, have much greater potential to help explain the creation of the Korean social security within the context of an "illiberal capitalist" society. In contrast to the society-centered approaches, the state-centered approaches ascribe explanatory importance to the interests and objectives of the state itself (Skocpol 1985; Weir & Skocpol 1985). The state is treated as an autonomous actor with its own financial and bureaucratic resources which it uses in pursuit of its objectives. The extent to which it is successful in achieving its objectives depends on its internal capacity and the capacity of society to resist its efforts. This approach clearly goes the farthest in taking into account the authoritarian character of Korean politics. It permits us to hypothesize that it was the objectives of the state which were paramount in the establishment and design of social security in Korea. It will be argued that social security in Korea was designed to complement the state's industrial strategy, and at the same time to legitimize its authoritarian rule in the face of challenges posed by the spread of democracy and trade unionism. Societal pressures were significant only to the extent they were obstacles the state sought to neutralize through establishing social security, among other measures.

The fact that society-centered theories are inappropriate for explaining policy evolution in non-democratic societies does not mean we cannot draw on them to shed light on certain aspects of Korean politics relevant to the development of social security in the country. Thus, in line with the main thrust of the labor mobilization approach, trade unions in Korea, while weak and state-controlled, were repositories of a potential threat which the state had to take into account and devise measures for containment and appeasement. Similarly, as predicted by the public choice theory, even Korean politicians were not oblivious of the need to work at promoting acceptance of their rule by the public. No state lives by repression alone. Indeed, we will give considerable attention to the fact the Korean state introduced social security partly to blunt opposition to the regime.

One reason for studying the emergence of social security in Korea is simply the fact that it has not been satisfactorily done before. Apart from publications by the economists associated with the Korea Development Institute (KDI), which provide economic accounts of social welfare programs, there is no study that systematically investigates the political and sociological factors underlying their emergence. Such a study would broaden our understanding of politics under late-industrializing capitalism, especially of the illiberal variety. Korea is an especially interesting case because it is one of the few economic success stories of the 1970s, and it would be useful to know the social and political character of its economic success.

SOCIAL SECURITY PROGRAMS IN KOREA

While some social security programs had been established in the 1960s, it was not until the mid-1970s that social development assumed priority with the government in Korea. This shift in priority was reflected in the Fourth Five-Year Development Plan (1977–1981), and re-confirmed in subsequent plans. Until then, social assistance had been provided to the needy on a limited and ad hoc basis. The sequence of adoption of social security programs in Korea has followed broadly the pattern found in the industrialized nations. In western Europe, the order of adoption of welfare programs was: industrial accident insurance, sickness insurance, old age insurance, and unemployment insurance (Flora & Alber 1982: 50). In Korea, industrial injury insurance was established in 1964, medical insurance in 1977, and finally old age pensions in 1988. Unemployment and family benefits available in nearly all industrialized nations are still not available in Korea.

Industrial Injury Insurance

Industrial injury insurance was the first significant social security program to be adopted in Korea. When it was first established in 1964, the program covered only mining and manufacturing firms employing a minimum of 500 workers. The eligibility was decreased to firms employing 200 workers in 1965, which was decreased further to 50 workers in 1969. The coverage continued to be gradually expanded throughout the 1970s, and eventually by 1982 all workers except those in self-employment, in certain service industries, or in firms with less than five workers had been covered. However, despite the expansion in coverage, the program covers only about 26 percent of the work force, largely because the excluded sectors are those consisting mainly of small firms which together employ a very large proportion of the workforce (Chang 1985: 209).

The program is funded entirely out of contributions from employers. The rate of contribution ranges from 0.2 to 4.0 percent of wages, depending on the level of risk in the industry. In 1983, the average rate was 1.24 percent of the wages (Chang 1985: 191). In addition, the government pays for a portion of the administration costs. The benefits cover medical expenses in full if the period of treatment exceeds four days. The program also provides for 60 percent of the wages during the recuperation period. In case of permanent, total, or partial disability, a lump-sum payment is paid equal to between 50 and 1,190 days' wages, depending on the extent of the disability (Park 1975: 37). The program also provides lump-sum payment equal to 1,000 days' wages to the survivors of covered workers who die as a result of industrial accidents.

Health Insurance

On July 1, 1977, Korea established a new health insurance program consisting of two parts: a compulsory program for the employees (and their dependents) of firms employing 500 or more workers and a voluntary, community-based program for all others. The compulsory program was extended to firms with at least 300 workers in 1979, and further to firms with at least 16 workers in 1983. Government officials and school teachers were brought under coverage in 1979, military personnel in 1980, and pensioners in 1981 (Yeon 1989: 10–11). The program was extended to the self-employed in the rural areas in 1988, and to the urban self-employed in 1989. As a result of the expansion in coverage, health insurance has covered 90 percent of the population since July 1989 (Kwon nd: 1). The remaining 10 percent is covered under Medical Assistance, which is a public assistance program for the poor.

The funding for health insurance comes from payroll taxes levied on employers, supplemented by co-payments by beneficiaries, and by government contribution from tax revenues. The average premium rates for industrial workers, civil servants, and the self-employed is 1.7 percent, 2.3 percent, and 1.5 percent, respectively, of their wages. The effective co-insurance rate is very high, as direct payments by patients accounted for 51.2 percent of total health care expenditures in 1989, even though it was a decline from 83.6 percent in 1980 (Kwon nd: 7). Government subsidies (which are mainly earmarked for the regional programs and Medical Assistance) are expected to account for nearly 28 percent of all public expenditures on health care (Kwon nd: 8). The premiums, combined with co-payments and government subsidy, are more than enough to pay for the average annual benefits disbursed. In fact, in 1988, the funds for civil servants and industrial workers showed an average surplus of about 20 percent, while those for the self-employed showed an average surplus of about 5 percent (Kwon nd: 22).

Old Age, Invalidity, and Survivors Pensions

All public employees have been covered by a civil service pension program since 1960. Military personnel were separated from the main plan in 1963 and brought under a separate program established especially for them. The programs provide for annual pensions equivalent to 50 percent of the final year's salary for those who have been in public service for 20 years (Park 1975: 37). In 1973, a similar program was established for university and private school teachers (the public school teachers were covered under the program for the civil servants). Despite the expansion in coverage, in 1975 pension programs covered only 5.2 percent of the working population. These are insurance programs financed from equal contribution by the employer (that is, the government) and employees.

In 1973, the government adopted the National Welfare Pension Act, but the Act was not implemented because of economic difficulties at the time (National Pension Corporation nd: 2). In 1986, thirteen years after the earlier attempt, the government passed another similar act, which was fully implemented in January 1988. The program covers all persons between the age of 18 and 60 who are not covered by previously existing programs. Participation in the program is compulsory for employees of workplaces employing 10 or more persons. Those working in firms employing between five and nine workers will be covered in 1991. Participation in the program is voluntary for persons in self-employment.

The basic old age pension is payable from age 60 to those who have been insured for 20 years or more. Invalidity pensions, ranging from 60 to 100 percent of the old-age pension, are paid to those who have contributed for at least a year and become disabled as a result of sickness or injury. The exact amount of the invalidity pension is determined by the degree of disability. The program also provides a pension to the survivors of insured persons ranging between 40 and 60 percent.

The benefits payable under the National Plan consist of two parts: an income equalized and an income proportional components. The former is calculated as a proportion of the average monthly remuneration of all insured persons in the year preceding the year of pension payment, and the latter is based on the average standard monthly remuneration during the aggregate insured term of the insured person. The pension benefits for civil servants, military personnel, and school teachers are strictly income proportional.

Under the National Plan, the average level of benefit payable to those insured for 20 years is approximately 40 percent of the last monthly remuneration (National Pension Corporation nd: 7). While the plan replaces a higher percentage of the income for low income earners than for high income earners, in absolute terms, those with higher pre-retirement income receive higher pensions. The income replacement rate in Korea, though comparable to the average in the OECD nations, is far below countries like Austria (68 percent), Italy (69 percent), and Sweden (68 percent), but higher than such nations as Canada (34 percent), Denmark (29 percent), and the United Kingdom (31 percent) (Gordon 1988: 61).

The National Plan is funded from equal contributions by employers and employees as a percentage of their salary. Between 1988 and 1992, the employer and employee each pay 1.5 percent of the salary, but from 1993 they will each pay 6 percent, which will be subsequently raised to 9 percent in 1998. The contribution of those participating in the voluntary plan is calculated according to the average income of all wage earners, and they pay the whole amount themselves. The premiums for the plans for civil servants, military personnel, and school teachers are substantially higher than that for the National Plan. The government bears the costs of administering the programs. The programs also benefit from returns to investments from the accumulated fund.

Public Assistance

Besides the social insurance programs for the sick and the old, the state also provides need-based public assistance. The Livelihood Protection Act of 1961, which provided for income maintenance for the poor, has been expanded over the years. The recipients as a percentage of the population increased from 3.8 percent in 1975 (a year of exceptionally high economic growth rate, which was reflected in lower incidence of poverty) to 8.7 percent in 1982 (a year of recession), after which it declined gradually, and in 1988 it was 5.4 percent (Yeon 1989: 15).

Assistance under the Act is available to two groups of people: those unable to work (because of age or physical or intellectual disability) and the working poor. To be eligible for benefits, the applicants must have an income below an annually set limit; in 1980, it was equivalent to 19.2 percent of the average wage (Fisher 1987, 212). There has been a growing trend toward making the able-bodied beneficiaries work at low-paying seasonal work projects (Fisher 1987: 213). Beyond a doubt, the eligibility criteria and the meagre benefits make it difficult for anyone but the economically destitute to claim benefits.

The Medical Assistance Program, established in 1977, is designed specifically for those unable to pay for medical care. Recipients are divided into three categories: first, the poor and those unable to work (the disabled, the aged, and so forth with a monthly income of less than 44,000 Won); second, the able-bodied persons with low means (with a monthly income of less than 44,000 Won and assets valued at less than 3.2 million Won); and third, the able-bodied persons with marginal means (with a monthly income of less than 54,000 Won and assets valued at less than 5.4 million Won worth of assets) (Kwon nd: 34). All medical services are free for those in the first category. The program pays for all outpatient expenses and 40 percent of the inpatient rates in big cities, and 20 percent in other areas for those in the second category. For those in the third category, it pays for two-thirds of the outpatient expenses and 50 percent of the inpatient rates in big cities, and 40 percent in other areas. Between 1978 and 1980, about 6 percent of the population benefited from the program, which increased to about 10 percent during the 1986–88 period (Yeon 1989: 9). The program is paid out of general government revenues, supplemented by co-payments in some cases.

THE MARKET-REINFORCING CHARACTER OF
KOREAN SOCIAL SECURITY

If Korean social security is judged, following Esping-Andersen, by the degree to which it permits people to make their living independently of pure market forces, then the Korean arrangement does not go very far (Esping-Andersen 1990). As will become apparent in the subsequent discussion, it does not provide an alternative to the market for income. Using Titmuss's distinction between residual and institutional welfare states, the Korean social security system clearly falls in the former category (Titmuss 1958). In residual systems, the state assumes responsibility for the welfare of the citizens only when the family and the market fail. Korean social security is explicitly designed to maintain the family and market as the primary mechanisms for assisting those in need.

The total public expenditure on social development underscores the point that economic development, and even defense, are matters of higher priority with the state. The share of the total (central) government expenditures on social development in 1988 (excluding education) was 17.2 percent (Lee 1990: 10). While this was an increase from 11.7 percent in 1975, it was still low by international standards (Lee 1990: 11). It was also considerably lower than the share of the expenditures devoted to defense (21.2 percent) or economic development (24.4 percent) (Lee 1990: 10). Yeon has calculated that given Korea's level of economic development, Korea's social development expenditure should be more than twice what it is if it were to be comparable to the international trend (Yeon 1989: 6).

The low expenditure on social security is partly a result of the social insurance strategy adopted by the Korean state. Health, old age, survivors, and invalidity benefits are for the most part available only to those who have contributed to the relevant schemes during their period of employment. The problem here is that those outside the work force are left out and therefore must resort to means-tested public assistance.

Moreover, by tying benefits to wages, the social insurance strategy adopted by the state serves to perpetuate wage differentials during the period of employment. In the case of pensions, for example, by providing higher pension benefits to those who had higher income in their working life, and are hence likely to have saved more, the system contributes more to the preservation of social status of the aged than to satisfying needs arising from reduction in income after retirement. The insurance strategy is, of course, eminently suited to capitalism because it only slightly tampers with the market process, yet is able to address the eventualities when working individuals cannot participate in the market.

The public assistance component of Korean social security also does not undermine the market system, for it is available only to those suffering from acute poverty. Even then, it provides them with only meagre assistance, which ensures that reliance on the market for one's livelihood is not undermined. That the state wants to discourage the use of public assistance is confirmed further by the fact that between 1975 and 1987, government expenditures on social insurance programs, which depend on contributions and hence are less income redistributive, increased at the expense of public assistance programs, which are more redistributive (Yeon & Kim 1989: 8).

Similarly, the high rate of co-payment in the case of health insurance is intended to force the sick to continue to act rationally in seeking health services, even though they are covered by insurance. The need to ensure that the social security system does not reduce the incentive for active participation in the market was stated clearly in one of the KDI documents:

A welfare program may give beneficiaries the wrong impression that the state should provide benefits for the needy at all times. Furthermore, excessive welfare outlays resulting from an overly rapid expansion of social welfare programs may dampen people's desire to work and the private sector's drive to grow, thus adversely affecting the vitality of the national economy. Therefore, Korea is trying to pursue a social security policy of gradual improvement. (Kwon 1989: 22)

The unmistakable objective of Korean social security is to prevent the establishment of a welfare state that might undermine the market.

Even the establishment of social security programs indicates that equity was not their primary concern. Instead of beginning with social security for the weakest sections of the society, Korea began with the economically stronger sections employed in the public service and in large firms. Moreover, high co-payment for health services means the higher-income earners are able to make greater use of it. Similarly, the industrial injury insurance is not available to those who arguably need it the most. The workers in the smaller firms, which are less likely to adhere to occupational safety standards and thus expose their employees to greater risk, are excluded from the program.

FACTORS UNDERLYING THE ESTABLISHMENT OF
SOCIAL SECURITY IN SOUTH KOREA

Any discussion of the emergence of social security in Korea must include both the technological conditions that create the need for it and the political factors that lead to meeting the need. It was the industrialization and modernization of Korea that created the pre-conditions for the establishment of social welfare programs. But it was the state's industrialization strategy, and its efforts to legitimize harsh measures necessary for the success of the strategy in the face of the spread of democracy and trade unionism, that precipitated the establishment of social security.

Economic Development in Korea

No discussion on the emergence of social security can be complete without considering the role of economic development in general and industrialization in particular. Migration to urban centers in the wake of capitalist industrialization weaken family and community ties and increase workers' exposure to insecurities of the market. Those that cannot participate in the market process, and hence have no or inadequate income, are left without support, unless it is provided by charities or the state. At another level, industrialization is accompanied by decreases in birth rates and longer life expectancy, which result in an increase in the number of the elderly as a proportion of the total population. The increase in the elderly population, who have a reduced or no income, generates pressures for public programs to address their health and income needs.

By any measure, the 1960s and 1970s were a period of extraordinary growth in the industrialization of Korea. Between 1963 and 1980, real GNP grew annually at an average rate of 8.7 percent (Yeon 1989). Between 1960 and 1976, the share of the Gross National Product (GNP) accounted for by manufacturing and mining almost doubled, increasing from 15.7 percent to 31.1 percent (Chung 1979: 498). Relatedly, the size of the work force engaged in production, in percentage terms, doubled between 1963 and 1979. In terms of absolute numbers, production workers more than doubled from 1.15 million in 1963 to 1.96 million in 1971, and then doubled again to 4.11 million in 1979 (Bognanno 1987: 128). As a result of these developments, by the mid-1970s, the pool of salaried workers was large enough to support self-financing insurance schemes on actuarial grounds.

With rapid industrialization came rapid urbanization. The share of the urban population increased from 28.0 percent in 1960 to 48.4 percent in 1975, and increased further to 57.2 percent in 1980 and 65.4 percent in 1985 (Kwon 1986: 3). The figures do not include the population in townships, which grew especially quickly. As a result of urbanization, the ratio of the number of extended families to that of nuclear families in Korea as a whole declined from seven to three in the early 1980s (Chang 1985: 203). As a result of the break-down of extended families, which had traditionally played the strongest role in providing economic security to needy individuals, the only practical alternative was for the state to bridge the gap if widespread poverty was to be avoided.

The low life expectancy of the population, coupled with a high birth rate, up to the 1960s made for a youthful population and, as a result, less pressure for public policies to address the income and health needs of the elderly. But the birth rate declined sharply in the 1960s and 1970s. The total fertility rate declined from 6.0 in 1960 to 4.2 in 1970, 3.1 in 1975, and 2.7 in 1980 (Kwon 1986: 7). At the same time, the average life expectancy increased from 52.6 years in the 1955–60 period to 67.4 years in 1975 (Chung 1979, 518). As a result, the proportion of those over 60 years old increased from 5.2 percent in 1973 to 6.8 percent in 1986, and is expected to increase to 10 percent by the year 2000 (Min 1988: 200). In terms of numbers, the elderly increased from 1.8 million in 1973 to 2.8 million in 1986. The average annual growth of the elderly population during the 1970s was 3.4 percent (compared to only 1.9 percent for the population as a whole), and this was expected to increase in subsequent decades.

The Need for Public Support for the Sick

Despite the rapid economic growth and improvements in the standard of living, the poor in Korea have inadequate access to health care. A government survey showed that the proportion of the residents who went without medical services for economic reasons was 16 percent of the population in large cities, 26.7 percent in medium and small cities, and 41 percent in rural areas (Chung 1979: 522). In 1971, 58.5 percent of the population in large cities, 64.4 percent in medium and small cities, and 46.1 percent in rural areas relied on pharmacists rather than doctors for medical treatment (Chung 1979: 529). It would be reasonable to assume that they were avoiding treatment by qualified doctors for economic reasons.

The high private costs of medical and hospital services was reflected in the under-utilization of health facilities. The occupancy rate for both government (49 percent) and private (55–61 percent) hospitals was low (Park 1980: 108). Physicians were also under-utilized, as they saw on average only 15 patients a day. The problem was lack of purchasing power among the populace, not that they did not need a physician or hospital services. Subscription to private health insurance, which could potentially bridge the problem, was negligible. The churches, which in the past had played an important role in providing health services, had been cutting back their activities because of growing costs. The employers in Korea had never played any significant role in providing health services to their employees (Park 1980: 118–19).

The Need for Public Support for the Elderly

A large number of people in Korea, as elsewhere, reach retirement without accumulating sufficient reserves to support themselves in their retirement years. The average personal savings rate for the Koreans between 1960 and 1972 was 3.6 percent (Park 1975: 27). This could hardly be sufficient to provide for housing, education, and other necessities, and yet leave enough for use after retirement. In addition to personal savings, there were voluntary, mutual aid societies for farm workers, fishermen, and teachers that provided income maintenance against retirement and other contingencies to the subscribers. But these covered only a small section of the population. Private life insurance provided another mechanism for income maintenance for the retired, but again, it covered only 11 percent of the population in 1972 (Park 1975: 33). Even for those covered, the value of policies was frequently substantially below what was required to pay for living expenses during retirement. Given these inadequacies, in 1983, more than 78 percent of the elderly in Korea depended on their children for support. This form of support, of course, was being eroded by the spread of the nuclear family.

State and Industrialization in Korea

While the rapid rate of industrialization, economic growth, urbanization, an aging population, and the fact that a large number of people had inadequate access to health services or had insufficient reserves to see them through their retirement were serious problems, these factors did not make the establishment of social security in Korea inevitable. Many other developing countries, especially the other Asian NICs, were going through similar experiences that did not translate into the emergence of social security. The establishment of social security in Korea, as elsewhere, was a conscious political action that requires a political explanation to account for it. The political context surrounding the action was the authoritarian character of the Korean state and the key role it played in industrialization.

The "strong state" in Korea and the critical role it has played in the industrialization process has been a prominent theme in the literature on the country. The strong state machinery was inherited from the Japanese, who had overdeveloped the bureaucracy and police for their own colonial purposes between 1910 and 1945. The American occupation forces at the end of the Second World War had further reinforced the state apparatus as a check against the spread of communism. The military coup of 1961, and the subsequent wholesale disbanding and reorganization of all political and social organizations that could potentially pose political threats, strengthened the state even more. The declaration of emergency in 1971 and the institution of the authoritarian Yishun constitution in the following year extended the strength of the state.

The Korean state at the time of independence (1948) was not only strong, it was also considerably autonomous from the civil society. The bourgeoisie and the working class were an insignificant force as a result of Japanese colonization, which had stifled industrialization and thus retarded their emergence. The landed class, which was powerful at the time of independence, had its back broken by land reforms in the 1940s and 1950s that imposed low ceilings on land ownership. The state thus enjoyed an unchecked dominance over civil society.

Rapid industrialization after the mid-1960s no doubt created a significant domestic bourgeoisie, but this was a class completely dependent on the state for survival (Deyo 1989: 46). The state controlled it through generous loans and subsidies (or their denial to recalcitrants), protection from imports, and light taxation. The trade unions could have been potentially strong due to rapid industrialization and the resulting expansion of the working class, but were ruthlessly controlled to ensure their subordination. The state played a direct role in selection of trade union leaders and could count on their support for its policies. In addition, there were numerous legal and extra-legal restrictions limiting the role of trade unions.

In conjunction with measures to weaken potential political opposition, the state took measures to reward the bureaucracy and military, whose support was crucial for the survival and success of the regime. As such, it directed a large portion of the public spending on social development at the relatively well-paid civil servants and military personnel. Pensions were first made available to the civil service and the military, and these two segments of the ruling alliance were also the first to be covered by health insurance. In fact, social security in Korea until the mid-1970s meant social security for the civil service and military, and even now they are looked after better than the rest of the population (Park 1975: 46).

The primary objective of the Korean state between the mid-1960s and the mid-1980s was export-oriented industrialization, which has had a pervasive impact on political and social development of the country. The success of the strategy is contingent upon low wages and industrial peace, which are necessary for the country to be attractive to foreign investors and for the domestic producers to be competitive in the world market (Deyo, Haggard & Koo 1987: 46). In Korea, it was the state that played the pivotal role in securing these conditions.

Ensuring low wages was, of course, easy in a labor-surplus situation, which characterized the Korean economy until the mid-1970s. The migration from rural areas and the increasing participation of women in the workforce exerted constant downward pressure on wages. The annual wage guidelines set by the government further ensured that wage increases did not get out of hand. Wage costs were also kept down by the generally low occupational health and safety standards (Teal 1988: 252).

The situation, however, changed when the government initiated the strategy of chemical and heavy industrialization in the mid-1970s. The industries involved in this phase of industrialization were generally capital-intensive and relied on relatively more skilled, yet cheap, labor and could ill afford labor unrest. This was of course difficult to achieve in a tightening labor market. Yet it was crucial for the state to ensure labor peace without allowing excessive wage increases, for a great deal was at stake in the success of this strategy. Between 1977 and 1979, 80 percent of the total investments in manufacturing were directed at such industries, largely in the form of cheap "policy loans" (Haggard & Moon 1983: 217). The strategy's failure would have had severe repercussions on the economy and eventually the state.

The state was sponsoring the transition toward heavy industries at a time when the economy was experiencing a shortage of skilled labor and wages were rising at an unprecedented rate. The official unemployment rate had decreased from 8.2 percent in 1963 to 3.9 percent in 1976 (Chung 1979: 499), and the past practice of suppressing or ignoring labor's demands could not continue in the same form. At the same time, allowing wages to rise excessively would have threatened the competitiveness of Korean exports and the country's attractiveness to foreign investment. As it was, wage increases in the mid-1970s had been unusually high—real wages (at 1975 prices) increased by 17.5 percent, 19.9 percent, and 18 percent in 1976, 1977, and 1978, respectively (Bognanno 1987: 130)—and there was a perceived need for action to contain them.

The task before the state was to hold the line on wages, and at the same time create conditions for the development of skills and human resources. It was largely successful in accomplishing these seemingly contradictory objectives through a mixture of repression and concessions. Between 1971 and 1981, while the real wages had increased at an average annual rate of 7.8 percent, they were still less than the increase in labor productivity, which increased annually by an average rate of 11.12 percent (Launius 1984). As a result of productivity increasing faster than wages, the relative payment share of manufacturing workers fell from 24.8 percent of the GNP in 1961 to 16.5 percent in 1982 (Lim & Paek 1987: 29). This is not surprising given that Koreans worked, according to a study by the International Labor Office, the longest hours of any nation surveyed: men employed in industry worked 52.8 hours, and women 53.5 hours per week. (Launius 1984). Yet, surveys have shown that the average wage in the early 1980s (and most likely during the 1960s and 1970s as well) was significantly less than the minimum necessary for a family (Launius 1984).

The dilemma of improving labor skills to meet the needs of the targeted sectors without allowing excessive wage increases was resolved through a two-pronged strategy of increasing the level of control over the trade unions and the labor market, and at the same time addressing some of labor's needs through social programs. Thus, social security and repressive labor laws were established simultaneously in the 1970s. That explains why industrial workers were the first to bear the brunt of anti-labor laws and were also one of the first to benefit from social security programs. This was after all a tried and tested strategy that had worked well in Germany in the 1880s and in Japan in the 1930s.

In contrast to the 1973 law providing for pensions, which was never implemented, the health insurance law adopted in 1976 was put into effect immediately. Cho has argued correctly that this was largely because the latter was both less costly and more directly helpful for the maintenance of healthy workers, and hence more conducive to productivity growth (Cho 1989: 469). This was especially important for capital-intensive industries that required skilled labor, which was in short supply and not easily replaceable. That explains why manufacturing workers in large firms were the first beneficiaries of industrial injury and health insurances (Flynn & Chung 1990: 242).

However, the social security system that was eventually established also displayed the state's determination to ensure that the benefits to industrial workers did not reduce the producers' competitiveness. The system was required to be self-financing, paid for equally by the employers and employees. That way the state could address the social security needs without jeopardizing its industrialization strategy.

Democratization and Trade Unionism in Korea

Strong and authoritarian as the Korean state was, it was not above the need to take measures to build support among the ruled. Indeed, unlike liberal democracies, which can take a modicum of legitimacy for granted, authoritarian states generally must make greater efforts to garner support for the regime and its policies in order to be successful in the long run. This is especially so in the presence of elections and trade unionism which, no matter how state-controlled, impose an imperative on the state to devise measures to win popular support. All these have been cited as reasons for the early emergence of social security in Germany, and we will argue that they were important in the case of Korea as well (Flora & Alber 1982: 22; Rimlinger 1971: 9; Wilensky 1985: 40).

By giving people a chance to voice their opinions on the performance of the government, elections force states (authoritarian or otherwise) to heed the wishes of the people. While opposition parties in Korea operated under severely restricted conditions and elections were subject to state interference, the very fact there were elections meant the government could not entirely ignore the wishes of the people. No doubt, the tremendous economic growth rate went a long way toward winning support for the government, but it was not sufficient to eliminate opposition. This was evident in the 1971 election when President Park Chung Hee almost lost to Kim Dae Jung despite the fact he was undisputedly credited with engineering Korea's economic success. Soon after the election, his government increased social programs and income support for farmers. This was followed by the adoption of a national pension plan in 1973 and national health insurance in 1977. That the government did heed election results was also evident in the events following the 1985 election in which the ruling party received only 35.3 percent of the popular vote and was able to rule only because of the appointed legislators (Koh 1985: 883–97). The election was followed by a series of reforms in the form of relaxation of trade union laws, greater political freedoms, and expanded social security programs, the most important of which was a new national pension plan.

Another point relevant to the establishment of social security is the fact that the process of democratization was taking place at a time when it was becoming increasingly apparent the fruits of rapid economic growth were not being shared equitably. Table 4.1 shows clearly the increasing disparities in income distribution during the 1970s.

After decreasing in the late 1960s, the income inequality increased markedly in the 1970s, and declined only marginally in the 1980s. The state's industrialization strategy, which disproportionately rewarded big businesses and their senior officials, had played the primary role in increasing the disparities in income distribution (Koo 1984). Democracy, by giving every voter an equal vote, made it difficult for increasing income disparity to continue without some remedial measures. The establishment of social security thus can be seen as the state's effort to gain electoral support while still pursuing its industrial strategy.

Like elections, trade unionism was severely restricted, but even the limited room for political maneuvering was a cause of concern for the state. So long as trade union membership was legal, there was the possibility workers would join them and exert collective pressure on the state and their employers. The expansion of trade union activities in the 1970s was not immediately threatening to the state, but could become so if not handled carefully. As was mentioned earlier, between 1963 and 1979, the size of the work force engaged in production had doubled in terms of percentage and almost quadrupled in terms of absolute numbers. According to one estimate, by 1980, the working class formed 44.7 percent of the population (Lim & Paek 1987: 28). Thus the basic ingredients for class-based politics were already evident by the mid-1970s, and the government could not prevent its emergence by repression alone. As is evident from Table 4.2, the level of unionization in Korea, while low, was not insignificant.

It is noteworthy that trade union membership throughout the two decades was at least 20 percent of the work force. The level of unionization increased, particularly in the mid-1970s, which is significant given that this was a time when the size of the work force itself had expanded rapidly. Of course, what concerned the state most was the possibility of expansion of trade unionism to the extent it might upset its industrial strategy.

Even more dramatic than the increase in trade union membership was the progressive increase in registered labor disputes throughout the 1970s. By 1979, more than half of the collective bargaining had to be resolved through government intervention (Bognanno 1987: 120). Since these are

Table 4.1
Trend of Income Distribution in Korea

PERCENTILE	1965	1970	1976	1980	1985
Upper 20%	41.82	41.62	45.34	45.39	43.71
Lower 40%	19.34	19.63	16.85	16.06	17.71

Source: Lee 1990: 5.

Table 4.2
Trade Union Membership, Labor Disputes, and Work Actions in Korea

Year	Trade Union Membership, %	Registered Labour Disputes	Number of Work Actions
1965	22.2		
1967	22.0		
1969	21.1		
1971	19.6		
1972	20.1	452	
1973	20.2	566	
1974	21.7	942	
1975	22.8	1,139	133
1976	23.0	1,448	110
1977	24.1	2,042	96
1978	23.8	2,131	102
1979	23.4	2,038	105
Jan.–Apr., 1980			848

Sources: Kim 1985: 775; Bognanno 1987: 121.

figures for registered disputes, it is reasonable to assume that the actual numbers were much higher. The figures are all the more remarkable given that the 1971 Special Law on National Security severely limited the subjects open for collective bargaining.

The figures for work action confirm that by the mid-1970s trade unions were a significant force in Korea. While the numbers appear small, it should be remembered that most forms of job actions were banned or severely restricted and, as such, posed significant personal threat to the organizers. Moreover, work actions in non-unionized firms, which are not included in these figures, are likely to have experienced an even greater degree of labor unrest. Bognanno has estimated that during the 1970s, about 12 percent of the contract negotiations involved some form of work action (Bognanno 1987: 122).

The surge in work action in the four months of 1980 following relaxation in the enforcement of labor controls after the assassination of President Park provided a glimpse of the latent labor unrest, which had been concealed by restrictions imposed by the state. After dropping sharply in 1981 and 1982, subsequent to the imposition of harsh controls on trade unions by President Chun, labor unrest started increasing again in 1983. The trend became even more apparent after the liberalization of controls on labor in 1987. In the two months between July 4 and September 4 of 1987, there were more labor disputes than had taken place in the previous ten years. The increase in trade unionism and labor unrest was reflected in the unions' emerging strength in extracting wage and other concessions from the state and employers. In 1987 and 1988, wages increased annually by 15 percent to 20 percent (*Far Eastern Economic Review*, 1990, 16 (March): 84). It is significant that 1988 was also the year when the pension plan for private sector workers was implemented.

CONCLUSION

This chapter first examined the social security programs that have been established in South Korea since the mid-1970s. It found that the programs are designed primarily to benefit the civil servants, military personnel, and workers employed in large and medium-sized firms. Furthermore, they are intended to cause least distortion in the market place and impose minimal burdens on the state. At the same time, by providing for those in society whose support is crucial to the survival of the regime and the success of the economy, they legitimize and reinforce, rather than undermine, the state and market in Korea.

This chapter then examined the factors underlying the establishment of social security in Korea. It found that while rapid industrialization and the accompanying processes of urbanization, atomization of families, and aging of the population created the need for social security, the latter was actually established to address the imperatives of the state's industrialization strategy. The very success of the export-oriented industrial strategy in the late 1960s and early 1970s became a source of problems by the mid-1970s, when the state embarked upon the strategy of promoting heavy industries. The surplus labor had been exhausted by then, and it was becoming increasingly difficult to maintain low wages and industrial discipline. The state took a series of social security measures to ease pressures on wages as well as to legitimize its policy of favoring owners of large firms in targeted sectors. Such a policy was becoming increasingly difficult to continue in the face of increased democratization and trade union militancy.

The theoretical conclusion to be drawn from this analysis is that state-centered explanations are clearly superior in explaining the emergence of social security. They avoid the shortcoming of technological determinism, which assumes that social security automatically follows upon industrialization and economic development. The society-centered explanations have the virtue of giving due importance to political factors, but they suffer from another shortcoming, which is that they assume the presence of liberal democracy and tolerance for free trade unionism. In Korea, both democracy and trade unionism were heavily circumscribed and posed no immediate threat to the state.

Focusing on the objectives and actions of the Korean state itself allows us to avoid these shortcomings. Even then, a nuanced investigation of various factors is necessary, for the interplay of state and societal variables is quite complex in such regimes. Autonomous from control by either the capitalist or working classes, and unencumbered by liberal institutions and procedures, the Korean state could take whatever measure it deemed necessary to accomplish its ultimate goal of rapid industrialization. Repression and concessions were thus but two sides of the same strategy utilized by state managers to obtain compliance with its wishes. In this sense, the state in Korea was merely following in the 1970s what the Germans invented a century earlier and the Japanese refined in the inter-war years: the politics of illiberal capitalism.

REFERENCES

Ashford, D. E. (ed.). 1986. *Nationalizing Social Security in Europe and America* (Greenwich: JAI Press).

Bognanno, M. F. 1987. "Collective Bargaining in Korea: Laws, Practices, and Recommendations for Reform" in Il S.-K. (ed.) *Human Resources and Social Development Issues* (Seoul: Korea Development Institute).

Chang, I.-H. 1985. "Korea, South" in Dixon, J. & Kim, H. S. (eds.) *Social Welfare in Asia* (London: Croom Helm).

Cho, S. 1989. "The Emergence of a Health Insurance System in a Developing Country: The Case of South Korea" *Journal of Health and Social Behaviour* 30 (December): 467–71.

Chung, I.-Y. 1979. "Transition in the Substance of Poverty in Korea" *The Philippine Economic Journal* 18(4): 493–540.

Cutright, P. 1965. "Political Structure, Economic Development and Social Security Programs" *American Journal of Sociology* 70: 537–50.

Deyo, F., Haggard, S. & Koo, H. 1987. "Labor in the Political Economy of East Asian Industrialization" *Bulletin of Concerned Asian Scholars* 19(2) (April–June): 42–53.

Deyo, F. C. 1989. *Beneath the Miracle: Labor Subordination in the New Asian Industrialism* (Berkeley: University of California Press).

Esping-Andersen, G. 1990. *The Three Worlds of Welfare Capitalism* (Oxford: Polity Press).

Fisher, P. 1987. "Social Security in Korea in the Eighties" in Il S. K. (ed.) *Human Resources and Social Development Issues* (Seoul: Korea Development Institute).

Flora, P. & Alber, J. 1982. "Modernization, Democratization, and the Development of Welfare States in Western Europe" in Flora, P. & Heidenheimer, A. J. (eds.) *The Development of Welfare States in Europe and America* (New Brunswick: Transaction Books).

Flynn, M. L. & Chung, Y.-S. 1990. "Health Care Financing in Korea: Private Market Dilemmas for a Developing Nation" *Journal of Public Health Policy* (Summer): 238–53.

Gordon, M. S. 1988. *Social Security Policies in Industrial Countries* (Cambridge: Cambridge University Press).

Gough, I. 1979. *The Political Economy of the Welfare State* (Basingstoke: Macmillan).

Haggard, S. & Moon, C.-I. 1983. "Liberal, Dependent, or Mercantile?: The South Korean State in the International System" in Ruggie, J. (ed.) *The Antinomies of Interdependence* (New York: Columbia University Press).

Jackman, R. 1975. *Politics and Social Equality: A Comparative Analysis* (New York: Wiley).

Kim, K.-D. 1985. "Social Change and Societal Development in Korea since 1945" *Korea and World Affairs* 9(4) (Winter): 756–88.

Koh, B. C. 1985. "The 1985 Parliamentary Election in South Korea" *Asian Survey* 25 (September): 883–97.

Koo, H. 1984. "The Political Economy of Income Distribution in South Korea: The Impact of the State's Industrialization Policies" *World Development* 12(10): 1029–37.

Korpi, W. 1983. *The Democratic Class Struggle* (London: Routledge, Kegan, Paul).

Kwon, S.-W. No Date. "Distributional Consequences of National Health Insurance in Korea" (Discussion Paper) (Seoul: Korea Development Institute).

Kwon, S.-W. 1989. *Review of Current Social Development Policy and Planning* (Seoul: Korea Development Institute).

Kwon T.-H. 1986. *The Trends and Patterns of Mortality and Health in the Republic of Korea* (Bangkok: Economic and Social Commission for Asia and the Pacific)

Launius, M. 1984. "The State and Industrial Labor in South Korea" *Bulletin of Concerned Asian Scholars* 16(4) (October December): 2–10.

Lee, K.-S. 1990. "A New Role of Fiscal Policy and Tax Finance for Social Development in Korea." Paper presented at conference on Tax Policy and Economic Development Among Pacific Asian Countries, Taipei.

Lim H.-C. & Paek W.-S. 1987. "State Autonomy in Modern Korea: Instrumental Possibilities and Structural Limits" *Korea Journal* 27(11) (November): 19–33.

Min J.-S. 1988. "Korea's Pension Scheme: Major Policy Issues." Paper presented at the Joint Conference on Policy Issues in Social Security, October 26–27, Korea Development Institute, Seoul.

Myles, J. 1989. *Old Age in the Welfare State: Political Economy of Public Pensions* (Lawrence, KS: University Press of Kansas).

National Pension Corporation. No Date. *The National Pension Program in Korea: System and Operation* (Seoul: National Pension Corporation).

Park, C.-K. 1975. *Social Security in Korea: An Approach to Socio-Economic Development* (Seoul: Korea Development Institute).

Park, C.-K. 1980. "The Organization, Financing, and Cost of Health Care" in Park, C.-K. (ed.). *Human Resources and Social Development in Korea* (Seoul: Korea Development Institute).

Rimlinger, G. V. 1971. *Welfare Policy and Industrialization in Europe, America and Russia* (New York: John Wiley).

Skocpol, T. 1985. "Bringing the State Back In: Strategies of Analysis in Current Research" in Evans, P. B. Rueschemeyer, D. & Skocpol, T. (eds.) *Bringing the State Back In* (Cambridge: Cambridge University Press).

Teal, G. 1988. "The State, the Labor Process, and Industrial Health and Safety in South Korea" *Labor, Capital and Society* 21(2) (November): 238–69.

Titmuss, R. M. 1958. *Essays on the Welfare State* (London: Allen & Unwin).

Van Velthoven, B. & Van Winden, F.A.A.M. 1985. "Towards a Political-Economic Theory of Social Security" *European Economic Review* 27: 263–89.

Verbon, H. 1988. *The Evolution of Public Pension Schemes* (Berlin: Springer-Verlag).

Weir, M. & Skocpol, T. 1985. "State Structures and the Possibilities for Keynesian' Responses to the Great Depression in Sweden, Britain, and the United States" in Evans, P. B. Rueschemeyer, D. & Skocpol, T. (eds.) *Bringing the State Back In* (Cambridge: Cambridge University Press).

Wilensky, H. L. 1985. *Comparative Social Policy* (Berkeley: Institute of International Studies).

Wilensky, H. L. 1975. *The Welfare State and Equality* (Berkeley: University of California Press).

Yeon H.-C. & Kim K.-Y. 1989. *Major Trends Likely to Influence Future Social Development Patterns* (KDI Working Paper 8929) (Seoul: Korea Development Institute).

Yeon H.-C. 1989. *Social Development in the Republic of Korea: Considerations of Equity Versus Efficiency Issues in Policy-Making* (Seoul: Korea Development Institute).

III.

NATIONAL OVERVIEWS

5

Rural Populations, Social Security, and Legal Pluralism in the Central Moluccas of Eastern Indonesia

Franz von Benda-Beckmann and
Keebet von Benda-Beckmann

In all societies, people's provision with goods and services for their social security stems from a multiplicity of sources. Individuals, or groups of individuals, receive them on the basis of social relationships with other individuals, networks, or groups of individuals, associations, companies, and institutions of the government. Of course, people differ both in the total amount of goods and services that they receive, in the composition of sources from which they derive their social security, and in the extent to which they contribute to the social security of others, but they will typically be connected to several of such sources. There is thus, in nearly all contemporary societies, a multiplicity of social relations on the basis of which individuals provide and receive such goods and services. The sum total of what is received is a mix of social security provisions. In studies of social security, both in Third World and Western industrialized nations, this phenomenon has increasingly been recognized (Bossert 1985; von Benda-Beckmann et al. 1988). While the discussion has largely been carried out in terms of the closely related concepts of social protection, welfare, or support systems (Johnson 1987; Rose 1989), and less in terms of social security, the notion of "welfare pluralism" has gradually won acceptance.

However, this insight has not always led to adequate presentations of the social security arrangements available in a country, or in parts of a country. This is due to the fact that the variety of arrangements is not properly conceptualized. Distinctions between different forms or sectors of social security are often too crude and misleading. Moreover, too much emphasis is usually put on institutions and too little on the people, their needs, and their actual social security situations (for such a view see Rose 1989: 131). In this chapter we shall try to present a description of social security in Indonesia that tries to overcome some of the common short-comings. Since our account follows different lines than usual, it seems useful to set out our approach first at some length before we deal with the situation in Indonesia. We then shall describe the kinds of relationships that people enter into or mobilize to receive or to provide social security and we will demonstrate that many arrangements are governed by different types of norms at the same time, as a result of which there is not only a plurality of social security arrangements, but legal pluralism at the same time. The social security provided through the three main systems—government, "adat" (the local customs and traditions), and religious arrange-ments—will be discussed in their interdependence. For reasons of space we shall have to confine ourselves considerably. In the first place we shall deal with rural populations only. These include not merely people working in the agrarian sector, but also civil servants, traders, and so forth. Since there is enormous economic and legal ("adat" and religious) variation through-out Indonesia, we shall limit ourselves further and concentrate on the Islamic part of the Central Moluccas in eastern Indonesia, an area that we know well from our own field research.[1] We shall start with a brief overview of the types of social security that the Indonesian state has made available and that are of any relevance for its rural populations. Then we shall shift our attention to one particular area, Ambon, and look at the needs for social security of various categories of people and describe the arrangements of social security that are available to people living in rural areas.

SOCIAL SECURITY PLURALISM

In recent years, there has been an increasing interest in the variety of social security arrangements in the literature about both the Third World and industrialized societies.[2] Usually, authors express this mixture of rela-tionships in terms of a dichotomy and distinguish, for example, between formal and informal, or between public and private social security. With respect to Third World countries in which state regulation and provision of social security is a more recent and a less developed phenomenon, another well-known dichotomy, the distinction between traditional and modern, has been employed to indicate that not all social security is provided for by the state. The most recent invention is the distinction between "conventional" and "unconventional" social security, in which "conventional" denotes state regulated or provided social security (Getubig

& Schmidt 1992). Such general classifications of different "sectors" and institutions have had the merit of warning those who think that the state—in whatever society—is the sole provider of social security and that it has not completely smothered private activities and responsibility. One of the main insights from studies in Western societies has been that non-state forms of welfare, largely in-kind in character, do exist, and that in some fields of need they are even more important than the formal sector.[3] But these distinctions have at the same time contributed to some serious misunderstandings by distorting the ways in which the spectrum is perceived and analyzed.[4] The reason for this is that the classification is ambiguous, for it confuses the dimensions of the organization of social security: institutions, legal regulation, and actual relationships. Usually, the sources of regulation and sources of provision are not systematically distinguished, both in what is considered to be the "formal" and the "informal" sector.[5] This distinction also carries important connotations concerning the relationship between the formal/informal characteristics and the social and economic conditions that they refer to. As Connolly mentions, the poverty situation usually implied by informality is immediately explained by the lack of formality (1985: 64), while the formal presupposes a correspondence between certain production relations and good employment conditions and social security services (1985: 78). In this way, the formal/informal terminology not only reinforces the mutually exclusive dichotomy between modern progress and wealth on the one hand and traditional backwardness and poverty on the other, it also diverts attention from the immediate causes of poverty from the modern sector to the non-modern sector (Connolly 1985: 64, 65). The triple distinctions introduced more recently to overcome some of the shortcomings of the earlier dichotomies, such as the distinction between state, market and household (Rose 1989; Pradhan 1990; Fuchs 1985) constitute a significant advance. However, these categories are also problematic because here again no systematic distinction is made between source of provision and regulation, and social relations and institutions are too easily collapsed.[6]

Simple distinctions that collapse sources of providers and sources of regulation into one-dimensional categories are therefore misleading. This is all the more serious, since many relationships within which transfers of goods and services take place are subject to a parallel or duplicatory (plural) normative constitution and regulation, varying from government law, local traditional non-state law, religious law, or unnamed forms of self-regulation of groups or networks of individuals. That is, in addition to a pluralism of social security, there is also "legal pluralism," but plurality of social security institutions and of law and regulations do not necessarily run parallel. This is particularly evident in most contemporary Third World countries such as Indonesia, where different institutionalized systems of legal regulation provide institutions and normative constructions of social security regulation for the population.[7] The conceptions of need and risk embodied in the distinct legal systems may vary.[8] Multiple regulation, stemming from different sources, usually also have different scopes of operation. The state system is set up to provide social security for selected categories of persons all over the state territory, and religious social security regulations may have the same pretension. Local systems based upon tradition on the other hand operate in small-scale networks or groups of people.

A more nuanced perspective at the plural institutional forms of regulation and provision of social security, however, is not sufficient for an understanding of actual social security organization, in particular for understanding the position of people. Taking their departure from the institutional level, analysts tend to "translate down" institutional definitions of providers and receivers to the level of individuals, which then are identified by one distinctive normative-institutional category. It is easily overlooked that such people are involved in other social security relationships at the same time. Social security for civil servants, for example, is regulated by state social security laws. That does not mean, of course, that they are not also relatives, neighbors, friends, and perhaps also participants in private insurance schemes (see also Benda-Beckmann, F. von 1987; Benda-Beckmann, F. von & Benda-Beckmann, K. von 1989). However, these other relationships are rarely discussed in connection with civil servants' entitlements from the state regulations. The combinations of relations, in particular at the receiving end, the social security mixes resulting from such combinations, and the changes therein, must also be studied at the level of individuals and concrete relationships. Since people are involved in various arrangements of social security, based on various legal systems, and involving various goods and services, changes in one arrangement usually have implications for the other arrangements as well. It is only through a study of these mixed forms of social security that one can begin to understand what certain changes in one system may mean for the overall situation of people's social security position (see also Rose 1989).

In order to understand the way people make use of institutions and mobilize potential sources, an interactive perspective is necessary as well. It is through the interactions of people that goods and services are transferred, concrete relationships created and changed, interwoven, or distinguished. Institutions and relationships, whether they are relationships with state social security agencies or with kinsmen, do not work by themselves. They provide no more than options, which may or may not be mobilized and which may be more or less accessible (see Benda-Beckmann, F. von 1987). The simple fact that different social security options are available should not lead us to assume that people have equal access to all types of arrangements. On the contrary, in analogy to Breman's analysis of the Indian labor market, we should presume that the social security market in Third World countries is highly fragmented and to a great extent particularized, with the consequences of domination and suppression (Breman 1987b: 17–18, 21). Even where certain provisions are clearly prescribed by law—whether by state, religious or other law—they still must be mobilized. Failing to recognize that people for various reasons make different use of available options, and that the options are unequally distributed among people, would seriously hamper a proper insight in the actual situation of social security in any area.[9]

Taking such an approach, we cannot follow the common way of defining social security at the institutional or policy level, using classifications of contingencies that are (institutional approach) or should be (policy approach) covered by provisions as exemplified by the ILO definition (ILO 1984) in consequence of the ILO Convention 102.[10] Instead, we prefer to conceive of social security as an abstractly and functionally defined field of problems and try to identify which policies, institutions, relationships, and interactions form the social organization in this field of problems.[11] We take as a point of departure that the field of social security covers all arrangements through which members of a society who are unable, or are threatened to become unable, to make a reasonable living, including food, shelter, health, care, and education according to standards recognized in that part of the society, are to be provided for. Of course, the question of the reasonable standard of living is a normative one, one which may differ in time and space (see also Partsch 1983; Hirtz 1989). Rather than defining such standards ourselves, we think that it should be part of research to inquire how such standards are conceptualized in different societies. Even within one society, there will usually be more than one standard for different categories of people, and different standards may be defined in different normative relations. Moreover, at the institutional level, we must assume that we meet with a great variety in the degree to which social security relations are institutionalized. Some institutions, such as municipal social service departments, have a great degree of bureaucratic organization and are organized as functionally differentiated "institutions of social security." Others are less organized, and the social security aspect of social relations or institutions may not be differentiated from other aspects, integrated or bundled within the relationships. This usually is the case in multiplex or many-stranded relationships such as kinship or neighborhood (see also Partsch 1983). Last but not least, certain transfers, investments, and so forth, which in general bear no relevance to social security, may in specific cases acquire this additional function and become part of a social security package of people involved. Not only governments, but also individuals or groups of people may make their own social security policies. An interactional perspective is crucial here.

Taking these remarks seriously, we do not think that the range of phenomena that we consider to be relevant for an understanding of the social organization of social security could be captured in an institutional definition. Rather than trying to refine the existing definitional approaches, we prefer to identify the whole complex of institutions, relationships, and interactions and their interrelations, and see what their combined operation means for the social and economic life of people.[12]

SOCIAL SECURITY IN INDONESIA: THE LEGAL FRAMEWORK

It is difficult to generalize about the state of social security of the rural population in Indonesia, because there are enormous differences in the composition and the social and economic organization of the rural population, in wealth and income, and in government presence. What can be said is, that on the level of relevant legal ideas and regulations, elements from three distinct systems play a role: the locally developed "adats," which are intermingled with, but distinguished from, religion (for while about 85 percent of the population follow Islam, there are Christian and Hindu minorities), and the Indonesian state legal system. Each of these systems contains ideas about need and distress and defines the conditions under which certain categories of people are to receive or to give support. Each establishes its own institutions or assigns a social security role to existing institutions. But the ways in which the actual relationships and practices of social security combine elements from these regulatory systems vary considerably. Whereas the state legal system has a distinct set of institutions and regulations pertaining to social security, a largely undifferentiated social security function is characteristic of the continually changing "adat." social organization. There are few specifically differentiated institutions of social security in "adat." Transfers of goods and services are mainly embedded in relations of kinship, neighborhood and friendship, both in the organization of "normal" life and in situations or periods of crisis and distress.[13] Provisions of the national state basically are applicable to the whole population, although most schemes are set up for specific groups, such as industrial employees, civil servants, and military. Islamic provisions apply in principle to the whole community of believers. But as will become clear in the next section, there is also considerable local variation in the concrete working of Islamic institutions, since their provisions are interwoven with and partly shaped by local ("adat") forms of social security.

Since the social, economic, and political structure of the various ethnic groups and regions in Indonesia differs substantially, little more can be said here about "adat" forms of social security. We will discuss one region at length, the Islamic part of the Central Moluccas, more in particular the island Ambon. Ambon differs quite considerably from other rural regions in Indonesia, for it is not a rice-producing region, but one in which sago and vegetables are produced in horticulture. An important consequence is that the central Moluccas do not know the yearly recurring periods of severe food shortage shortly before the new rice harvest, which often afflicts people in western Indonesia ("musim pacekelik").[14] It has a distinct "adat" based upon the particular agro-economic setting of the area, and which varies from village to village.

THE STATE SOCIAL SECURITY SYSTEM

The first large-scale state organizations, the Dutch East India Company and the colonial state, have been a constant source of insecurity rather than providing security to the rural population throughout history. Those who staffed the state administration and controlled economic enterprises were more set on exploiting the indigenous natural and human resources for their own benefit than attempting to provide social security to the indigenous population. Where the state or European settlers engaged in production, working conditions were largely abominable (see Breman 1987a). While the establishment of a state political organization and the spread of the money economy seriously affected the local social organizations, including the local mechanisms of social security, the local populations remained dependent on these mechanisms. After Independence in 1949, some important changes were initiated. The Indonesian state adopted general principles of responsibility toward its subjects, in which welfare rights took an important place. Social justice ("keadilan sosial") became one of the five "pillars" of the state philosophy ("Panca Sila").

The Indonesian state has started to develop a system of social security. It regulates and provides social security in different ways in which different ministries are involved. The general policy ideas and the concrete institutionalized forms are heavily influenced by the development of the official, institutionally differentiated forms of social security that have emerged in Western industrialized states. In the first place, the state system offers income substitution in case of adversity to certain categories of the population. The development of an official system of social security in Indonesia, in the sense of the ILO Convention 102, has been relatively slow if compared to other developing countries.[15] Social security long remained more or less restricted to civil servants and members of the armed forces and the police. Recently, the state, by the Ministry of Labor, has issued laws and regulations concerning income substitution in case of adversity for the private sector as well (Soepomo 1983: 142 ff).

Civil servants and members of the armed forces receive at present comparatively good pensions in case of sickness, invalidity, or old age.[16] Old age pensions amount to 2.5 percent of the basic salary per year in service, with a minimum of 40 percent and a maximum of 75 percent (Prawotosoediro 1982: 95). Given the retirement age of 55, payments may have to be made for up to 30 years. Civil servants pay 10 percent of their salary to social security funds. From this, five percent are paid into the pension fund to which the government contributes from its own budget; the rest is divided among the provident fund and the health insurance scheme (Esmara & Tjiptoherianto 1986: 60).

The schemes for the private sector are of the insurance type and involve regular monthly payments by registered workers who have more or less regular work. The programs ("Asuransi Sosial Tenaga Kerja" [ASTEK]) include widows' and orphans' pensions as well as payments in case of accidents, but no old age pension or health insurance. There is a provident fund for old age allowances.[17] Until 1983, social insurance programs were obligatory for companies with more than 100 workers and a capital of 5,000,000 rupiah, but the scope has now been expanded. Since 1983, companies with more than 25 workers and a capital of at least 1,000,000 rupiah have been required to participate. While reliable statistical data are not available, there is no doubt that the majority of companies falling under these requirements do not in fact participate fully (see also Joenoes 1982; Esmara & Tjiptoherianto 1986: 64; ILO 1985; Benda-Beckmann, K. von 1988). In 1992, new and ambitious social security legislation was passed, which considerably extended coverage.[18] It includes a full scale of benefits to workers, and in principle every worker is entitled to coverage, although participation will be phased in over time.[19] "Worker" is defined to include those who are self-employed and would in theoretical principle also comprise the large masses of people working in what is considered to be the "informal" sector in small enterprises who still live without any form of insurance regulated by the state, as well as the rural population mainly engaged in agriculture as farmers or agricultural laborers.

Apart from income substitution schemes, the Ministry of Social Affairs had in the 1980s started to set up social security projects for four categories of needy persons: widows, orphans, the disabled, and the aged.[20] These projects are directed at income-generating activities for the participants who are to set up small-scale trading or productive enterprises. The Department of Social Affairs provides a non-refundable input lump sum of 300,000 rupiah as a starting capital, which may be provided in money and goods. The subsidy is meant as a stimulus to set up projects that will become self-supporting and, after some time, will make profits enabling participants to send their children to school.

Furthermore, the government finances various kinds of institutions and projects that aim at increasing the general level of income of those with a "weak economic situation" ("ekonomi lemah"), in order to overcome some of the main risks of falling into poverty. Among them are the village cooperatives ("kooperasi unit desa" [KUD]), which are strongly controlled and firmly built into the administrative hierarchy of the government. They are linked via provincial Centers of Cooperatives ("Pusat Kooperasi Unit Desa" [PUSKUD]) to the Ministry of Labor, Transmigration and Cooperatives. The activities of the village cooperatives are geared at the improvement of production through collective and subsidized provision of technology (fertilizer, new varieties, new agricultural knowledge) and marketing. In the Central Moluccas they are mainly involved in clove trading.

Finally, there are basic services to increase the welfare but which are not primarily directed at increasing the level of income. To this category we count the family welfare movement ("pembinaan kesejahteraan keluarga" [PKK]), started in 1973 and the program for the improvement of women's roles to achieve a healthy and prosperous family ("peningkatan peranan wanita menuju keluarga sehat dan sejahtera" [P2W-KSS]). The PKK is directed at women as a channel through which the government may set up various programs to increase human resource management, to enhance social welfare of women, and to gain support for government policies in general (Sajogyo 1988: 229). It is funded by the regular budgets of the national, provincial, and local governments, to which the women add their labor and some cash. The organization is in the hands of the wives of the highest administrative official at each level of government (Sajogyo 1988; Wieringa 1988; Suryakusuma 1988).

Village health centers may be counted among the category of social security provisions. Health centers have been set up in many villages throughout Indonesia. In most areas, basic health care is available within a day's travelling.

RELIGIOUS LAW

With the Islamization of most parts of rural Indonesia, the ideas of social justice and duties of assistance to the poor and needy of the Islamic religion and law came to Indonesia. Several passages in the Koran refer to the desirability of charity. The most prominent institution that embodies social security and charity functions is "zakat," the alms-tax. There are two forms of "zakat"; "zakat mal," a property tax, and "zakat al fitrah," the personal "zakat," which has to be given by every believer at the end of the fasting month in the form of a specified amount of agricultural produce. Islamic law specifies eight categories of beneficiaries of "zakat," among which the poor and the needy ("fakir miskin"), converts to Islam, and the collectors of "zakat" are the most relevant ones in the Indonesian context. According to the Shafi'ite school, generally followed in Indonesia, the "zakat" must be distributed equally among the categories after a reduction in the form of a reward for the collectors of "zakat." The ways in which "zakat" has been incorporated into Indonesian social and political organizations varies widely, and we shall discuss the situation on Ambon later. The general impression one gets from the scarce sources is that property "zakat" is rarely paid according to the official Islamic rules. "Zakat al fitrah" seems to be given in most Islamic areas in Indonesia. However, how "zakat" is collected and distributed varies. In some areas, most "zakat" is given to the religious leaders (mosque officials, religious leaders) who then do, or do not, redistribute. In other areas, people prefer to give their "zakat" directly to whom they consider to be poor and needy (see Benda-Beckmann, F. von 1988).

In a more general sense, Islamic law obliges blood relatives in the direct patri-line (descent/ascent) to support each other and, if necessary, to provide each other with the means of livelihood ("nafakah") (Juynboll 1925: 223). Besides food and housing livelihood comprises clothing and care in case of sickness (Juynboll 1925: 199). Only those who themselves are not capable of providing for their own nuclear family are excepted from this obligation. The provision of livelihood is also a strict obligation of a husband towards his wife. After divorce, this obligation extends during the "iddah" period, four months and ten days (see Juynboll 1925: 205).

SOCIAL SECURITY ON AMBON

The population in Ambonese villages is not homogeneous. The large majority is formed by ethnic Ambonese, who earn their living through agricultural and horticultural activities, as fishermen or petty traders. Many villages have a considerable immigrant population, mainly Butonese, who have migrated from the southeast of Sulawesi to the Central Moluccas in search of land and working opportunities. Increasingly also, villages have become the residence of civil servants, of Ambonese, or those of other ethnic origin. In the village of Hila, a sub-district capital village at the northern coast of the island, of a population of about 4,400 inhabitants 1,700 are of Butonese origin. There are about 20 retired government officials, mostly from the police and military. In addition, about 50 civil servants live and work in Hila, in the sub-district administration, the health center, in the two primary schools, and in the lower and higher secondary school. Hila has a health center with a number of trained nurses, a trained midwife, a birth control officer, and a young doctor visiting twice a week from Ambon city. Most villagers make frequent use of these services. They consider them to be a welcome addition to more traditional health care, to be used alternatively or additionally. Together with a neighboring village, Hila has a village cooperative (KUD) with about 250 members. The women's social welfare project (P2W-KSS) never came off the ground in Hila. The social projects set up by the Provincial Department of Social Affairs will be discussed below. The social security mixes of Hila villagers vary considerably. They are substantially different for Ambonese and Butonese, but vary also within the ethnic groups for civil servants and farmers, according to the degree to which people are plugged into the different sets of relationships through which goods and services were transferred.

BASIC MECHANISMS OF LIVELIHOOD
AND SOCIAL SECURITY

For most Ambonese villagers, goods and services required for daily needs and in situations or periods of distress are produced and distributed through general social and economic relationships. In the "adat"-based social organization, there are no differentiated institutions with a specific social

security function. Nuclear families form the most important cluster of
people and relations. In Hila, about 50 percent of the nuclear families live
in one-family houses; the other houses are used by two or more nuclear
families. Adult sons with their wives may live with their parents, but most
young couples regard that as a temporary arrangement, though it may last
for many years. In theory, the youngest son remains in the parental house
and is expected to take care of his parents when they grow old. However,
most elderly people, especially women, prefer to live with and be taken care
of by a daughter. Often a widowed or divorced brother and sister move in
together and provide for each other. Women over 35 years often do not
want to remarry because they consider themselves beyond the age of
childbearing and prefer to stay on their own. Elderly people without
children or grandchildren often adopt young relatives as "adopted children" ("anak angkat") or foster children ("anak piara") (see Strijbosch
1988; Benda-Beckmann, K. von 1991). Living in the same house does not
always mean pooling all resources for food preparation and consumption.
Thirty percent of the two or more nuclear family houses have more than
one kitchen and consumptive unit. If a relationship between mother and
daughter-in-law is good, they may share a kitchen, but often adult women
each have their own kitchen. There are still some traditional family (clan)
houses, which function as a "reserve" living space for individuals or couples
who want to move out of their parents' home but have not yet been able
to build a house for themselves. Besides, family ceremonies may be cele-
brated there.

The care of children, the elderly, the sick, and the disabled is primarily
a task for the closest co-residing relatives, or else for parents, children,
especially daughters, grandparents, and grandchildren. It is this circle of
persons to whom one can always turn. Within this circle it is difficult to
deny a request for help even if there are no additional ties of friendship or
co-residence. Neighbors play an important role in the provision of help,
but only if they maintain friendly relations or if they are kin. More distant
kin usually hardly play a role, unless they are also friends or a special
relationship of reciprocity has been established earlier. The basic circle of
kin who bear the main responsibility for each other thus is quite limited,
especially if several children have migrated. Only during special occasions,
such as big weddings, funerals, and other big ceremonies, do people coop-
erate and support each other on a large scale (Benda-Beckmann, K. von
1991; Bartels 1989). The cooperation on such occasions is not institutionalized in the form of mutual help associations ("muhabat") like in Christian
Ambonese villages (see Cooley 1962: 105; Strijbosch 1988: 171). It is

organized ad hoc on the basis of kinship, friendship, and neighborhood. For exceptional expenses or services, such as paying a hospital bill, one may turn to more distant kin, but even then the mere fact of being kin is not enough, and special relationships, especially and preferably with relatives in government service, are required.

For the provision of basic food, sago, vegetables, root crops, and fish a family needs little help. Although land is not equally distributed, most Ambonese villagers usually have access to and work upon land that they either have inherited, brought in cultivation, or purchased, rented, or pawned (see also Taale 1991). Most adult couples have a garden in which they grow cassava and vegetables for their own consumption. In former times, the gardens were rather close to the residential area. During the past 20 years, however, the residential center of the village has become filled up with houses, and the distance between people's houses and their gardens has become greater. This has led to problems for those elderly people whose garden land is at some distance in the hills. Going and working there becomes too burdensome, and they no longer can maintain a garden by themselves. They then depend on the gifts from their relatives and friends. A healthy adult does not need much help, apart from the first clearing, which is mostly the work of men, although women have done it on their own. Sometimes two sisters, mother and daughter, or two friends will cultivate adjacent gardens, but each has its own fence, even though they may always work together.

Nearly all people own or have at least easy access to sago palms. Sago can be harvested all year round and thus provides a constant source of basic food. Cooperation in food production is very much done on an ad hoc and voluntary basis. Sago palms are usually harvested by teams of three friends or relatives, but if necessary a single man can grind and wash the pith, and a single woman can bake bread or cook porridge. Fish may be caught individually, but many prefer to buy it.

Traditionally, housing provided little problems. The traditional Ambonese houses were constructed from materials that were easily accessible: wood, coral stone, and sago leaf stalks. They were built in mutual cooperation on the basis of labor exchange (masohi). Nowadays, the building of modern stone houses requires many more materials that can only be acquired with money, such as concrete, bricks, and zink plates for the roof. Also, the building process has changed. Modern concrete houses are built in a combination of masohi and work by professionals (tukang). Because the village center has no open spaces left, new houses are increasingly built outside the village core, and it has become more difficult to acquire the land. One's clan may not have land in the preferred area close to the coast and the main road; besides, there is increasing competition between agricultural and residential land use. Sales of land have become more frequent over the past two decades. It is, however, still possible to build simple houses with wood and sago palm materials, if necessary, without much help from other people.

Though it is possible to acquire shelter and food with relatively little money, cash is required for a normal existence, in particular for clothing, food (rice, sugar, flour, salt, soap, and so forth), for the education of children, and for health care. Education especially has become of eminent importance for villagers, and only the very poor will not let their children get more than primary education. One of the reasons education is valued so highly is that it promises access to a job in public administration, or, even better, in the army or police. Educating one's children has become a major strategy in social security: it is believed to safeguard support at old age, and it is hoped that the children become civil servants and can then act as brokers in all kinds of governmental and private services. It also has become a risky strategy, because the great expansion of the state apparatus in the 1970s has come to halt (see for more details Benda-Beckmann, F. von & Benda-Beckmann, K. von 1989).

Much of the life of the rural population thus turns around "finding money." Cloves and nutmeg are currently the most lucrative cash crops. Though cloves do not need much tending over the year, harvesting is hardly possible without assistance, because the buds have to be picked within a very brief period of time. There are traditional arrangements of picking (panta bakul), in which the pickers are invited from among relatives, neighbors, or friends to help in exchange for one basket of cloves (about one-fifth of the harvest) and a meal, coffee and tea, and cigarettes. People who have no young close relatives and who have no money of their own therefore cannot plant and maintain clove trees, because they are unable to clear land on their own, cannot buy the seedlings, and have hardly the means to recruit pickers and supply them with a meal and cigarettes. Nowadays, some people prefer to have their trees picked by wage labor, either by Ambonese or by Butonese migrants who come to the island when they hear there is a good harvest. Those who do not have enough cash use the traditional arrangements. Since cloves yield a full harvest only once or twice out of four years, and because of the great price fluctuations, they do not form a stable and reliable source of income. And not every villager has clove trees, notably many Butonese and elderly Abonese. Thus, other sources of income have to be developed. Many women make and sell snacks along the road. During the fruit seasons they bring the fruit to the market in Ambon. There are some professional sago grinders, and some men try to find odd jobs at road construction or house building. Every village has a few small shops, and some women specialize in selling clothes. There are few full-time traders. Most traders and shopkeepers combine trading with horticulture or work as civil servants. In short, people try to develop and keep open as many options for earning income as possible.

THE BUTONESE

The situation for the Butonese immigrants is quite different. Access to agricultural and residential land is subject to Ambonese adat, and the Butonese have no adat rights on Ambon (see Benda-Beckmann, F. von 1991). They therefore depend on the Ambonese for land to cultivate and to build a house. Temporary rights to house sites and vegetable gardens have been given rather freely in the past, but on the basis of adat the Butonese were not allowed to plant cloves or nutmeg trees. Allowing them to plant trees basically means a transfer of the land upon which the trees have been planted. At present, there are several disputes about the question of rights to land on which Butonese have planted trees. Because these problems do not play a role with annual crops, Butonese have specialized in vegetable gardens and often produce for the market, in contrast to Ambonese, who grow vegetables for private consumption only. There is, however, considerable variation among the Butonese. Some Butonese families, who have lived for generations on Ambon, have established stable and permanent links with Ambonese clans upon whose land they live. They have been able to buy land to build a permanent house upon, and some also have acquired clove trees. This stands in contrast with the newcomers, who often live for several years illegally in the hills where they clear some land and build a shack in permanent fear of being chased away. After some years they may try to establish a relationship with an Ambonese clan and may be allowed to build a sago-leaf house. They are often extremely poor, but Ambonese have little sympathy with these squatters, and the government programs are not meant for them. There is similar variation in the extent to which Butonese can draw upon kinsmen for help. Butonese families who settled in Hila three generations ago have a fully developed set of kin. Newcomers lack a full set of close kin.

ZAKAT

The daily social security is provided mainly through adat mechanisms. The principles of Islamic law concerning mutual assistance between ascendants and descendants in the male line are not stressed as a set of particular obligations, but have been incorporated into the wider set of kinship obligations as circumscribed in adat. The institution of zakat has also been modified and largely adatized in Ambon. The Islamic rules concerning zakat are of a quite different nature from the adat rules concerning (mutual) support. The giving of zakat in Islamic law is conceived of as a duty toward God. It is a form of sacrifice that purifies wordly goods and that, according to God's wish, must be channelled toward the community of believers (umma), which transcends ethnic, social, and spatial boundaries. The giving of zakat does not presuppose any preexisting social relation between giver and recipient.

The Islamic rules have been adapted to adat conditions. Besides the poor and needy (orphans, widows, sick, the disabled, elderly, and recent converts) adat has added two more categories: the traditional midwife, who receives the zakat of the children whom she has delivered during the first three years of their life, and the marriage guardians. Local ideas of need and poverty do not fully correspond with the classic Islamic ones. Sickness, disability, old age, or being a widow by itself does not constitute need according to adat, but they do according to Islam. In Hila, the Islamic categories and the nature of the zakat obligation are largely reinterpreted in adat terms. The community of believers is quite strictly seen as being constituted by the Ambonese co-villagers. The ethnic division between Ambonese and Islamic Butonese co-villagers are rarely crossed through zakat distribution.

In Hila, large amounts of zakat rice are being redistributed at the end of the fasting month, the monetary value of which well exceeds the yearly amount of direct taxes paid in a village or the "development subsidy" that villages receive from the government (Benda-Beckmann, F. von 1988). Between 10 and 20 percent is given to the mosque officials, but direct transfers are the rule.[21] Every person is free to choose for himself or herself to whom to bring it, as long as the receiver falls under the categories of rightful recipients. Most people give their zakat to someone who falls within an Islamic category but to whom they are obliged in an already existing social relationship. So most zakat is given to relatives or neighbors, and only about 50 percent of the zakat reaches persons who are really poor.

Most zakat thus remains in a relatively small circle of kin, and much of the potential redistributive effect is mitigated.

CIVIL SERVANTS AND MIXED PROVISIONS

The civil servants living in the village are in yet another situation. Most civil servants on the Moluccas are recruited from rural areas. Many spend a considerable time away from their home village, but they may be lucky enough to be stationed there. Schools usually have a number of teachers from the village itself, and even secondary schools have some teachers who were born there. Moreover, young teachers often marry someone from the village where they are stationed. In many villages there live at least a few civil servants who were born there or are married to a partner from the village.

Civil servants receive a more or less regular monthly salary, and an additional 10 kilograms of rice per family member (provided for several years but only for up to three children). They can also rely on state social security services, as described above. However, they cannot live on their salary alone and need substantial additional income. The lowest echelons in particular, such as beginning teachers, do not even earn enough to pay for their own expenses, let alone to maintain a family. Those who come from other regions often live as a foster child (anak piara) with a host family. They are often given a small garden or may receive vegetables and root crops from neighbors or relatives. In the beginning of their career they are thus recipients of care and support from relatives or neighbors. The balance usually changes when they advance in the administrative hierarchy and have more access to extra income via better salaries and, more importantly, by their position to direct and to profit (officially and unofficially) from project funds. They then are also in a better position to help their village relatives, friends, and clients with information and connections in the outside world, in the world of the city, the administrative system, schools, hospitals, and banks. This also means, however, that their relatives' and friends' demands on their help and support increase, and it is difficult to resist these demands. Civil servants who have not spent their lives in their home village have not had the opportunity to invest in social relationships that would enable them to fall back upon in case of need. Assisting village relatives with money and contacts may establish and maintain such relationships, but it also puts a heavy financial burden upon them, which usually exceeds their income from their salary. All civil servants therefore need substantial additional income, and often they start a commercial enterprise of some sort together with relatives.[22]

The increasing presence of civil servants in villages has led to new forms of social and economic cooperation between civil servants and other villagers in which resources from different livelihood and social security structures are merged. The normative structure for these new forms of cooperation and mutual help is a complex self-regulatory mix of elements from "adat," state law provisions, and new elements. Villagers usually bring in their labor and access to natural resources; the civil servants bring in money, their knowledge, and relationships to other government agencies. Especially in the case of teachers, their status as civil servants also allows them to control some economic activities in the village. As we have described elsewhere, the sale of sweets and snacks is a relatively lucrative business. School children are the greatest consumers, and the place in front of the schools the best place to sell. Gradually a new piece of economic village law developed according to which the sale of snacks in front of the schools became the monopoly of the teachers/headmasters. Some organized the production and sale of sweets by themselves with a limited number of relatives, also allowing a poor widow (a distant relative) to earn some money. Other secondary schoolteachers, who were strangers, let neighbors use their right to sell snacks in front of the higher secondary school and received vegetables or some domestic services in return.

If civil servants are stationed far away on a different island, they will also maintain relations with their home village. They are well aware of the near certainty that after retirement they will not be able to exist from their pension alone. They thus attempt to provide for their life after retirement by securing a place to live in and sources of additional income. Some will build a house for which they pay the materials, food, and some additional money to local people who do the work. We have described such a case in more detail elsewhere (Benda-Beckmann, F. von 1987) where such a project was launched by a judge who lived in Ambon town and visited his native village in the weekends. He built a house using the unpaid labor of his wife and his wife's relatives. When the house was completed, one of his wife's relatives could stay in the house and look after it. After some time, they started an ice factory for which the judge bought the freezers and the material, and his village relatives produced and sold the ice. About 20 relatives, mainly poorer women and children, participated in and profited from this new source of income. The judge and his wife also earned a welcome extra income, but, more importantly, it meant an investment for the time after retirement. He and his wife were considered sociable and generous patrons who often paid poor relatives' bills and provided them with necessary contacts with government and private institutions.

The value that such projects have for the parties concerned differs, and it also varies with the deficit phases of their life cycles. For the villagers, such projects are an immediate way of earning additional income and of avoiding or reducing the chances for destitution. They are thus in the position of recipient of social security in relation to the civil servant. The younger ones are potential prospective providers in case the civil servant will be in need of care. For him, it means additional income, which is needed to provide his relatives with services. The provision of these services in turn may be regarded as an investment in the future, to avoid coming into a situation of destitution when the civil servant becomes old and needs support. He is thus at the same time a provider of social security and a potential prospective recipient. Thus, although they are mutually both provider and recipient of social security, the effectuation may take place at different periods.

Participation in such cooperation is not equally distributed among villagers. The socially higher clans have been longer involved in formal education than the lower clans, and thus have now more and higher civil servants among them. Butonese rarely get a position in the government. Besides, they usually do not have such an extended network of relatives as most Ambonese have, especially the more recent migrants. The chances that they will develop this kind of cooperation therefore is lower than for Ambonese. They also have a smaller and therefore more unstable set of adat relationships. Thus, this form of social security, though profitable for those who have access to it, is at the same time a source of social stratification.

MIXED PROVISIONS: DUAL INSTITUTIONS

Village Cooperatives

The success of the village cooperatives (KUD) varies greatly throughout Indonesia and may fluctuate considerably over time. In the late 1980s, not many KUD were doing well on Ambon. The KUD in Hila was an exception. The chairman, also a civil servant at the PUSKUD in Ambon, had transformed the KUD into a private enterprise and patron-client network and extracted from the cooperative large amounts of money for his personal use. Although his political opponents disapproved of the way he ran the KUD, he was backed by the majority of the members, because as a patron and broker he was generous, and many KUD members profited from his support. Even those who did not want to cover him in his function as chairman did admit that he helped a lot of villagers by paying bills, sending children to school, and so forth (Benda-Beckmann, K. von 1987). His disregard of official regulations was only tolerated because the parallel system worked.[23] As a patronage system the KUD served its social security function well. This "success" was based upon its official status as a KUD, which gave access to the facilities under the official regulations, the main ones being credits from the Bank Rakyat Indonesia in order to buy cloves, and the monopoly on tax-free auctioning of cloves to the interinsular traders. The leaders of the cooperative violated the state regulations by auctioning far more cloves than the village produced, although only cloves produced in their own village were exempt from taxes. No member would protest against this violation, because it was in the interest of all that as much clove as possible be sold. The funds for the KUD thus came in part from the government, through the bank and the tax offices. They came, of course, also from the labor of the members in the shop run by the cooperative. The distribution of the profits was regulated on the one hand by state regulations, which allowed for a yearly payment of the proceeds. There was considerable dissatisfaction among the members about these payments, because the board wanted to "reserve" far more than they thought necessary. But there were enough clients of the chairman among whom he distributed a part of these reserves as a patron.

The patronage system, with its own norms, was the other way in which distribution was regulated. The difference between the two kinds of distribution is that—theoretically—all members profit equally as a member of a cooperative, whereas the support of a patron is always particularistic. Though a certain balance probably must be reached, some clients profit far more than others, and not all KUD members were clients.

Social Security Projects

The Provincial Department of Social Affairs of the Moluccas started, in 1983, social security projects for four categories of needy persons: widows, orphans, the disabled, and the aged (see Benda-Beckmann, F. von 1988). All projects were directed at income-generating activities for the participants. The Department of Social Affairs provided a non-refundable lump sum of 300,000 rupiah as starting capital, which was used to build a small store and buy the first stock. Of the four projects set up in Hila, only one, the widows' shop, turned out to be successful. The other three either did not really start, or stopped because of differences between the leaders and the members or because the managers were incapable of running a business. The stock of one of the projects disappeared under the hands of the village secretary. "The mice filled their stomachs," people would say.

The widows' shop started with 30 widows and divorcees, adjusting the term "widow" to the local interpretation. Not all participants were needy in local terms. Most of them had either adult children or relatively healthy parents. And some were quite wealthy, owning up to 100 clove trees. The latter participated in part out of solidarity and in part because they found it awkward to refuse participating in government projects. The shop sold the same goods as all other 15 odd village shops. The manager, a son and nephew of two participants, took care of the supplies and went to town to buy new stock. Most of the daily work was done by the secretary and the treasurer of the project, both energetic women, well versed in financial matters and in high esteem for their reliability. All important decisions regarding the organization of the provisioning were taken by the three. The fact that they were capable, reliable, and went along well was one of the important reasons for success.

Although a modest profit was made, the main advantage for participation was that the shop provided its participants with short, small, but important credits for their vending activities. Whereas normal customers, with the exception of school teachers and the village secretary, had to pay up front, members were allowed to take the necessary ingredients and pay without interest after having sold the snacks, three days later at the latest. These short-running credits were a welcome facility for their individual economic enterprises and made participation interesting (compare Bouman 1989). However, as a result, the neediest profited least, although they got their full share of the yearly proceeds, because they were unable to prepare and sell snacks and therefore could not make use of these credits. There were signs of deterioration in 1988, because the village secretary had started the habit of buying extensively without paying. There was an unwritten rule that civil servants and the village secretary were allowed to buy on credit and outstanding debts were running up dangerously high, but it was extremely difficult to withstand such an "attack."[24]

The examples of the KUD and the widows' project show that it is crucial to look not only at the official purposes and rules of such institutions; the parallel ways in which they function deserve equal attention. Other sets of norms are used besides or instead of the regulations issued by the government, and these other norms may be as important in the contribution to social security. The paradoxical result is that the success of the enterprise may depend on those rules that make the level of the participants' welfare rise differentially and that have an uneven redistributive effect among the participants, as a result of which the poorest profit least of all.

PLURAL DEFINITIONS OF
NEEDS-DIFFERENTIATION IN PROVISIONS

Studying the actual organization of social security in a Third World country requires, even more so than in a Western welfare state, an approach that can look at the different types of need of rural people, the complexities of normative regulation of social security, and the relationships and transfers through which the necessary resources are provided. As we have seen, on Ambon actual situations of need and distress vary among the different categories of rural people, and they are differently conceptualized in the three main normative systems, although there is some overlap. Local interpretations of need and poverty are mainly given in adat terms, in which the situation of individuals is seen within the context of their actual social and economic relationships.

The fact that land is sufficiently available for most Ambonese villagers means that for them the factor of labor is more problematic than land. For the Butonese, lack of access to land may be an additional cause for poverty. Civil servants do not depend on land and labor to the same extent as peasants do. The greatest risk for them is losing their job and income, both official and that which they may generate alongside on the basis of their position.

Having land without being able to work on it is of little use. Since the circle of people primarily responsible for each other's well-being is quite small, the "really poor" people are those without close relatives and elderly people without children. Both are referred to as "orphans" (yatim piatu). As the example of zakat shows, Islamic definitions of need and poverty which abstract from these social relations are largely translated into adat terms and become embedded into the existing social relationships. The same attitude is extended to civil servants. A civil servant who falls ill, for example, would be considered needy according to the classification in the state system, but not necessarily according to adat, provided he has close relatives. On the other hand, a young unmarried teacher coming to live in a strange village is needy according to adat standards, but not according to the state system. Widows and widowers as such are not considered poor in adat terms, because they can and largely do provide for themselves as long as they are healthy. As all Ambonese women, widows have access to pusaka land in their own right and may well cultivate their own vegetable garden.

But the category of widows, which officially means women whose husbands have died, is taken to include also divorced women in the village, including the widows' project. Villagers use the terms "janda mati" and "janda hidup" (widows whose husbands are dead and widows whose husbands are alive). Converts, a lawful category of zakat recipients in Islamic law, would not be treated as "poor" in terms of state law. However, there is a good reason to include converts as needy persons also in adat terms. For it is expected, and not without ground, that a convert will have lost all contacts with his or her family and therefore is de facto an orphan. Hence, converts are also considered needy in adat terms. In fact such a convert usually lives as a foster child (anak piara) with the Moslem family, which has guided him or her to conversion and takes care of the convert, so that he or she rarely is in a needy position. Zakat is as much paid out of joy over the conversion as for the reason of the convert's needy situation.

While there are many ways in which need and destitution are defined, there are also many different ways in which funds and services are made available and distributed. The systems of social security are distinct, but many villagers make combinations and derive their social security from different sources, and are themselves involved in different networks to provide help and support. Often it is difficult to establish what the precise source of a particular provision is. This is especially the case where civil servants enter into a patron–client relationship with relatives and other villagers, thereby acting as brokers and business partners at the same time.

Their services are possible because of their official position, but not all of them are part of the performance of the official job. The distribution of government funds and services may be equally complex. The example of the KUD and the social projects have shown that there may be parallel ways of distribution, one on the basis of equality, the other fundamentally particularistic in character. The patron-client-like forms of cooperation and distribution have many advantages, both for the social security of the clients and the civil servants themselves. Where peasant villagers profit from such cooperation because it gives access to services and immediate financial gain, the civil servants profit in two ways: the business provides additional income, but is also an investment for their old age care. However, such a system tends to be more profitable for some participants than for others. The very needy tend to gain least of all. They may lack the physical capacities to make use of available resources, as the widows' shop has shown. They may also lack the necessary contacts, because they have few relatives at all, or because they have no prominent government officers among their close relatives.

AN OUTLOOK INTO THE FUTURE

The fact that the systems are so interwoven and interdependent means that changes in one system will affect the other mechanisms. It is on the basis of this assumption that the authors want to take a cautious look into the future development of the social security organization on rural Ambon, following what we see as three important trends.

First, the provisions for civil servants will in all likelihood be changed. It has become clear that the accumulated contributions that civil servants pay into the pension funds will not be sufficient to pay all pensions in the near future, regardless of the problems of maladministration and corruption. There are plans to convert the pension fund into a social insurance fund through which "the burden could be shifted completely to the civil servants themselves" (Esmara & Tjiptoharianto 1986: 60). What that will mean for the level of pension payments is not yet clear, but it is likely that pensions will be reduced substantially in the not all too distant future. Civil servants will then increasingly need additional sources of income, which may well lead to a sharp increase in the kind of cooperation with relatives in their home villages.

Second, the strategy of sending children to school to ensure one's own social security at old age has become increasingly risky, for it is not at all sure that these youngsters will obtain a permanent job either in government service or in the private sector. The expansion of public administration has come to a halt, and there are plans to reduce the civil service apparatus. Thus, a large amount of money and potential labor invested in a general education of children flows away from the village, without any certainty that it will pay off. To ensure access to lucrative jobs, brokers are more than ever needed. The pressure upon those who are in a position high enough to act as successful brokers will increase, because more relatives will lay a claim upon them. The civil servants will need even more resources than before and will have a greater interest in commercial cooperation. It is very likely that this will lead to a sharper division between those who will be included in patronage relationships and others who will remain excluded and stay largely dependent upon help and support from others who also lack the more profitable contacts. For them the circle of support may contract to alarmingly small proportions.

Third, the plans to introduce social insurance schemes for the rural population have in 1992 been addressed in the new social security legislation. Scheduled for those in active production, this policy is strongly based upon what Macarov (1980) has called the "unholy alliance between work and welfare" (see Chhabra 1980; Stanboel 1986). The target group for such an extension of social insurance are those rural people whose work situation is seen to come closest to those in the "modern" economic sector (see in general Fuchs 1985: 63; McGillivray 1980). In Indonesian planning, self-employed farmers are presumed to be faced with the same risks as agricultural wage laborers. Both categories are therefore treated equally. The farmers will have to pay monetary contributions into a fund that has to cover payments and administration of the scheme (Stanboel 1986: 12). Payments will be made once a year in a lump sum, for the sake of administrative "simplicity." In order to avoid the risk of failure, the program is planned to start in the most developed villages and will be administered by the village councils, the cooperatives, and/or the PKK organization. The central government realizes that the introduction of social security schemes in rural areas will be faced with problems, mainly administrative in character. These problems include registration, the collecting contributions, adjudicating claims, payments and administrating funds (see Stanboel 1986: 12; see also Esmara & Tjiptoharianto 1986: 64).

This extension of state-regulated social security is not very promising, considering the rural conditions in Indonesia. Already the technical-administrative problems with which the local administration is faced are enormous. Maladministration is a serious problem in many regions. Moreover, these funds will be faced with the risks of inflation, for which little provisions have been made. But there are more basic problems. There is little awareness of a need to differentiate according to the different social and economic positions within the prospective clientele. Only the conventional catalogue of risks, such as sickness, invalidity, and old age, are taken into account. Self-employed farmers are presumed to be faced with the same risks as agricultural wage laborers and are treated equally.[25] The program does not take into account basic differences among the participants in the kind and extent in land rights, differences in income from land and labor, differences in the life and enterprise cycle, seasonal fluctuations in income, and differences in knowledge and capability to gain access to the provisions. Because the first two differences are not taken into account, the system is bound to be regressive in character and thus discriminate against poorer families. The last two factors will in all likelihood cause problems with yearly payments and may eventually eliminate the most needy participants from the program. The program thus provides for a fund for which the poorer pay relatively more but gain relatively less than the wealthier, and which is extremely susceptible to abuse by local leaders and officers. It is a mechanism to extract rural savings that could otherwise be invested in other, local mechanisms of social security and that probably will provide little security in exchange (see McLeod 1993.)

All three trends point to a similar conclusion. The trends identified are likely to weaken the resource base upon which villagers can draw in their social security arrangements, and they will reinforce already existing forms of social and economic differentiation. The social security projects and the planned social insurance schemes, with their emphasis on income generation and the link between work and welfare, will not reach those who are not able to engage in these activities. As long as the government concentrates on income-generating activities and does not manage to set up programs that really reach the poorer villagers, Ambonese and Butonese, the future of the rural poor will look bleak.

NOTES

1. The project was carried in 1985 and 1986 by the authors, who concentrated on the social organization and social security arrangements, and by Tanja Taale and Arie Brouwer in 1987–1988, who studied the agricultural aspects of social security issues. The project was sponsored by the LIPI, the Indonesian research council.

2. See Partsch 1983; Midgley 1984; Bossert 1985; Fuchs 1985; Connolly 1985; Benda-Beckmann, F. von et al. 1988; Hirtz 1989; Ferman, Henry & Hoyman 1987; Rose 1989; Johnson 1987; Wheelock 1990; Ahmad et al. 1991.

3. Thus Johnson (1987: 91) states categorically: "The evidence that the informal sector provides more care than the statutory, voluntary or commercial sectors is incontrovertible." See also Pahl 1984, Redclift & Mingione 1985.

4. For an excellent critique of the assumptions and the ideological and political implications of the formal/informal distinction, see Connolly 1985. Connolly stresses the powerful character of the distinction in political and development-oriented debate and argues that this force is in direct relation to the importance of the social issue they refer to. "For . . . in Third World countries . . . the informal sector is not really about minority groups, anomalies or exceptional cases but rather touches on the fundamental problems of development, employment and poverty" (1985: 56).

5. This distinction was originally developed as a characterization of the labor market (see Breman 1987b: 4, Connolly 1985, Pahl 1984). The protection of workers within specific labor arrangements by *state regulation* was then taken as the basis for formal social security from which "the rest" of social security and protection is distinguished as "informal." When states increasingly took over the role of providers of social security services, such state regulated provisions were also classified as "formal." Formal social security thus came to refer both to the *sources* of social security provisions, or rather the providers of funds, and to the

normative *organization* of *distribution* of goods and money and the provision of services. In conceptual practices, the source of regulations mostly provides the last handhold for the formal/informal distinction (see Fuchs 1985 & 1988). For a critique see Connolly 1985: 59.

6. Rose distinguishes between the household, the market, and the state. In addition, he adds another dimension, that is the ways in which such provisions are transferred, in monetized or non-monetized form (1989: 133). No systematic distinction, however, is made between the sources of provision and regulations, and social relations and institutions are too easily collapsed. But there are other problems with his distinctions. The concept of household is both too narrow and too broad. It is too broad because it departs from an institutional notion, in which the household is identified with kinship relations and treated as the basic social unit. Members of one household do not necessarily pool their sources and may stand in different networks that cannot be reduced to a household. The term is also too narrow, because it excludes household–external kin relations, as well as relations of neighborhood and friendship, which do not belong to the market or the state, yet are important relationship sets through which social security may be provided or received. The market is also a problematic category. The sharp distinction between state and market suggests that the state does not interfere with the market and leaves regulation open to private negotiation. Yet some market institutions are highly regulated by the state, such as insurance companies, and so are many transfer relations, especially if they pertain to the field of social security. Using the term market in opposition to household also suggests that only what happens within the household is outside the money economy and operates on a different logic, whereas what happens between households is also largely or fully part of the market economy and works according to the market mechanisms. (Wheelock 1990: 157). Neither of these propositions is true.

7. This is perhaps not so evident in European and American industrialized states. Non-state forms of regulation are usually not regarded as law or law-like forms of regulation. For instance, household internal and external relations of kinship are also subject to duplicatory regulation. The nature of such legal regulation may be obscured by the fact that family members perceive the social security relationship as governed by love and affection. While the affective loading of these relationships undoubtedly plays a role in its functioning, the obligations of help and assistance cannot be reduced to it (see Benda-Beckmann, F. von et al. 1988: 12).

8. What the "family" is, in Indonesia, what kinds of relations involve what kinds of obligation, may also be differently defined in terms of state law, Islamic law, and village adat regulations. The members of a household or relatives thus may be obliged to provide social security services on the basis of three normative regulations. These regulations may differ and may pose different requirements upon the same persons; they also may constitute the interconnected units of the relationship in different ways.

9. See Midgley 1984 for a discussion of the disastrous problems for the rural population in Third World countries in acquiring access to state-provided social security.

10. See Savy 1972: 2–5; Zacher 1977: 38; Fuchs 1985. For critiques of the ILO definition see Partsch 1983; Woodman 1988.

11. See also Partsch 1983; Benda-Beckmann, F. von & Benda-Beckmann, K. von 1984; Benda-Beckmann, F. von et al. 1988. For a similar approach see also Hirtz 1989.

12. For a similar approach to "work" see Pahl 1984: 128, who stresses that work can only be understood in relation to the specific social relations in which it is embedded.

13. For a general treatment see also Partsch 1983.

14. See for example Hüsken 1989, Alescander and Alescander 1982 for the organization of rice harvesting and its consequences for social security of the Javanese rural population. See Benda-Beckmann, F. von 1990 for sago production.

15. For overviews see Mesa Lago 1978; Midgley 1984; Fuchs 1984. For Indonesia see Chhabra 1980; Esmara and Tjiptoharianto 1986; Joenoes 1982; Stanboel 1986.

16. There is no unemployment scheme for civil servants.

17. For overviews see Mesa Lago 1978; Midgley 1984; Fuchs 1985. For Indonesia see Chhabra 1980, Esmara & Tjiptoharianto 1986, Joenoes 1982; Stanboel 1986.

18. The Jamsosetek law, Undang Undang Republik Indonesia Nomor 3 Tahun 1992 rentang Jaminan Sosial Tenaga Kerja (see McLeod 1993).

19. The benefits comprise: workers' compensation insurance for work-related accidents and illnesses, life insurance, retirement (provident fund) benefits, and free health care for workers, their spouses, and up to three children (see McLeod 1993).

20. The general policy assumptions of the Department of Social Affairs are laid down in the Directives for the Enhancement of the Social Potential of the Rural Community (Appendix A 2 of the Basic Design). Briefly, they can be summarized as follows: in the present stage of national development, not all rural communities have yet been able to identify the existing problems of welfare and social security and to solve them in accordance with the demands of the development process. There is insufficient capacity to identify and mobilize potential resources. The situation in the villages is the result of an underdevelopment of social abilities, insight, and mobilization of potential resources. Therefore, social conditions have to be created, enabling the population to do so. Social workers have to be trained to act as dynamic stimulators in cooperation with the village council and instruct the population.

21. The Ministry of Religious Affairs tries to gain control over zakat payments. In some areas on Java, it has become quite successful, but not in Ambon. Where the involvement of the government is successful, the government has

incorporated the Moslem definition of need, where it concerns zakat, in its own legal system (see Benda-Beckmann, F. von 1988: 358). For an overview of the ways in which governments have attempted to incorporate zakat into their official social security regulation (see Midgely 1984: 198; Siddique 1972; Rosenthal 1965.

22. The headmaster of the secondary school in Hila developed a great many economic activities with a more or less strong component of social security. He started cooperatives of various sorts, ranging from a fishing cooperative to small shops, which were for a longer or shorter period profitable. Many villagers borrowed money from him, repaying in cloves, which he stored until prices in Ambon were good. His wife sold gold jewelry. She also organized a group of poor women who made snacks to sell in front of the school. Besides, the couple was considered very generous and could consequently mobilize a lot of support and help when they needed it (Benda-Beckmann, K. von 1988).

23. Chairmen of KUDs in other villages also violated the official regulations. One was forced to resign, because he looked too much after his private interests only and did not do enough for his clients, who then ceased to support him (Paassen 1986).

24. Personal communication by Tanja Taale and Arie Brouwer.

25. See, however, some cautious remarks by McGillivray 1980.

REFERENCES

Ahmad E., Dreze, J., Hills, J. & Sen, A. (eds.). 1991. *Social Security in Developing Countries* (Oxford: Clarendon).

Alescander, J. & Alescander, F. 1982. "Shared Poverty as Ideology: Agrarian Relationships in Colonial Java" *Man* 17:597–619.

Bartels, D. 1989. *Moluccans in Exile: A Struggle for Ethnic Survival* (Leiden: Centrum voor Onderzoek naar Maatschappelijke Tegenstellingen).

Benda-Beckmann, F. von. 1987. "De ijsjes van de rechter: een verkenning van complexe sociale zekerheidssystemen" *Recht der Werkelijkheid* 1987/I: 69–82.

Benda-Beckmann, F. von. 1988. "Islamic law and Social Security on an Ambonese Village" in Benda-Beckmann, F. von, Benda-Beckmann, K. von, Casino, E., Woodman, G. R. & Zacher, H. (eds.) *Between Kinship and the State: Law and Social Security in Developing Countries* (Dordrecht: Foris).

Benda-Beckmann, F. von. 1990. "Sago, law and food security on Ambon" in Bakker, J. I. (ed.) *The World Food Crisis: Food Security in Comparative Perspective* (Toronto: Canadian Scholars' Press).

Benda-Beckmann, F. von. 1991. "Ambonese adat as Jurisprudence of Insurgency and Oppression" *Yearbook of Law and Anthropology* 5: 25–42.

Benda-Beckmann, K. von. 1987. "Overheidscooperaties als Particuliere Ondernemingen: Sociale Zekerheid op Islamitisch Ambon" *Recht der Werkelijkheid* 1987(1): 54–68.

Benda-Beckmann, K. von. 1988. "Social Security and Small-Scale Enterprises in Islamic Ambon" in Benda-Beckmann, F. von, Benda-Beckmann, K. von, Casino, G. R., Woodman, E. & Zacher, H. (eds.) *Between Kinship and the State: Law and Social Security in Developing Countries* (Dordrecht: Foris).

Benda-Beckmann, K. von. 1991. "Developing Families: Moluccan Women and Changing Patterns of Social Security in the Netherlands" in Claessen, H., Engel, M. van den & Plantenga, D. (eds.) *Liber Amicorum Els Postel* (Leiden: University of Leiden, Faculty of Cultural Anthropology and Research Centre for Women and Autonomy).

Benda-Beckmann, K. von. 1992. "Joint Brokerage of Spouses on Islamic Ambon" in Bemmelen, S. van, Djajadiningrat-Nieuwenhuis, M., Locher-Scholten, E. & Touwen-Bouwsma, E. (eds.) *Women and Mediation in Indonesia* (Leiden: KITLV Press).

Benda-Beckmann, F. von & Benda-Beckmann, K. von. 1984. "Recht en Sociale Zekerheid op Ambon" *NNR* 5/2: 262–81.

Benda-Beckmann, F. von & Benda-Beckmann, K. von. 1989. *Where Structures Merge: State and "Off-State" Involvement in Rural Social Security on Ambon, Indonesia.* Paper presented at the EIDOS conference, Amsterdam.

Benda-Beckmann, F. von, Benda-Beckmann, K. von, Bryde, B. O. & Hirtz, F. 1988. "Introduction: Between Kinship and the State" in Benda-Beckmann, F. von, Benda-Beckmann, K. von, Casino, G. R., Woodman, E. & Zacher, H. (eds.) *Between Kinship and the State: Law and Social Security in Developing Countries* (Dordrecht: Foris).

Benda-Beckmann, F. von & Taale, T. 1992. "The Changing Laws of Hospitality: Guest Laborers in the Political Economy of Legal Pluralism" in Benda-Beckmann, F. von & Velds, M. van der (eds.) *Law as a Resource in Agrarian Struggles* (Wageningen: Pudoc).

Bossert, A. 1985. *Traditionelle und Moderne Formen Sozialer Sicherung in Tanzania* (Berlin: Duncker & Humblot).

Bouman, F.J.A. 1989. *Small, Short and Unsecured: Informal Rural Finance in India* (New Delhi: Oxford University Press).

Breman, J. 1987a. *Koelies, Planters en Koloniale Politiek* (Dordrecht: Foris).

Breman, J. 1987b. *The Informal Sector in Research: Theory and Practice* (Rotterdam: Erasmus University, Comparative Studies Program).

Chhabra, H. R. 1980. "National Strategies for the Provision of Rural Social Security in Developing Countries in Asia" *Report of the Asian Regional Sound Table Meeting on Social Security Protection of the Rural Population in Developing Countries, Kuala Lumpur 1–4 July 1980* (Social Security Documentation: Asian Series, 5) (New Delhi: Regional Office for Asia and Oceania, International Social Security Association).

Connolly, P. 1985. "The Politics of the Informal Sector: A Critique" in Reclift, N. & Mingione, E. (eds.) *Beyond Unemployment: Households, Gender and Subsistence* (Oxford: Basil Blackwell).

Cooley, F. L. 1962. *Ambonese Adat: A General Description* (New Haven: New York University).

Esmara, A. & Tjiptoharianto, F. 1986. "The Social Security System in Indonesia" *ASEAN Economic Bulletin* (Special Issue) (July): 53–67.

Ferman, L. A., Henry, S. & Hoyman, M. 1987. "Issues and Prospects for the Study of Informal Economies: Concepts, Research Strategies, and Policy" *Annals AAPSS* 493: 154–72.

Fuchs, M. 1985. *Soziale Sicherheit in der Dritten Welt–Zugleich eine Fallstudie Kenia* (Baden-Baden: Studien aus dem Max-Planck-Institut fur Auslandisches und Internationales Sozialrecht).

Fuchs, M. 1988. "Social Security in Third World Countries" in Benda-Beckmann, F. von, Benda-Beckmann, K. von, Casino, G. R., Woodman, E. & Zacher, H. (eds.) *Between Kinship and the State: Law and Social Security in Developing Countries* (Dordrecht: Foris).

Getubig, I. P. & Schmidt, S. (eds.) 1992. *Rethinking Social Security: Reaching out to the Poor* (Kuala Lumpur/Eschborn: APDC & GTZ).

Hirtz, F. 1989. *Managing Insecurity: State Social Policy Family Networks in the Rural Philippines, Past and Present* (Unpublished Ph.D. Thesis, University of Bielefeld, Bielefeld).

Hüsken, F. 1989. *Een dorp op Java: Sociale Differentiatie in een Boerengemeenschap, 1850–1950 (Amsterdam: ACASEA)*.

International Labor Organization (ILO). 1984. *Introduction to Social Security* (Geneva: (ILO)).

International Labor Organization (ILO). 1985. *Report to the Government of Indonesia on the Planning and Administration of Social Security: Project Findings and Recommendations* (Geneva: (ILO)).

Joenoes, M. 1982. *Readings in Social Security, the Indonesian Case* (Jakarta: Sentano Kertonegoro and the Social Insurance System "Astek" Research and Development Board).

Johnson, N. 1987. *The Welfare State in Transition: The Theory and Practice of Welfare Pluralism* (Brighton: Wheatsheaf Books).

Juynboll, Th. W. 1925. *Handleiding tot de Kennis van de Mohammedaansche Wet Volgens de leer der Sjafi'itische School* (Leiden: Brill).

Macarov, D. 1980. *Work and Welfare: The Unholy Alliance* (London: Sage).

McGillivray, W. R. 1980. "Observations on the Provision of Social Security Protection to Rural Workers and their Dependents" in *Report of the Asian Regional Sound Table Meeting on Social Security Protection of the Rural Population in Developing Countries, Kuala Lumpur 1–4 July 1980* (Social Security Documentation: Asian Series, 5) (New Delhi: Regional Office for Asia and Oceania, International Social Security Association).

McLeod, R. H. 1993. *Workers Social Security in Indonesia.* (Unpublished manuscript).

Mesa Lago, C. 1978. *Social Security in Latin America: Pressure Groups, Stratification and Inequality* (Pittsburgh: University of Pittsburgh Press).

Midgley, J. 1984. *Social Security, Inequality and the Third World* (New York: John Wiley & Sons).

Paassen, A. van. 1987. *Sociale Zekerheid: Recht op Bestaan* (Unpublished Masters Thesis, Agricultural University, Wageningen).

Pahl, R. E. 1984. *Divisions of Labor* (Oxford: Basic Blackwell).

Partsch, M. 1983. *Prinzipien und Formen Sozialer Sicherung in Nicht-industriellen Gesellschaften* (Berlin: Düncker und Humblot).

Pradhan, R. E. 1990. *Family, Inheritance and the Care of the Aged: Contractual Relationships and the Axiom of Kinship Amity*. (Unpublished manuscript).

Prawotosoediro, P. 1982. *Pegawai Negeri Sipil* (Jakarta: Pradnya Paramita).

Redclift, N. & Mingione, E. (eds.). 1985. *Beyond Unemployment: Households, Gender and Subsistence* (Oxford: Basil Blackwell).

Rose, R. 1989. *Ordinary People in Public Office: A Behavioural Analysis* (London: Sage).

Rosenthal, E.I.J. 1965. *Islam in the Modern National State* (Cambridge: Cambridge University Press).

Sajogyo, W. 1988. "Local Level Organization in Planned Development: An Analysis of Women's Participation in Rural Java" in Quarles van Ufford, Ph., Kruijt , D. & Downing, Th. (eds.) *The Hidden Crisis in Development: Development Bureaucracies* (Amsterdam: Free University Press).

Savy, R. 1972. *Social Security in Agriculture* (Geneva: International Labor Organization).

Siddique, S. 1972. *Some Malay Ideas on Modernization, Islam and Adat* (Singapore: University of Singapore Press).

Soepomo, I. 1983. *Pengantar Hukum Perburuhan* (Jakarta: Djambatan).

Stanboel, M. I. 1986. *The National Experience of Indonesia in the Field of Social Security Protection for the Rural Population* (Report to the International Social Security Association Asian Regional Round Table Meeting on Social Security Protection for the Rural Population, Jakarta, April 8–10) (New Delhi: Regional Office for Asia and Oceania, International Social Security Association).

Strijbosch, F. 1988. "Molukse Adopties in Nederland" *Nederlands Juristenblad* 7: 218–25.

Suryakusuma, Y. 1988. "PKK: The Formalization of the Informal Power of Women." Paper presented at the International Workshop on Women as Mediators in Indonesia, September 6–30, Leiden.

Taale, T. 1991. *Looking For a Livelihood in Hila: Continuity and Change in Land Use and its Implications for Social Security in an Ambonese Village* (Unpublished Masters Thesis, University of Wageningen, Wageningen).

Wheelock, J. 1990. *Husbands at Home: the Domestic Economy in a Post-Industrial Society* (London: Routledge).

Wieringa, S. E. 1988. "Women as Mediators in two Mass Organizations." Paper presented at the International Workshop on Women as Mediators in Indonesia, September 6–30, Leiden.

Woodman, G. R. 1988. "The Decline of Folk-Law Social Security in Common-Law Africa" in Benda-Beckmann, F. von, Benda-Beckmann, K. von, Casino, G. R., Woodman, E. & Zacher, H. (eds.) *Between Kinship and the State: Law and Social Security in Developing Countries* (Dordrecht: Foris).

Zacher, H. 1977. "Vorfragen zu den Methoden der Sozialrechtsvergleichung" in Zacher, H. F. (ed.) *Methodische Probleme des Sozialrechtsvergleichs. Schriftenreihe für Internationales und Vergleichendes Sozialrecht*, (Vol. 1) (Berlin: Düncker & Humblot).

6

An Examination of the Roles of the State, Networks, and the Family in Philippine Social Security

Frank Hirtz

In studies concerning social welfare in Third World countries, it is usually posited that basically weak, poor, and rudimentary state institutions are interlocked with strong, elaborate, and sophisticated kinship organizations that care for the individual (Partsch 1983; Bossert 1985; Zacher 1988). This chapter will critically examine this conventionally held dichotomy using the Philippines as an example. Based on an empirical study in the rural Philippines, the author found neither a weak state nor a strong kinship organization. The author did find, however, that among the rural population, neither the state nor kin can be counted upon in times of need. In this chapter, the author examines state institutions and local kinship practices of assistance, with particular attention to the majority of the Philippines population, the rural poor. This investigation will illustrate some of the issues and problems that stem from studying social welfare in a developing country.

ON STATE AND SOCIAL WELFARE

Social welfare, social policy, and social security systems have emerged and developed side by side, yet not without conflicts in the industrialized world. These systems play a specific and very different role within a given industrialized country as well as in bilateral and multilateral relations, as in the case of the European Community. The roles of welfare can be defined by overlapping spheres of interests (business, economics, and politics). The varied social and political background in each nation contributes to the emergence of distinctly different forms of institutions along the public-private sector spectrum. Additionally, diverse social philosophies that have to be understood as part of the varied history of nation states increase the difficulty of reaching a common understanding and an agreed-upon definition of what either social policy, welfare, or security denote.

A further complication arises if the scope of observation is extended to the Third World. Condensing the highly varied historical experiences of these countries, then two important features emerge: the dependent development of national economies and state formation on the basis of specific colonial and post-colonial definitions, heritages, and interferences. However, the colonial legacy alone cannot be taken as the yardstick against which specific conditions in a specific country can be measured. The history and social conditions prior to the conquest played and, though transformed, continue to play an important role. This is referred to as a country's indigenous heritage. Hence, the merger of each unique indigenous heritage with the colonial past adds a further dimension to the already complex and varied understandings of what a Third World nation is all about. It is within this general context that the contemporary problems of social welfare in the Third World are situated. Indeed, social policies themselves are very often part of the colonial heritage, yet simultaneously the expression of approaches to contemporary problems. The Philippines is no exception.

Welfare matters in Third World states are defined by a peculiar mixture of interference, dependency, and self-definition. The emergence of institutions that base their existence on constitutional mandates are supposedly governed by laws and regulations and executed by civil servants. This attempts to follow the paths of the industrialized nations and often perpetuates the policies of their colonial masters. In essence, it is the legacy of the state in social welfare with which one has to contend. One of the colonial heritages is the creation of social security and social welfare systems. With allowances for difficulties of definition, social welfare relates to a quality of life, free from economic, political, and social constraints. A welfare state is a political system in which its inhabitants are secured against individual risks through a system of private and public insurances and subsidies, which are distributed in accordance with pre-defined circumstances.

Social security, in its broadest sense, is not only a subset of organized public and/or charitable activities within a given country but denotes all those activities that are focussed at safeguarding an acquired standard of living. This includes efforts to prevent a further deterioration of living conditions. It encompasses all respective actions of individuals, groups, and state agencies alike. The difference between state and private efforts in social security is simply an analytic distinction (Hirtz 1988b).

THE PHILIPPINES CASE

It is important, first and foremost, to gauge the Philippines' varied colonial and post-colonial history, which left a lasting imprint on its social welfare institutions. The Philippines was ruled by the Spanish Crown for about 350 years, while subjugated by a combination of Roman Law and the (often not so) social services of the Catholic church. The country was then inspired by an abortive national war of liberation from 1892 to 1898 (the Katipuneam Insurrection) and then totally transformed in its public sector by American involvement from 1898 (Spanish American War) until 1946, with a three-and-a-half-year brutal interruption by the Japanese occupational forces. With this long period of colonialism, an indigenous development of government institutions and a national public ideology in the Philippines have never taken place. The declaration of independence, several elite governments (Lande 1965; Wurfel 1988), the 14 years of Martial Law under President F. Marcos (1972–86), and the world-captivating change of government by Aquino and "people power" in 1986 were all events that contributed their share to the irregular understanding of state obligations and state performance in general, and with regard to the state's social obligations in particular.

Social welfare as a state obligation has been amply reflected in the many constitutions of the Philippines, which were promulgated between 1898 and 1986. The more important documents in which the social obligations of the Philippines state were legislated are the constitutions of 1936, 1973 (the Marcos constitution), and 1986 (the Aquino constitution). The 1935 constitution forms the basic blueprint that all following basic laws adopted. The entire structure of government and political representation, civil service, military, and judiciary embraced the American model, not too surprisingly since the United States was administering the Philippines at that time.

All three constitutions entailed wordings with regard to the obligation of the state to promote social justice "to insure the well-being and economic security of all the people" (Article II, Section 5, 1935 Constitution), with more specificity in the Marcos constitution, which included regulations regarding the social obligations to "equitabl[y] diffuse property ownership and profits" (Article II, Section 6, 1973 Constitution). The Aquino constitution simply stated: "The State shall promote social justice in all phases of national development" (Article II, Section 10, 1986 Constitution). Differentiation as to how this social justice ought to be achieved is spread in several articles over this very wordy and long document.

The present constitution of the Philippines displays a wide array of social obligations of the state, either under the heading of "Social Justice and Human Rights" (Article XIII)—where 19 sections deal in generalities with (among other things) labor, agrarian and natural resources reform, urban land reform and housing, health, women, role and rights of people's organizations, and human rights. Other more specific provisions regarding social obligations (for example, the rights and obligations of cultural minorities, the disabled, and so forth) are well dispersed over the 60 or more pages. Generally, the new constitution has left vague which form to be used to meet these obligations. The constitution has, however, established social services as one form of dealing with the notion of social policy:

The State shall promote a just and dynamic social order that will ensure the prosperity and independence of the nation and free the people from poverty through policies that provide adequate *social services*, promote full employment, a rising standard of living, and an improved quality of life for all. (Article II, Section 9, 1986 Constitution, emphasis added)

This discussion demonstrates that the idea of social justice is well embedded in the notion of Philippines statehood and is operationalized in the administration through various institutions. The Philippines notion of social justice in constitutional, legal, and official political thinking pertains to a wide array of topics and concerns. It shows, however, that the Philippines constitution could have been the constitution of any country in the world, were there not a few hints such as "poverty" or "land reform" that remind the reader that one is dealing with a developing nation. Suffice it to say, any social policy intervention from the state to achieve and to safeguard welfare seems to be not only permissible but in fact commanded. The Philippines compare favorably with its neighboring countries in the ASEAN (Association of South East Asian Nations) region in regard to its constitutional history and the content of its constitutions.

Favorable comparison of constitutional, legal, and administrative institutions pertains equally to those institutions in the Philippines that administer social security and social welfare programs. Early in the American colonial period, employees' compensation and rather enlightened labor laws were inaugurated (which does not say anything about their implementation), pension schemes for government employees were introduced, and in 1937, unified in the still existing Government Service Insurance Service

(GSIS). Additionally, the present Department of Social Welfare and Development (DSWD) traces its uninterrupted mandate back to the Public Welfare Board established in 1915 (Hirtz 1988a). Since the beginning of the century—and partly in continuation of efforts during the Spanish colonial period—social services were rendered by a variety of organizations and institutions, governmental and non-governmental. Some of these organizations operate on a sectoral basis: health, nutrition, housing, labor and industry, community development, family planning, and education, which in the Philippines understanding is part of the social services (Mendoza 1981; Pangalangan 1985).

Social Security Administration

The single most important institution providing social security for the majority of the employed (compulsory) and for self-employed (partly compulsory, partly voluntary) is the Social Security System (SSS), which began operations in 1956. With a membership of some 11.5 million (SSS, 1993), the SSS provides virtually all the services of a modern social security administration. The benefits and services of the SSS (and with some variation in scope and amount also of the GSIS) are disbursed for the following reasons: sickness, disability, maternity, retirement, survivors (death), and funeral. Additionally, both the SSS and the GSIS grant their members certain privileges like housing loans and salary loans. In the case of the GSIS the civil servants are granted additional privileges, including optional life insurance loans, policy loans (against life insurance), and educational loans. The funds for these benefits and services are collected in the form of compulsory contributions, which are part of the salary (slightly over eight percent), whereby the employers' and employees' exact share is dependent on the salary bracket of the employed. In the case of the self-employed, an equivalent premium is collected. These contributions are divided between the Philippines Medicare Fund and the Employees' Compensation Fund. Both Funds provide separate services and benefits yet are fiscally administered by the GSIS and the SSS. All benefits are given under certain qualifying conditions, which are spelled out in various laws and internal circulars. The important exclusions are domestic servants, family labor, and virtually all agricultural laborers. There are no unemployment benefits and family allowances known in the Philippines social security policy. Both institutions are government entities and managed by professional administrators. Each of them is controlled by a board of directors, which is composed of the secretaries of some departments (ex officio) and representatives of labor and employers.

Social Service Administration

With regard to social services for those who are not contributing directly to any social security program (excluding general taxation as a contribution), a highly complex and virtually indescribable array of policies, programs, projects, pilot projects, special considerations, targeted disbursements, and different regional emphasis are rendered by an equally constantly changing diversity of institutions and organizations (see Hirtz 1990: 109–76). The single most important government entity is the DSWD. The Aquino government reemphasized the importance of this department, and through Executive Order No. 123 (1987) declares in Section 3:

The State is committed to the care, protection, and rehabilitation of that segment of the country's population (individual, family and community) which has the least in life and needs social welfare assistance and social work intervention to restore their normal functioning and participation in community affairs.

Presently, the DSWD is involved in six major programs: assistance to socially disadvantaged communities; assistance to socially disadvantaged families; promotion of welfare of socially disadvantaged women; care, protection, and rehabilitation of children and youth under difficult situations; disability prevention and rehabilitation of disabled persons; and relief and rehabilitation of victims of natural calamities and social disorganization. The programs are executed within specialized segments of the department, the bureaus, which are in accordance with the program thrusts. The following bureaus are established: Bureau of Emergency Assistance; Bureau of Family and Community Welfare; Bureau of Disabled Persons; Bureau of Women's Welfare; and Bureau of Child and Youth Welfare.

In all of the programs, aside from relief and rehabilitation services, which have a different demand structure, the DSWD set its target at 60 percent of the identified problem areas, which were supposed to be achieved by 1992. From the 40,000 barangays (the smallest local government unit) of the country, the DSWD attempts to focus on 24,000 barangays, helping to erect 36,000 community structures and anticipating to have trained and organized some 540,000 barangay volunteers. The target with respect to the socially disadvantaged (poor) families is equally haunting: there are 5.8

million disadvantaged families targeted for DSWD assistance out of the total of 9.6 million such families nationwide. The services of self-employment assistance, parent effectiveness service, family case work, and social services for single parents are also part of the DSWD program, whereas planned parenthood service and marriage counselling are mandated by the Philippines civil code and family planning statutes. The program for socially disadvantaged women limits its operation to those women between the ages of 25 and 59. There are an estimated 5.6 million women who are potentially clients for the following social communication skills: self-employment assistance, maternal and child care skills, self-enhancement skills, community participation, and substitute home care. All together, the magnitude of these tasks meant that the targets or goals could probably never be achieved, but especially not by 1992.

All of these major programs cater to a highly impoverished nation. In other words, all the benefits that the social security and social welfare institutions are able to disburse are in heavy demand, given the level of rural and urban poverty. The term "poverty" denotes the many faces of deprivation suffered by the majority of Filipinos. Their lives are characterized by malnutrition and under-nutrition; extremely unequal distribution of wealth and access to work in the urban and rural areas alike; victimization through civil-war-like conditions in many parts of the nation, as well as the victimization by natural calamities (typhoons, droughts, floods, earthquakes), all of which regularly assault the lives of the poor majority. By all accounts, two-thirds of the society are constantly under some form of economic, social, and political stress (Canlas 1988; World Bank 1988). This must be compared with the fact that, at the same time, the Philippines has a comparatively high standard of education and an impressive history of a skilled administration (Corpuz 1957).

The Role of Social Networks

In analyzing the problems of social welfare in the Philippines, or any other Third World country, it is important to remember that the networks of the extended family and the neighborhood do, in fact, provide the necessary security to survive under adverse circumstances. This idea is fueled by a conjectural history of the past in industrialized countries, where one similarly assumed that closely knit communities, neighborhoods, and extended families were in fact the functional equivalent of modern day social security networks. Even though this interpretation of (at least European) history has been skilfully demystified (Mitterauer 1980), it is still widely presumed to be the predominant mode of cooperation and provision of an economic and social threshold in times of need in the Third World (Midgley 1984; Zacher 1988). Methodologically, this assumption follows the approach of modernization theory, which assumes (among other things) that societies develop from stages of mechanical to organic solidarity in concert with the theory of the development of higher differentiation and the division of labor in societies (Durkheim 1926; Smelser 1968).

Yet, when considering indigenous forms of social security, it is necessary to clearly appreciate two factors. The first is to recognize that when people must survive without the support of state institutions they do so with all the means available, whether from kin, friends, or other associations. The second is to understand over a given time period what kind of income or other financial transfers are occurring, under what conditions, and between whom. To label the indigenous networks as a functional equivalent to state intervention (or vice versa) becomes under these considerations a glimpse of the obvious. People have no other choice but to cope anyway. The question is how to assess this seemingly widespread network of help and assistance, solidarity, or generalized reciprocity within the realm of kinship and the family, which is assumed to be available.

Mangapit: The Results of a Field Study

To answer this question, the author conducted an empirical research in a comparatively well-to-do village (with electricity) in Northeast Nueva Ecija. After 10 months (1985) of field study in Mangapit—as the author calls this village—a mixed picture with regard to indigenous solidarity emerged. The results of can be summarized by four basic observations. First, while some sort of solidarity between people and/or households is available, it is not forthcoming in a predictable manner. Second, the extended Filipino family does not provide the ultimate safety net for what is often labelled the informal social security. Instead, kinship serves as a legitimizing communication network, like other networks (friends, church, "barkada," and so forth), but it cannot be considered as a reason for mutual aid. Third, a number of social networks operate along the different class alliances within the village, providing assistance to only a few households. Exchange between individuals or family members of different classes seems to occur only occasionally. Finally, the basis of social interaction is a high tolerance for ambiguity, which results in a low level of pursuing one's entitlements, either those granted by social customs or by state laws.

These observations are based on an analysis of the various networks available within the rural population. The unit of analysis was—in accordance with the local usage—the household ("bahay"). An interrelated web of several group formations exists, which include the "local kin group," a term coined by Murray (Murray 1970, 1973a & 1973b); the "compadrinazgo"; the "angkan" (clan), as well as several village-wide associations and local sources of credit such as the "sari-sari" (neighborhood store) and the "kabesilya" (agricultural laborers' groups).

The local kin group can be subdivided into three further elements, which are the "kasambahay" (housemate), "kapitbahay" (neighbor), and "kamg-anak" ("special relative"). Within this group, constant visiting and sharing takes place. However, local kin groups are quite unstable. The composition changes over time, its "members" do not possess "membership security"; and its activities are highly seasonal. The bilateral kinship system (real or attributed) is constantly (re)negotiated and depends upon the perception of needs and ability, of obligations and a continuous exchange of services, gifts, and goods. It is rare that entitlements are enforced; rather, the norm is best described as a high level of ambiguity in expectations and in promises. Additionally, norms like "hiya" (shyness, shame, saving face) can very well produce a stalemate at a time of need; one person cannot ask and the other cannot offer. Cheating, disappointments, personality clashes, differences over local and national politics, and so forth (real or imagined), all can lead to a disintegration of the local kin group (Kaut 1961), which consists of both the biological as well as the ritual kinship relationship.

Units covering the greater family system—like the "angkan" (or clan)— are mainly utilized for assistance in political matters or in demands beyond the boundaries of the village (Wolters 1984). In other words the "angkan" serves more as a general communication network. It can be perceived as a formation that exceeds the satisfaction of everyday needs. "Compadrazgo" (or "compadrinazgo") (the relationship between sponsor and sponsee) serves similar functions as does the angkan. There is one important variation: one can choose a "kumpare" and "kumare" (godfather and godmother of one's child), while one cannot, save some interesting exceptions, choose one's family.

How people assist each other can be assessed in several ways. First, an attempt can be made to gauge if acts of mutual assistance occur predominantly between closely related households. One way to measure mutual assistance is to quantify all exchanges between households that occur over a period of time. The aggregation of such give and take, comparing a group of closely related to non-related households, would then allow a judgment to be made as to whether preferential treatment of kin members could be established. Alternatively, the effects of such exchanges could be concentrated upon.

If such exchanges are assumed to take place preferentially between households that are closely related, then there should be a statistically significant correlation in the socioeconomic rankings of these selected households. For this purpose, a social class analysis was undertaken, based on indicators of the population itself. The results of this empirical inquiry supported the perception of households as basically individual units. Households were ranked into four classes: very poor (26.5 percent), poor (33.3 percent), rather well-off (32.5 percent), and rich (7.7 percent).

The hypothesis based on the perception of an enduring solidarity among kin members would expect that households whose members were consanguineously closely related would show a significant rank correlation. A close kin relationship was defined as one between parents and children, or sisters or brothers, of one couple in a household to a couple in another household. The rankings of individual households in relation to the rankings of its close relatives showed no statistical significant relationship, which confirmed the author's anecdotal observations (see Hirtz 1990: 292–395).

One such observation was made during a typhoon that ravaged the village during the author's field research and the treatment of the elderly. An assessment of the actions of the villagers before, during, and after the typhoon showed no refusal of cooperation but also hardly any provision for those affected by the typhoon. Despite good prior meteorological information in radio and TV, hardly any effort was made to alert neighbors, relatives, or other villagers. Shelter was offered not along family lines, but rather determined by the safety provided by a particular house for refuge and the proximity of it to their own dwelling. After the typhoon, those with destroyed houses were eager to return to their own sites, to live in their make-shift shelter, cooking in the open air until they had reconstructed their place, rather than working their way back to normalcy from a protected place among relatives or friends.

The other pertinent anecdotal observation concerns the treatment of the poorest in the village: the seven widows. They were living alone, and though they were assisted by those relatives living in the village, they were basically dependent on their own meager incomes, which they created by selling their labor whenever they were still physically capable. They generally cooked for themselves, and after the above-mentioned storm, all of them went back to their low quality "kubo" (make-shift house). There was only one three-generation household in the village, and, significantly, this was the only Protestant household in the Mangapit.

The view that "the family" is not of prime importance for the villagers is further supported by survey data from 117 members of the village. The answers to the following question were revealing: How do they prepare for times of financial hardship? First, there was a high diversity of answers, suggesting that different perceptions are at work when people judge their capacity to positively influence future events. These ranged from "saving" (actual savings or would save if possible) to "investments in farm product diversification" to "trust in social networks" to "faith in cultic practices (prayer, trust in God)" to "no preparations." Further qualitative research is needed to ascertain the different models of coping within the rural classes. Second, all answers show a curvilinear correlation between mode of preparation and class status. This indicates that one cannot employ arguments such as: "The poorer (or richer) a family the more (or less) it saves, invests, prays." The only exception is the category: "Trust in Social Network," which has an equal linear correlation, but scored too few absolute numbers to allow a generalizable judgment. Those who answered that friends and neighbors will assist in times of need were recorded under this category. Only one respondent specifically mentioned that one needs to maintain a good relationship with the neighbors. However, none of the richest ever mentioned social networks as a remedy for misfortunes. From this survey it is clear that the households in Mangapit preferred the individuals to cope with whatever adverse situation they might encounter.

CONCLUSION

It should not be concluded from this study that people in the rural Philippines are purely selfish and egoistic and that they do not care for each other. People in Mangapit muddle through and they do this cheerfully. This is difficult enough given the living conditions in the Philippines. One important finding is that mutual assistance is not structured along strong kinship relations. Instead, networks of help and support consist of an unstable mixture of relatives, friends, and working arrangements. On the other hand, people in need are not supported by state institutions even though the institutions of social welfare are well entrenched. This leaves rural Filipinos in a precarious situation where they are ignored by the state yet cannot depend upon kin or other local groups for help.

Rural Filipinas and Filipinos live in a contemporary world, and they are very aware of the social welfare achievements of their own country and of the advanced industrialized societies. They rightly claim access to social welfare institutions whose admission is denied to them. The argument that "modern" social systems destroy the "traditional" ties of solidarity, disrupting compassionate relations of assistance, is challenged by this case study in the Philippines, where such indigenous solidarity and assistance is not readily forthcoming. Clearly, the dichotomies in the social welfare literature on the Third World do not represent the more pluralistic reality that exists.

REFERENCES

Bossert, A. 1985. *Traditionelle und Moderne Formen Sozialer Sicherung in Tanzania* (Berlin: Düncker & Humblot).

Canlas, M. et al. 1988. *Land, Poverty and Politics in the Philippines* (London: Catholic Institute for International Relations).

Corpuz, O. 1957. *The Bureaucracy of the Philippines* (Manila: University of the Philippines).

Durkheim, E. 1926. *De la Division du Travail Social* (5th edition) (Paris: Gallimard).

Hirtz, F. 1988a. "Zur Entwicklung des Sozialrechts und der Sozialpolitik auf den Philippinen und in den Vereinigten Staaten, 1900–1935. Ein Vergleich" *Zeitschrift für Ausländisches und Internationales Arbeits-und Sozialrecht* 2(2): 125–38.

Hirtz, F. 1988b. "Coping with Adversity in the Philippine Lowlands" in Benda-Beckmann, F. von, Benda-Beckmann, K. von, Casino, G. R., Woodman, E. & Zacher, H. (eds.) *Between Kinship and the State: Law and Social Security in Developing Countries* (Dordrecht: Foris).

Hirtz, F. 1990. *Managing Insecurity–State Social Policy and Family Networks in the Rural Philippines. Past and Present* (Unpublished Ph.D. Thesis, University of Bielefeld, Bielefeld).

Kaut, Ch. 1961. "Utang na loob: A System of Contractual Obligation among Tagalogs" *SouthWestern Journal of Anthropology* 17(3): 256–72.

Lande, C. H. 1965. *Leaders, Factions and Parties. The Structure of Philippine Politics* (New Haven: Yale University Press).

Mendoza, T. L. 1981. *Social Welfare and Social Work. An Introduction* (Cebu City, Philippines: Q. Cornejo & Sons).

Midgley, J. 1984. *Social Security, Inequality and the Third World* (New York: John Wiley & Sons).

Mitterauer, M. 1980. "Der Mythos von der Vorindustriellen Grofamilie" in Mitterauer, M. & Sieder, R. (eds.) *Vom Patriarchat zur Partnerschaft. Zum Strukturwandel der Familie* (München: Beck).

Murray, F. J., Jr. 1970. *Local Groups and Kin-groups in a Tagalog Tenant Rice-farmers' Barrio*. (Ph.D. Dissertation, Dept of Anthropology, University of Pittsburgh) (Ann Arbor: University Microfilms).

Murray, F. J., Jr. 1973a. "Lowland Social Organization I: Local Kin Groups in a Central Luzon Barrio" *Philippine Sociological Review* 21(1): 29–36.

Murray, F. J., Jr. 1973b. "Lowland Social Organization II: Ambilineal Kin Groups in a Central Luzon Barrio," *Philippine Sociological Review* 21(2): 151–68.

Pangalangan, E. A. 1985. "Philippines" in Dixon, J. & Kim, H. S. (eds.) *Social Welfare in Asia* (London: Croom Helm).

Partsch, M. 1983. *Formen Sozialer Sicherung in Nicht-Industriellen Gesellschaften* (Berlin: Duncker & Humblot).

Smelser, N. 1968. "Toward a Theory of Modernization" in Smelser, N. (ed.) *Essays in Sociological Explanation* (Englewood Cliffs, NJ: Prentice Hall).

Social Security System of the Republic of the Philippines (SSS). 1990. *Facts and Figures* (Quezon City: SSS).

Wolters, W. 1984. *Politics, Patronage and Class Conflict in Central Luzon* (Quezon City: New Day Publishers).

World Bank. 1988. *The Philippine Poor: What is to be Done?* (Country Studies) (Washington: World Bank).

Wurfel, D. 1988. *Filipino Politics: Development and Decay* (Ithaca: Cornell University Press).

Zacher, H. F. 1988. "Traditional Solidarity and Modern Social Security: Harmony or Conflict?" in Benda-Beckmann, F. von et al. (eds.) *Between Kinship and the State: Law and Social Security in Developing Countries* (Dordrecht: Foris).

7

Social Security Reforms in China

Nelson W. S. Chow

The social security system in China is in need of major revisions. In February 1985, the then Premier of the State Council of the People's Republic of China (PRC), Zhao Ziyang, was reported to have remarked that the Chinese social security system must be looked into and revised in accordance with the economic reforms carried out in recent years (Ma 1986). Since then, local and overseas social security experts have expressed their views on how best to reform the Chinese social security system (Xu & Chen 1986; Chow 1989). At the same time, experimental projects to improve the system have been tried out in various counties and townships of China, and some of the successful ones have now been implemented nation-wide.[1] While China is still groping its way toward a new social security system, it is the intention of this chapter to discuss the following three sets of questions. First, why does the system need revision? What changes have resulted from the economic reforms, and to what extent have they affected the operation of the existing social security programs? Second, what are the shortcomings and ideological constraints that surround the reform of the system? Third, what are the social security reform proposals? What are the possible future directions in which the system could develop?

With the suppression of the democratic movement in China in 1989, and the subsequent political turmoil, came the departure of some of the political leaders who had been supportive of social security reform (such as Zhao Ziyang), which must have slowed down the reform process. But recent happenings, such as the experimentation of social insurance in Hainan province and Shenzhen special economic zone, indicate that instead of becoming a dead issue, social security reform is still under active pursuit in China.[2]

WHY THE CHINESE SOCIAL SECURITY SYSTEM NEEDS REFORM

The existing Chinese social security system can roughly be divided into two parts: one covering the majority of the state and collective enterprise workers working in the cities, and the other helping the indigent in both the cities and the rural areas who lack the means of a basic living or are victims of natural disasters (Dixon 1992; Chow 1988).

State expenditures on social security are presently absorbed mostly by the programs provided for the state and collective enterprise workers and their dependents, with little left over for the peasants living in the villages. As four-fifths of the work force in China are living in the villages, this means that only a minority of the Chinese are beneficiaries of the state social security programs.[3] But even for this minority, the expenditures on their protection have been escalating so rapidly in recent years that social security costs have now become a matter of national concern.

The escalating costs of providing social security benefits for the urban workers have been attributed mainly to the increasing number of retired workers. By the end of 1989, 22 million workers in the cities were reported to have retired and were receiving old age pensions (State Statistical Bureau & Ministry of Labor 1990: 389). Other than the increasing number, the relatively high rates of old age pensions, equivalent to around 60 to 80 percent of the workers' last wages, is another reason for the financial burden to become unbearable, especially when wages have been on the rise in recent years (Chow 1989). As a result, expenditures on labor insurance and welfare benefits increased from a sum equivalent to 13.7 percent of the total wage bill of the urban workers in 1978 to 28.2 percent in 1989 (State Statistical Bureau & Ministry of Labor 1990: 397). Although the burden finally falls on the state in the capacity of the ultimate owner of most of the urban enterprises, it is still a heavy one.

In addition to the increasing costs, recent economic reforms in China have also revealed other shortcomings of the existing social security programs. First, with the development of free enterprise in the economy, individual or non-state enterprises have flourished in great numbers. While just over six million workers at the end of 1989 were reported to be working in such enterprises, over 70 million peasants were known to have left farming and were engaged in various commercial or industrial activities in the villages.[4] These "self-employed" workers are excluded from the protection of the Labor Insurance Regulations, which cover mainly the state enterprise workers. What these workers can resort to in times of difficulty is the relief provided by the Civil Affairs bureau. How to provide for this group of "unprotected" workers is now an issue urgently calling for a solution. Second, in order to attract foreign investments, China has since the early 1980s been establishing special economic zones along the coastal regions. The conditions of employment for workers working in these zones are different from the state enterprise workers, and they are generally excluded from labor insurance protection. Though in some cases, contracts directly negotiated between the workers and their employers might include coverage for sickness, injury, and survivors' benefits, a more uniform system is still to be worked out (Philipps & Yeh 1987). It is obvious that the existing provisions, especially the Labor Insurance Regulations first introduced in 1951 (Dixon 1981a), are no longer capable of meeting the challenges of the time. New arrangements or even an overhaul of the entire system are now necessary.

A further question related to the financial burden of providing the labor insurance benefits is the profitability of the state enterprises. In 1984, the Central Committee of the Chinese Communist Party (CCP) issued a decision to reform the economic structure of the cities, and one of the measures was to lessen the control of the state over the enterprises (*Decision. . . . 1984*). In simple terms, state enterprises had to become profitable. As labor insurance payments usually formed a substantial proportion of the outlays of the state enterprises, enterprise managers were put in an awkward position of trying to strike a balance between the profitability of their enterprises and the social security needs of their workers. Although changes have later been made for collective labor insurance funds to be set up instead of requiring individual state enterprises to be responsible for the payments, the conflict that arises from the dual role of the "protector" of the well-being of the workers and profit-making organizations have not been completely resolved (Ministry of Labor 1989).

The urban and rural indigent receive assistance provided by the Ministry of Civil Affairs. Before examining the need for reforms, it has to be realized that like their ancestors, Chinese peasants are today receiving most of their financial help from their kin and the village communities (Leung 1990). Immediately after the establishment of the PRC, villages continued their age-old practice of collecting charitable contributions from the more wealthy members and distributing them to help the sick and the indigent. Then came the commune system in 1958, and the practice, rather than coming to a stop, had been made mandatory with the establishment of welfare funds in every commune (Dixon 1982). The commune system was disbanded in 1982, and before that a "responsibility system" was introduced, allowing peasants a greater freedom to exercise control over their own piece of land (Oi 1990). Although the dissolution of the commune system has not resulted in a complete disappearance of the welfare funds, peasant families are now expected to be more self-reliant and to turn to the village communities or the Civil Affairs bureau for assistance only when they have exhausted their own financial means.

The extent of assistance that is currently provided by the Civil Affairs bureau can only be described as minimal or meager. So far as the peasants are concerned, the more permanent assistance program provided for them is known as the five-guarantee system ("wu bao hu"), which caters mainly for the needs of the orphans and the lonely elderly. In addition, the Civil Affairs bureau also provides temporary assistance for "difficult households," both in the cities and in the villages, and relief for victims of natural disasters. In 1988, 34.5 million peasants were reported to have been assisted by the Civil Affairs bureau with another 2.5 million provided for under the five-guarantee system (State Statistical Bureau 1989: 894). Compared with the over 1.2 billion population in China, those assisted represented only a small percentage, and what they could obtain is often nothing more than a basic living standard. It is also known that although stark starvation has largely been wiped out in China, poverty as measured by a living below the subsistence level still exists,[5] and a reform of the Chinese social security system must assume as a primary task the guarantee of the means of a basic living for everyone.

In summary, the Chinese social security system has been found to be on the one hand putting too heavy a financial burden on the state enterprises, and on the other failing to provide sufficient support for the needy and the indigent. As a result, reforms are necessary to redress the imbalance of the system both in terms of the distribution of state resources allocated for social security and the ranking of the needs that the system should strive to meet. But as China is such a big country with immense diversities, any proposal to revise a system that may affect the lives of more than 1.1 billion people must necessarily be an extremely complicated matter.

SHORTCOMING AND IDEOLOGICAL CONSTRAINTS OF THE CHINESE SOCIAL SECURITY SYSTEM

Before examining the various proposals to reform the Chinese social security system, it may be desirable to first look at the shortcomings of the system itself and the ideological issues surrounding the reform. First, the present social security system in China is extremely limited in its coverage since, strictly speaking, only state enterprise workers and some of those working in the collective enterprises are covered by social security in its modern connotation (Yan 1987). This has not posed any problem in the years before the introduction of the economic reforms in 1979, as migration of peasants into the cities was strictly forbidden (Dixon 1981b). Unlike other developing countries, which often experience a swelling of their urban population within a short period, China had been successful for 30 years after the establishment of the PRC in keeping its urban population at less than 20 percent of the total population. However, migration rules were relaxed after the introduction of the economic reforms, and the urban population speedily jumped from 20.2 percent of the total population in 1981 to 51.7 percent in 1989 (State Statistical Bureau & Ministry of Labor 1990: 4). Although the majority of the peasants who have left farming moved only to live in the nearby townships instead of big cities like Beijing, Shanghai, and Guangzhou, this migration has still given rise to very serious social and economic repercussions. It is obvious that, after leaving their villages, the peasants could no longer avail themselves of the assistance of the village communities (Chan 1990). On the other hand, they could not enjoy the labor insurance benefits provided for the state enterprise workers. The Labor Insurance Regulations in their present form could hardly be extended to cover all the workers working in different types of enterprises, as it is simply not feasible financially. New arrangements will have to be devised, but it will mean that the inequality in terms of social security protection that has long existed between the urban workers and the farmers will now be extended to workers employed in different types of urban enterprises (Davis 1988). Of course, those working in the state enterprises will remain the most privileged.

A second defect of the Chinese social security system that has existed ever since the days when it was first devised is that it is not geared to the special economic and social conditions of the country. So far as the labor insurance program is concerned, the Chinese government has never concealed the fact that it was patterned after the Soviet model and based on the principles laid down by V. I. Lenin.[6] As a result, the program could at its best only be representative of the socialist ideal, but in view of the predominantly agrarian economy of the country, it is obviously out of place. And as long as the program is regarded as a device to safeguard the interests of the state enterprise workers, there is little likelihood that it could be revised to take into consideration the financial capacity of the state enterprises and, more fundamentally, the level of social security protection that the country as a whole should provide for its workers (Zhao & Pan 1984). It is indeed rather unfortunate that the social security system in China has been viewed as a vanguard of socialism rather than a device to counteract the blind forces of a modern economy.

It is also tragic that the Chinese cultural heritage, particularly the traditional supportive networks of the family and village, has not always been acknowledged in devising social security schemes. It has been pointed out that the family system as well as the village communities remain until today the most important institutions to provide help and assistance for people living in the rural areas. Yet, although the village communities have sometimes been mobilized to organize help for the needy members, they have been treasured more for their political rather than welfare roles. At times, the welfare functions of the village communities have even been viewed as posing a challenge to the state in taking away the loyalty of the people from the latter. Hence, the village communities as well as the family system have often been seen as enemies rather than as allies of the state in safeguarding the people's well-being (Ministry of Civil Affairs 1987). Only in the last few years, and after the demise of the commune system, have the village communities been revived and acknowledged as occupying a proper place in the entire social security network (Chen 1990).

The Chinese social security system as an income-support measure is badly in need of improvement. But the revision of such a major social institution as social security in socialist China can never be a simple technical matter; it must also be justified on ideological grounds. The labor insurance program was introduced to vindicate the superiority of socialism. Hence, if there is any need to revamp that program, the first ideological question that would have to be answered is whether it would continue to safeguard the interests of the proletariat. In the words of the CCP, the system must remain "socialist" in nature. Thus in the Seventh Five-Year Plan for Social and Economic Development, it was stated that the aim was "to gradually put in place a socialist social security system with Chinese characteristics" ("The Seventh Five-Year Plan. . ." 1986: 136). Another ideological issue arising from the above statement is that the Chinese social security system must also be "Chinese." The word "Chinese" is of course open to interpretation, but the Seventh Five-Year Plan (1986: 136) further stated: "We shall continue to foster the fine tradition of mutual assistance among relatives, friends and neighbours." It is thus clear that as long as the system does not deviate from its "socialist" nature, which probably means the principles laid down by Lenin on social insurance, the Chinese communists are prepared to accept the contributions made by the traditional supportive networks to the protection of the livelihood of the people.

Another major ideological debate that has been carried out concerns the interpretation of the principles of "to each according to his work" and "to each according to his need" (Xu & Wang 1985; also Dixon & Kim 1992). Those advocating a complete revision of the social security system would argue that since China is at the early stage of socialism, it would not be possible for the state to satisfy all the income-support needs of the people. Hence it would be wrong to base the system on the concept of "to each according to his need" and to organize programs without regard to the past contributions of the beneficiaries. They would like to see the principle of "to each according to his work" adopted so as to wipe out the "eating from the same rice pot" syndrome and hence lessen the financial burden on the state. However, those insisting on the "need" principle would argue that social security provisions are by nature needs-based; though they would not advocate for a system to cover all the income support needs, neither would they want a social security system entirely divorced from the primary task of meeting needs.

To some people, the ideological debate on the "work" and "need" principles may be futile. The Minister of Civil Affairs, Cui Naifu, once suggested that as China was moving from a product economy to a commodity economy, it would be imperative for "the national [social security] reform program [to] include relevant mechanisms aimed at social stability" and one of the ways to do it was to establish "a system under which the state provides, in accordance with relevant legislation, security of existence to its citizens by means of distribution and redistribution of the national income" (Cui 1988: 171). In other words, what Cui wanted was a state social security system that guaranteed for everyone in China a basic living standard. The importance of such a system is obvious, as many of the Chinese in both the villages and the cities are still deprived of the minimum income support. Cui hoped that such a guarantee could come from the distribution and redistribution of the national income. The attention is therefore focused once again on what the state could do for her people, especially for the purpose of promoting social stability, rather than dwelling on the fruitless discussion of the interpretation of "work" and "need." While the introduction of a social security system that provides for every Chinese the security of existence is an immense task, it probably is the most suitable measure to achieve what is stated in the Chinese Constitution, that "Citizens of the PRC have the right to material assistance from the state and society when they are old, ill or disabled."[7]

In summary, the ideological issues discussed above indicate that the Chinese leaders themselves are at a loss about the direction that the social security system should develop in the future. What they have insisted on is that the system must remain socialist in nature and should be combined, if possible, with "the fine tradition of mutual assistance among relatives, friends and neighbours." But what exactly "a socialist social security system with Chinese characteristics" means is unclear, and the decision is made even more difficult with the debate on the meaning of "work" and "need" and their role within the provision of social security. After the political turmoil in China in 1989, there is no doubt that the Chinese leaders will now proceed slowly with the reform of social security, in order not to upset the superior position of the state enterprise workers in particular. But with the recent social and economic changes in China, more and more Chinese are badly in need of income support and they will continue to suffer while the leaders are considering an acceptable ideological basis for a social security program.

SOCIAL SECURITY REFORM PROPOSALS AND EXPERIMENTS

As the ideological debate goes on, proposals and attempts to reform the Chinese social security system have at the same time been made. Among the many proposals and attempts, those made by the Ministry of Labor and the Ministry of Civil Affairs are of special relevance here, as these two ministries are responsible for the administration of the different social security schemes. In brief, the Ministry of Labor is in charge of implementing the Labor Insurance Regulations and, not surprisingly, they have concentrated their suggestions on the reform of programs protecting the urban workers (Fu 1985). In making their suggestions, the Ministry has stressed that, first, the reform must be based on a realistic assessment of the financial conditions of the country; second, it must be conducive to production as well as the protection of the livelihood of the people; third, the future labor insurance program must be managed collectively and not by enterprises on an individual basis; fourth, the funding must come from different sources, including the state, the enterprises, and individual workers; and finally, the future program must be planned together with the reform of the wage system and other state subsidies. In addition, the Ministry held the view that the existing Labor Insurance Regulations must gradually be replaced by contributory insurance schemes.

The suggestions made by the Ministry of Labor could only be described as modest, but they already represent a radical departure from the existing practices. For example, one of the principles laid down by Lenin on social insurance was that the costs of financing the benefits must be borne entirely by the employers and the state, but the Ministry of Labor suggested that funding of the schemes must also come from the workers themselves. Partly as a result of this suggestion made by the Ministry of Labor, new workers joining the state enterprises after October 1, 1986 have been required to contribute a monthly sum equivalent to three percent of their wages toward an old age fund.[8] But the fact that the existing workers are not required to contribute reflects that it is also important to maintain the status quo.

Another radical suggestion of the Ministry of Labor is that labor insurance funds should be established at the county and city levels to replace the practice of having enterprises individually responsible for their labor insurance payments. When the suggestion was first put forward in the mid-1980s, it was strongly resisted by the new state enterprises, as it implied that they would have to share the funding burden of labor insurance with the old enterprises. However, notwithstanding the resistance and the criticism that the establishment of the funds would hinder economic progress as new enterprises would have less capital for investment, labor insurance funds were gradually set up in most of the cities and counties. It was reported that by early 1989, about 2,000 collective labor insurance funds have been established in more than 90 percent of the cities and counties in China (Fu 1990: 138). In other words, most state enterprise workers are no longer receiving their labor insurance payments, particularly old age pensions, from their employers; at the same time, contributions are now required of the employers toward the labor insurance funds.

As to the other suggestion of the Ministry that the wage system be reformed together with the labor insurance system, changes are only coming slowly. For the majority of the state enterprise workers, the distinction between "wage" and "labor insurance and welfare benefits" is still very unclear, as they tend to take them all as one package to support their living. The Head of the Insurance and Welfare Bureau of the Ministry of Labor was also worried about the confusion. He suggested that the two systems be distinguished by defining the labor insurance and welfare benefits as "a form of social security provided by the state and society for workers who have lost their working capacity" (Fu 1985, 463). What he meant was that labor insurance benefits should not be regarded as supplements to the generally low wages received by the workers; neither should they be used as incentives for increased production. Their purpose should remain as a compensation or safeguard for the living of those who have for one reason or another lost their working capacity. Nevertheless, as long as wages are kept absurdly low in China, it seems unlikely that the workers could totally rely on their wages as their sole means of living, and any reduction in labor insurance and welfare benefits would actually impoverish the majority of the workers (Zhao & Yang 1987). Given the present level of wages, it also seems unlikely that the workers could make a significant contribution toward their own protection.

As for the Ministry of Civil Affairs, their suggestions have concentrated on the income support needs of those who were not covered by the Labor Insurance Regulations (Xu & Chen 1986; Chan 1990). The suggestions of the Ministry consisted of the following: first, that different types of social insurance schemes be introduced to cover the various newly emerging needs, such as unemployment, workers employed on contract terms, and those arising from the increasing numbers of divorces and the enforcement of the one-child policy; second, that attention be given to the achievement of social equality by concentrating help on the needy, especially those living in the rural areas; and finally, that the introduction of any new measures take into account the possible contributions of the family, relatives, and local communities.

To implement the first suggestion, the Ministry of Civil Affairs has since 1985 been experimenting with various contributory social insurance schemes to cover natural disasters, medical care, and old age (Ministry of Civil Affairs 1987). Although only those who could afford the premium, like the more wealthy farmers and the better paid workers, are covered, the experimental schemes demonstrate that contributory social insurance schemes are not impossible in China. As for the second proposal that resources should be concentrated on helping the needy, the Ministry has been experimenting with various assistance schemes to relieve the plight of the poor and the lonely. It was reported that in 1988, 34 million people living in the villages and 7.2 million in the cities, respectively, were assisted by various relief programs (State Statistical Bureau 1989: 894). The Ministry has also been moving ahead with the plan of employing as many disabled persons in welfare factories as possible in order to promote self-reliance. But the major difficulty encountered by the Ministry is still the lack of funds, as it usually receives just over one percent of the total state budget.[9] In order to raise more funds for welfare, the Ministry has since the mid-1980s introduced the sale of lotteries,[10] although ideologically it appears to be rather unacceptable in a socialist country.

As for mobilizing the contribution of the relatives, friends, and neighbors, the Ministry of Civil Affairs has been placing a greater emphasis on the welfare functions performed by the rural collectives in the villages and the residents' committees in the cities.[11] Most of the lonely elderly in the villages are now taken care of by the rural collectives, and in the cities many residents' committees have also set up their own welfare factories and institutions for the disabled and the elderly.[12] The Ministry of Civil Affairs admits that its bureaus in the local districts are often supplementing what the rural collectives and the residents' committees are providing.

Other than the attempts made by the Ministry of Labor and the Ministry of Civil Affairs, the World Bank once sent a mission in 1989 to advise China on how to develop its social security system (World Bank 1989). In fact, before 1989, other World Bank missions visiting China have also expressed their concern about social security development in China. For example, a World Bank report published in 1985 commented that "continued heavy reliance on pensions paid directly by employers could be an obstacle to intensive growth"(World Bank 1985: 141). As for the special mission on social security, it recommended that in the short run, China should consider the introduction of pay-as-you-go old age pensions. In the long-run the mission hoped that China could set up old age pension funds with contributions equivalent to around 20 percent of the workers' wages to be paid jointly by the employers and the workers, with the latter contributing about three percent of their wages. The mission also recommended the extension of unemployment insurance with contributions solely collected from employers. Partly based on the recommendations of the World Bank mission, China introduced in the beginning of 1990 contributory social insurance in Hainan province and the Shenzhen special economic zone on an experimental basis (Liu 1993). Although results of the experiments are still to be assessed, it looks very likely that contributory social insurance would be the method to be adopted to meet the income-support needs of those who are presently not covered by the Labor Insurance Regulations.

FUTURE DIRECTION: A SOCIALIST SOCIAL SECURITY SYSTEM WITH CHINESE CHARACTERISTICS

Recent attempts to revise the existing social security provisions and to introduce new ones have already made the Chinese social security system very different from that at the time when China opened up its economy in the late 1970s. However, in revising its social security system, China is hampered in the following aspects: first, since the early 1950s China has instituted for the state enterprise workers one of the most comprehensive and also non-contributory labor insurance programs in the world (Yue 1985; Dixon 1981a). Any attempts to alter the arrangements and to require particular contributions from the workers would inevitably result in immense dissatisfaction and resistance. Second, as China is still a poor country with a Gross National Product per capita under US $400 a year, there would be few choices for the leaders but to concentrate a large portion of the resources on relieving the hardship of those who could not even afford a living above the subsistence level. Third, as a socialist country, China is bounded by the mandate, real or not, to maintain equality in the society (Fu 1990: 67–69). In other words, the design of any new programs must not aggravate social inequality and must also first consider the needs of those at the bottom layers. A fourth restriction is that in such a vast country with immense geographical as well as social and economic diversities, the application of a single system for all regions would be unacceptable. The Chinese social security system must therefore by necessity be a diffused one in order to suit the many different needs.

In 1986, when China announced its Seventh Five-Year Plan for Social and Economic Development, it had the following to say about social security development ("The Seventh Five-Year Plan . . ." 1986: 136).

During the period of the Seventh Five-Year Plan, we shall try to gradually put in place a socialist social security system with Chinese characteristics. We shall establish a social insurance system, promote social welfare undertakings, continue to give preferential treatment to families of servicemen and revolutionary martyrs and provide relief to the needy. Social security funds will be raised through various channels. We shall reform the social security management system by integrating socialised administration with work unit administration, but emphasizing the former. We shall continue to foster the fine tradition of mutual assistance among relatives, friends and neighbours.

With the constraints mentioned above, what was stated in the Seventh Five-Year Plan on social security is probably the most that the Chinese leaders were prepared to implement in revising its social security system. To carry out the mandate in the Plan, a number of reform measures were introduced including: the introduction of contributory social insurance for the more affluent farmers and selected groups of workers not covered by the Labor Insurance Regulations; the requirement of contributions from new state enterprise workers for their own old age pensions; the setting up of

unemployment funds by collecting contributions from employers; the establishment of collective labor insurance funds at the city and county levels;
the setting up of welfare institutions and factories through the efforts of the
rural collectives and the residents' committees; the strengthening of relief
and assistance programs for the indigent and dependents of servicemen.

By the early 1990s, after the implementation of the series of reforms, it
was obvious that social security benefits in China had gradually shed their
former image of being "gifts" given by the state. Although Chinese leaders
still insist that the system represents the superiority of socialism, people
have learned the hard fact that they too have to make their contributions,
not directly but through their own employing enterprises. The "eating from
the same rice pot" syndrome has of course not been completely wiped away,
as most of the urban enterprises are still state-owned and there is no
intention to change this basis, but benefits have been gradually reduced
and workers employed by non-state enterprises have also learned to rely on
their own resources.

The spirit of self-reliance is even more apparent in the villages, where
the main form of assistance still comes from the family and the village
communities. Though this is congruent with the emphasis of creating a
system with "Chinese characteristics," mutual assistance among relatives,
friends, and neighbors has long existed in Chinese society and is definitely
not the result of the deliberate effort of the present government (Chow
1990). What the CCP can best do is in fact not to destroy this fine tradition.
Indeed, what the CCP achieved in the past few years after the an-
nouncement of the intention to revamp the social security system was to
rectify some of its imbalances and shortcomings, which have arisen because
the CCP has for many years used it for purposes other than providing
income support for the people (Davis 1989). As long as the Chinese social
security system is given its legitimate place as a means to protect people
against the vicissitudes of life of a modern society, it would be performing
its primary functions of financial allocation.

NOTES

1. It was reported in *The Hong Kong Economic Journal* (January 27, 1991) that
the State Economic System Reform Commission had adopted seven strategies to
reform the social security system in China. These strategies were tried out in the
last few years and were proven successful.

2. The State Economic System Reform Commission announced in early
1991 that social security experiments were being carried out in the following

places: social insurance in Shenzhen special economic zone and Hainan province, medical insurance in Dandong, and rural old age insurance in Dailian (see *The Hong Kong Economic Journal*, January 27, 1991).

3. At the end of 1989, the work force in China numbered 553.29 million persons, and of this number 143.91 million, or 26 percent, were working in the cities and 409.38 million or 74 percent, were working in the villages (see State Statistical Bureau and Ministry of Labor 1990: 3).

4. The Ministry of Civil Affairs reported in 1986 that over 70 million people in the villages were engaged in commercial or industrial activities (see *Shehui Baozhang Bao* (Social Security News), No. 27, October 2, 1986).

5. According to a survey conducted in 1986, which defined a peasant household with annual per capita income of less than 200 yuan as being poor, 11 percent, or 88 million people, were found to be living in poverty (see *People's Republic of China Yearbook* 1987: 570).

6. The principles laid down on social insurance by V. I. Lenin can be found in Rimlinger 1971: 250.

7. See Article 45 of the Constitution of the People's Republic of China adopted in 1982.

8. The stipulation can be found in "Temporary Directive Regarding the Implementations of Labor Contract System in State-Run Enterprises" issued by the State Council in 1986.

9. It was reported that in 1988, total government expenditure amounted to 266.8 billion yuan, with 4.19 billion yuan, or 1.53 percent, allocated for social welfare purposes (see State Statistical Bureau 1989: 657 &. 666).

10. A Social Welfare Lotteries Committee was set up in 1987 to coordinate the sale of lotteries in various provinces of China. In 1988, the sale of lotteries amounted to 500 million yuan, and 150 million yuan were subsequently given to various social welfare projects (see the report in *Outlook Weekly* (Overseas Edition), January 9, 1989).

11. Community service centers have been set up in nearly all cities in China to provide services for the elderly, the handicapped, and the mentally ill. These centers, numbered 70,000 at the end of 1990, are run by the residents' committees with assistance from civil affairs bureaus (see the report of an interview with the Social Welfare Section Head of the Ministry of Civil Affairs in *Ming Pao*, December 7, 1990).

12. At the end of 1988, there were altogether 39,030 social welfare institutions and 40,496 social welfare factories throughout the country (see State Statistical Bureau 1989: 893).

REFERENCES

Chan, C. 1990. *Issues of Welfare Planning in the PRC in the Midst of Economic Reform* (Hong Kong: University of Hong Kong, Centre of Urban Studies and Urban Planning).

Chen, L. 1990. *Shehui Baozhang Jiaocheng* (The Content of Social Security) (Beijing: Beijing Knowledge Press).

Chow, N.W.S. 1988. *The Administration and Financing of Social Security in China* (Hong Kong: University of Hong Kong, Centre of Asian Studies).

Chow, N.W.S. 1989. "Modernization and Social Security Reforms in China" *Asian Perspective* 13(2): 55–68.

Chow, N.W.S. 1990. "Social Welfare in China" in Elliott, D., Mayadas, N. S. & Watts, T. D. (eds.) *The World of Social Welfare* (Springfield, Illinois: Charles C. Thomas).

Cui, N. 1988. "Reflections on a Social Security System with Chinese Characteristics" *International Social Security Review* 41(2): 170–5.

Davis, D. 1988. "Unequal Chances, Unequal Outcomes: Pension Reform and Urban Inequality" *The China Quarterly* 114: 223–43.

Davis, D. 1989. "Chinese Social Welfare: Policies and Outcomes" *The China Quarterly* 115: 577–97.

Decision of the Central Committee of the Communist Party of China on Reform of the Economic Structure 1984 (Hong Kong: Joint Publishing Company).

Dixon, J. 1981a. "The Workers' Social Assistance System in China: 1949–1979" *International Social Work* 21(1): 1–13.

Dixon, J. 1981b. "Community-based Welfare Support in China: 1949–1979" *Community Development Journal* 16(1) (January): 21–30.

Dixon, J. 1982. "The Community-based Rural Welfare System in the People's Republic of China: 1949–1979" *Community Development Journal* 17 (1) (January): 2–12.

Dixon, J. 1992."China"in Dixon, J. & Macarov, D. (eds.) *Social Welfare in Socialist Countries* (London: Routledge).

Dixon, J. & Kim, H. S. 1992. "Social Welfare under Socialism" in Dixon, J. & Macarov, D. (eds.) *Social Welfare in Socialist Countries*. (London: Routledge).

Fu, H. 1985. "Gaige Laobao Fuli Zhidu" (Reform of the Labor Welfare System) in *Laodong Gongzi Renshi Zhidu Gaige de Yanjin Yu Tantao* (A Study of the Reform of the Labor, Wages, Personnel System) (Beijing: Labor and Personnel Press).

Fu, H. 1990. *Shehui Baoxian de Lilun yu Shijian* (The Theory and Practice of Social Insurance) (Henan: Henan People's Press).

Leung, J. 1990. "The Community-Based Welfare System in China," *Community Development Journal* 25(3): 195–205.

Liu, L. 1993. "New Forms of Social Security in South China" *Social Security Bulletin* 56(1): 93–94.

Ma, C. 1986. "Shehui Baozhang Tizhi Gaige Fazhan Qushi Chutan" (A Preliminary Study of the Trend of Social Security Reform) *Zhongguo Minzheng* (Civil Affairs of China) 1: 13–14.

Ministry of Civil Affairs. 1987. *Nongcun Shehui Baozhang Tansuo* (An Enquiry into Rural Social Security) (Hunan: Hunan University Press).

Ministry of Labor. 1989. *Shehui Baoxian, Tuixiu Feiyang Shehui Tongchou* (The Collective Administration of Social Insurance and Retirement Fees) (Beijing: Ministry of Labor, Social Insurance and Welfare Section).

Oi, J. C. 1990. "The Fate of the Collective after the Commune" in Davis, D. & Vogel, E. F. (eds.) *Chinese Society on the Eve of Tiananmen* (Cambridge and London: Harvard University Press).

People's Republic of China Yearbook. 1987. (Beijing: Xinhua Publishing House).

Philipps, D. R. & Yeh, A.G.O. 1987. "The Provision of Housing and Social Services in China's Special Economic Zones" *Environment and Planning C: Government and Policy* 5: 447–68.

Rimlinger, G. V. 1971. *Welfare Policy and Industrialization in Europe, America and Russia* (New York: John Wiley and Son).

State Statistical Bureau. 1989. *The Chinese Statistical Yearbook 1989* (Beijing: China Statistical Press).

State Statistical Bureau and Ministry of Labor. 1990. *Zhongguo Laodong Gongzi Tongji Nianjian* (Annual Statistical Report on Work and Wages) (Beijing: China Statistical Press).

"The Seventh Five-Year Plan of the People's Republic of China for Economic and Social Development (1986–1990)." 1986. In *Documents of the Fourth Session of the Sixth National People's Congress* (Beijing: Foreign Languages Press).

World Bank. 1985. *China-Long-Term Development Issues and Options* (Baltimore: Johns Hopkins University Press).

World Bank. 1989. *Zhongguo Shehui Zhuyi Jingji Zhong Shehui Baozhang Zhidu Gaige* (The Reform of the Chinese Social Security System Within the Socialist Economy) (Beijing: The World Bank, Asia Office, China Unit).

Xu, C. & Chen L. 1986. "Tantao Xinde Shehui Baozhang Zhidu de Yuanze he Gouxiang" (A Construct of the Principles of a New Social Security System) *Shehui Baozhang Bao* (Social Security News) (Trial) 1 (6 March).

Xu, Y. & Wang Y. 1985. *Zhongguo Shehui Zhuyi Laodong Wenti* (The Problem of Labor in Chinese Socialism) (Anhui: Anhui People's Press).

Yan, Z. 1987. *Dangdai Zhongguo de Zhigong Gongzi Fuli he Shehui Baoxian* (The Wages, Welfare and Social Insurance for Workers in Today's China) (Beijing: China Social Sciences Press).

Yue, G. 1985. "Employment, Wages and Social Security in China" *International Labor Review* 124(4): 411–22.

Zhao, L. & Pan, J. 1984. *Laodong Jingii yu Laodong Guangli* (Labor Economics and Labor Management) (Beijing: Beijing Press).

Zhao, Lukuan & Yang Tiren. 1987. *Zhongguo Laodong Jingji Tizhi Gaige* (The Reform of the Chinese Labor Economic System) (Chengdu: Sichuan Scientific Press).

8

Social Security and Redistribution: The Case of Zimbabwe

Edwin Kaseke

The term "social security" is often interpreted differently, hence the variation in the nature and scope of social security schemes worldwide. However, despite such variations there seems to be some consensus that the objective of social security is to maintain income in the event of involuntary loss of income. In this chapter the International Labor Organization's definition of social security applies, viz: "the security that society furnishes through appropriate organization against certain risks to which its members are exposed" (ILO 1942: 80).

SOCIAL SECURITY IN ZIMBABWE

Zimbabwe does not have a comprehensive social security system but rather a number of fragmented schemes (Hampson & Kaseke 1987; Kawewe 1994a & 1994b). The existence of such a state of affairs must be understood within the context of Zimbabwe's political and economic history. It must be pointed out that the advent of colonialism and the resultant industrialization and urbanization necessitated dependence on a wage economy in order to meet basic needs. At the same time, it was recognized that dependency on a wage economy is associated with certain risks that curtail the ability of an individual to sustain himself and his family. On one hand, individuals may fail to derive their livelihood from the wage economy by virtue of the economy's inability to generate enough jobs for the people, and yet on the other hand they may fail to do so on account of such contingencies as old age, injury, sickness, and invalidity.

Unfortunately, in colonial Rhodesia this recognition of the relationship between individuals and their environment was only in respect of the white settler community. The indigenous population was excluded on the assumption that their needs were simple and that they could be met within the extended family network and the peasant economy (Kawewe 1994b). As Clarke (1977) notes, the peasant economy was viewed as an indigenous pension. Thus black individuals in an urban area were expected to return to their rural home at the cessation of employment.

Consequently, social security was primarily targeted at the white settler community and resulted in the reinforcement of inequality between the white and black population. Expressing his disappointment at the attitude of the colonial government Savanhu (1945: 3) explained: "It should not be supposed therefore that Africans working in towns could return to live in the native reserves which have already proved incapable of carrying the African population now domiciled there."

The various social security schemes will now be discussed before examining the extent to which they facilitate the redistribution of income or wealth.

Welfare Assistance

Welfare assistance, commonly known as public assistance, is a non-contributory social security scheme administered by the Department of Social Welfare, which provides state-financed, means-tested financial benefits to persons of limited means. For decades the provision of welfare assistance in Zimbabwe was not governed by an Act of Parliament, and it was only in 1988 that the Welfare Assistance Act was enacted.

In terms of the Welfare Assistance Act (1988), the Director of Social Welfare or any person acting on his behalf may grant social welfare assistance to a destitute or indigent person where he is satisfied that such a person "is over sixty years of age; or is handicapped physically or mentally; or suffers continuous ill-health; or is a dependent of a person who is destitute or indigent or incapable of looking after himself; or otherwise has need for social welfare assistance."

Welfare assistance is only awarded in circumstances where an applicant can prove that he is experiencing financial hardships and is unable to obtain assistance from his family or from any other source. The level of assistance awarded is usually Z $15 per adult or Z $5 Zimbabwe dollars per child per month, and a fuel and rent allowance is also payable. Assistance is usually granted for a period of 12 months but is subject to renewal if circumstances remain unchanged.

Workers' Compensation

Workers' compensation is provided under the Workers' Compensation Act (1976) (Chapter 296) and administered by the Department of Occupational Health, Safety and Workers' Compensation. The objective of Workers' Compensation according to this Act is "to provide financial relief for employees and their families where the employee is injured or killed in an accident which occurred in the course of and arising from his employment." This protection is extended to all workers earning up to Z $500 per month. However, this protection is not extended to domestic and casual workers.

Workers' compensation is financed from employer contributions only and at rates determined by the Commissioner of Workers' Compensation. An employer with a poor safety record is usually penalized by being required to pay higher premiums. Benefits provided under workers' compensation include medical treatment, rehabilitation, widow's pension, and a disability pension. A widow's pension is discontinued in the event of the widow remarrying, but a lump-sum payment equivalent to 24 months' pension is paid. In addition, children's allowances are also payable and calculated at 12.5 percent of the deceased worker's pension in respect to the first child and at five percent of the worker's pension in respect to the subsequent children, up to a maximum of five children. In the case of a widow having more than five children, the Commissioner will use his discretionary powers to determine appropriate rates.

State Services Disability Benefit

State Services Disability Benefits are provided under the State Services (Disability Benefits) Act (1980) (Chapter 274), which provides non-contributory benefits to civil servants in the event of work-related injuries or death occurring. According to this Act, protection is in respect to:

any injury to a member or former member the date of which is on or after the appointment date and of any aggravation to a material extent of any injury which aggravation occurs on or after the appointed date.

the death of any member or former member which is caused by an injury or organization of any injury referred to in paragraph (a) [above].

Claims are submitted to the Pension Officer, who in turn convenes a Disablement Benefits Board. The power to award benefits rests with the Board, which normally acts on the evidence of a Medical Board.

War Victims Compensation

The provision of war victims compensation is governed by the War Victims Compensation Act (1980), which is administered by the Department of Social Welfare. War victims compensation is a non-contributory social security scheme that is funded from government revenue. The scheme "provides for the payment of compensation in respect of injuries or death of persons caused by the war" (War Victims Compensation Act 1980). Compensation is in the form of a disablement pension calculated as follows:

forty-five percentum of his earnings immediately prior to the date of his injury which are not in excess of seven thousand and forty-one dollars per annum and thirty percentum of his earnings immediately prior to his injury which are in excess of fourteen thousand and seventy-six dollars per annum. (War Victims Compensation Act [1980])

The level of compensation is also dependent upon the degree of disablement as assessed by a medical board. In circumstances where an injury has necessitated a change of occupation, higher rates of compensation are paid. A widow's pension is also payable but it is withdrawn when the widow remarries.

War Victims Compensation is therefore a special arrangement created to meet the needs of victims of Zimbabwe's war of liberation. The state assumed responsibility for those whose earning capacity was impaired by war-related injuries or those whose breadwinners died as a result of the war.

Occupational Pensions

Occupational pensions have historically been a preserve of white employees. Black employees were not covered by occupational pensions on the assumption that their post-retirement needs would be met within the peasant economy. As Bourdillon (1976: 26) observed, "the belief that all black people have rural homes where they can be supported in childhood or old age on subsistence agriculture excused white controlled industries from taking responsibility for childhood or old age of their employees which in turn keeps wages low and labor cheap." Since Zimbabwe's independence, however, there has been a significant expansion in the coverage of occupational pensions, and those retiring in the next 10 years would be able to fall back on their pensions. The government will, however, need to ensure that occupational pensions are transferable from one employer to the other in the event of a worker changing jobs. This will be a necessary change if pensions are to provide meaningful social protection against old age or retirement.

THE REDISTRIBUTION QUESTION

While the major objective of social security is income maintenance, redistribution of income has become more important. There are two forms of redistribution—namely vertical and horizontal redistribution. According to Midgley (1984: 165) vertical redistribution entails "a resource flow between different income groups." Vertical redistribution therefore allows for the transfer of resources from the high income category to the needy persons to enable them to lead decent lives. This is particularly important in countries with significant inequalities in the distribution of income. Social security can therefore be used as a means for creating an egalitarian society. Midgley also points out that horizontal redistribution occurs when there is a transfer of resources within an income group. Horizontal redistribution therefore allows for the transfer of resources from insured persons not exposed to any contingency to those insured persons whose earning capacities have been impaired, whether temporarily or permanently.

The effect of redistribution is dependent upon the methods of financing social security schemes (de Aranjo 1972). Because of the fragmented nature of social security schemes in Zimbabwe, the redistribution effect is quite minimal. As Paukert (1968) observes, the scope and coverage of social security schemes in developing countries is limited, thus making meaningful redistribution unrealizable. The high unemployment rate in Zimbabwe makes it difficult for the government to extend coverage to the majority of the people.

Workers' compensation in Zimbabwe entails a pooling of resources and a sharing of risks on the part of employers, as employees do not make any direct contributions. This is based upon the recognition that individual employers may not be able to afford adequate compensation for their employees. While the workers' compensation redistributes resources to workers and their dependents, this redistribution, however, has limited impact because workers only constitute a small percentage of the entire population, given the fact that about 75 percent of the population lives in the rural areas and are wholly dependent on the land. It is also common for employers to pass on the costs of their goods or services to consumers, who include workers and peasants. Some companies go to the extent of creating artificial shortages of goods or services in order to force the government to agree to increases in the price of their commodities. The sad thing is that peasants who are, after all, not covered by the workers' compensation end up subsidizing the costs of social security through indirect taxes paid when purchasing goods and services, which also serves to reinforce existing inequalities that exist between the urban and rural people. This is also true of the State Services Disability Benefits, as peasants also contribute through indirect taxation. Because an employer with a poor safety record is penalized through increased premiums, many employers avoid reporting injuries to the Workers' Compensation Commissioner, thus denying the injured workers of their benefits. Under such circumstances, the objectives of workers' compensation are defeated, as workers cannot seek redress for fear of losing their jobs. This fear is quite real and legitimate given the high levels of unemployment in the country. Vertical redistribution of income is also hampered by the fact that rates of contributions are not determined by income but rather by the degree of risks involved in the operations of a given enterprise. The transfer of resources therefore is not in any way related to earnings. In fact, enterprises with large earnings only pay a small percentage of their earnings if their operations are not hazardous.

The welfare assistance program has the potential of facilitating vertical redistribution of income, as it is financed by the state from revenue accrued through taxation. In Zimbabwe those earning Z $40,000 and above per annum confront a marginal tax rate of 60 percent, which makes Zimbabwe one of the countries with the highest taxation rates in the world. Income accrued from this taxation can be transferred to the poor to enable them to meet their basic needs, but this is not always the case. For instance, such revenue is used in part to finance free tuition in primary schools, a privilege that is also extended to the high-income groups. Because Zimbabwe's tax base is small, a greater proportion of government revenue comes from indirect taxation. Thus the peasants contribute significantly to government revenue, yet benefits extended to them are minimal. There is therefore a regressive transfer of resources from the poor to the non-poor.

It must be pointed out that government allocation for welfare assistance constitutes a small percentage of its total allocations. This is so because the government in its allocation of resources gives a higher priority to sectors capable of generating more resources. Welfare assistance therefore receives a very low priority on the assumption that a person usually counts on the assistance of the extended family in the event of becoming destitute. There is generally an urban bias in the provision of welfare assistance, the major rationale being that peasants are usually self-sufficient except in cases of drought. This urban bias therefore means the great majority of the population have no access to welfare assistance. Under such circumstances vertical redistribution of resources cannot be realized, since coverage of welfare assistance is not extended to the most needy members of society, who also constitute the majority of the population.

The situation is exacerbated by the fact that many peasants are unaware of the existence of the welfare assistance program and are therefore automatically excluded on account of their ignorance. The other major factor that curtails the ability of welfare assistance to redistribute income is the inaccessibility of welfare offices. Most welfare offices in the rural areas are not within easy reach of peasants. They have to travel long distances to get to their nearest office, and many withdraw prematurely on account of the travel costs involved. Welfare assistance is rarely given publicity for fear of creating artificial demand, and this fear appears to stem from a recognition of Zimbabwe's inadequate resource base. The scarcity of resources has greatly compromised the redistributive aspect, as the government is forced to adopt strict eligibility conditions resulting in too few people being awarded assistance. The use of tight eligibility criteria means that a greater percentage of needy persons go without welfare assistance and are therefore unable to benefit from a transfer of resources from the rich to the poor. The scarcity of resources also means that the benefits paid under welfare assistance are too meager for purposes of meeting basic needs. The redistribution impact is therefore very minimal, as beneficiaries are often unable to sustain themselves and their families on welfare assistance.

The Welfare Assistance Act (1988) itself is a major impediment in the redistributive effort of welfare assistance in Zimbabwe. It restricts welfare assistance to those over the age of 60 years, the handicapped, and the chronically ill but excludes unemployed able-bodied persons, which has the effect of narrowing the transfer of resources.

On the question of occupational pensions, it is true that they facilitate horizontal redistribution by allowing a retiree to benefit from the totality of contributions from members of a given scheme. The redistribution of income is therefore from those who have not yet reached retirement age to those who have. This therefore enables retired persons to receive reasonably adequate benefits for their post-retirement needs. The benefits are usually earnings-related and therefore offer very little scope for vertical redistribution within income groups. The redistributive impact is further limited by the fact that it is not compulsory for employers to provide pension schemes for their employees. Consequently, the coverage of occupational pensions is very small. The redistributive impact can be enhanced by making the provision of occupational pensions compulsory and making the contributions transferable from one scheme to the other.

CONCLUSION

The discussion has revealed that Zimbabwe does not have a comprehensive social security scheme. The few social security schemes in operation rarely complement each other, and coverage is extended to a very small percentage of the population. It is this limited scope and coverage that curtails the ability of social security to redistribute income or resources. The impact of the Workers' Compensation, Occupational Pensions, and State Services (Disability Benefits) schemes is limited on account of the fact that the employed form a small percentage of the population. Welfare assistance, on the other hand, has limited impact on redistribution because of scarce resources at the disposal of the government. Because the income tax base is very small, the accumulated revenue is inadequate for purposes of financing welfare benefits. The revenue is used to finance a variety of social services, and only a small percentage of it is earmarked for welfare assistance.

The high demand on welfare assistance forces the government to spread welfare assistance thinly to needy persons. However, only urban destitute families appear to benefit from welfare assistance. This urban bias is symptomatic of the colonial attitudes toward the problems of poverty. As Midgley (1984: 171) observes, "colonial policy makers took the view that the urban poverty problem could be reduced considerably if the urban destitute were encouraged to return to their villages where they could earn a living in agriculture and be supported by traditional welfare institutions such as the extended family." The assumption that has been carried into independent Zimbabwe is that poverty is essentially an urban problem and that rural people are self-supporting and sustained by their agriculture. Consequently, there is a very limited flow of resources from high-income urban areas to low-income rural areas. It is ironic, however, that there is a flow of resources from rural areas to urban areas through indirect taxation. This therefore reinforces existing disparities in the distribution of resources between urban and rural areas.

Zimbabwe has enacted a new Social Security Act, which will cover such contingencies as old age or retirement, death, disability, and maternity. Because the scheme will be contributory, coverage will only be extended to those in formal employment. It will initially exclude domestic and casual workers and peasants. Although this new social security scheme will have the potential of redistributing income horizontally within the group of insured persons, the scope for vertical redistribution is nonexistent. In fact, the scheme has the potential of becoming elitist, as it will feed (albeit indirectly) on income derived from peasants and ultimately heighten the existing inequalities in the distribution of income or resources. Protection must be extended to all groups if redistribution is to be realized. Zimbabwe is a country with glaring inequalities in the distribution of income. If the distribution of income is to be more equitable, then Zimbabwe would need to transfer income from high-income groups (through progressive taxation) to low-income groups. The transferred resources would be used to finance welfare assistance benefits for the poor. Welfare assistance must be made accessible to the poor by loosening the rather tight eligibility criteria. The benefits paid must be adequate for purposes of meeting basic needs and must be processed and paid in a manner that does not compromise human dignity. Unless the scope of social security is broadened and coverage extended to the majority of the population, vertical redistribution will remain an unrealizable ideal.

REFERENCES

Bourdillon, M.F.C. 1976. *Myths About Africa* (Gwelo, Rhodesia: Mambo Press).

Clarke, D. 1977. *The Economics of Old Age Subsistence in Rhodes* (Gwelo, Rhodesia: Mambo Press).

de Aranjo, L. L. 1972 "Social Security as Instrument of Income Redistribution in the Developing Countries" *International Social Security Review* 25(3): 1–28.

Hampson, J. & Kaseke, E. 1987. "Zimbabwe" in Dixon, J. (ed.) *Social Welfare in Africa* (London: Routledge).

International Labor Organization (ILO). 1942. *Approaches in Social Security: An International Survey* (Series M, 18) (Geneva: ILO).

Kawewe, S.K. 1994a. "Social Welfare for Military Veterans in Zimbabwe" *Journal of International and Comparative Social Welfare* 10 (1 & 2): 45–67.

Kawewe, S.K. 1994b. "Social Welfare with Indigenous Peoples in Zimbabwe" in Dixon, J. & Scheurell, R.P. (eds) 1994. *Social Welfare with Indigenous Peoples* (London: Routledge).

Midgley, J. 1984. *Social Security Inequality and the Third World* (New York: John Wiley & Sons).

Paukert, D. 1968. "Social Security and Income Redistribution: Comparative Experiences" in Kassaloe, E. M. (ed.) *The Role of Social Security in Economic Development* (Washington DC: Government Printing Office).

Savanhu, J. Z. 1945. *Social Security: The Native Problem in Southern Rhodesia. The African View Point* (Bullawayo, Rhodesia: Rhodesian Printers and Publishing Company).

9

Social Security in Yugoslavia: Change or Continuity in the 1990s

Miroslav Ruzica

A PRELUDE

Yugoslavia was an impossible nation–state idea, the result of the existence of the three relatively independent centers of power (Serbia, Croatia, Slovenia), and the legacy of the Communist Party rule. The struggle over supremacy, the unitary, federal state concept, and diverse economic strategies have prevented from the beginning stability and integrity of a country. Current tensions have resulted not only in the disintegration of the state and the civil war, but in possible armed conflict in the region, and indeed throughout Europe.

An essential characteristic of Yugoslav society up to 1989 was the monistic structure of its political system characterized by the integration of its Communist Party into the state structure, the removal of any political pluralism, as well as a direct control of all political and other institutions by the party-state. Therefore, the society lost its functional differentiation as well as the autonomy and specialization of its parts at the political and other levels. The centers of social power were party and state leaderships at the federal, regional, and local levels.

Instead of a federal government at the pinnacle of the federal state there existed the so-called polycentric statism, which led to a high degree of independence of the member-states as well as to a complex system of decision making at the federal level. A further characteristic was the decentralization to a network of autonomous communes. This system evidenced a low degree of federal integration, whereas at the level of member-states, the structure of the Communist Party provided the monism of the system, both formally and informally.

The social system was shaped formally as a self-managed one. It was composed of a network of autonomous institutions and their various associations as well as of many functional and territorial forms of self-regulation, all independent of the state. The reality, however, was quite different. A jagged network of self-management turned into a quasi-state network. This was the expected outcome because of the monistic structure of the social system. A consequence of this was that the whole social system became inert and inefficient, for self-management offered just a subsequent and formal legitimatization to all decisions made outside at its own frame-work, which is what made all formal, professional,and other public participants passive outsiders.

Ideologically, collective forms of ownership, production, consumption, and other activities were emphasized. Various forms of collectivism were always introduced from the top; and traditional and self-managed forms were neglected. The individual became an invisible and de-personalized member of various collectives (such as family, school, enterprise, Party, local community, nation), and all individual and collective forms appeared in a mass, standardized, and impersonal manner that is bureaucratized, inactive, and inefficient. Any individualized action was evaluated and verified by some collective body in order to become legal. Any collective action was illegal unless verified and supervised by a higher political or administrative body.

THE FOUNDATIONS OF THE YUGOSLAV SOCIAL SECURITY SYSTEM

After the catastrophe of the Second World War and the disintegration of a state, the new Yugoslavia was reconstructed in accordance with the Soviet Union model, through the integration at the Communist Party into the state apparatus and through establishing an extremely strict hierarchical system, which was represented as one of "building of socialism." In reality, this meant imitating the Bolshevist model. The same process was true of the welfare system (Ruzica 1992; Ruzica et al. 1991).

The old Bolshevist concept formulated on the All-Russian Social-Democrat Congress in Prague in 1912 was accepted as a framework. Basically it was a part of the German Social-Democrat Party's program from the 1870s slightly re-formulated by V. I. Lenin. This model served as a basic model for the first comprehensive but utopian program in the 1920s in the Soviet

Union, and as a permanent frame of inspiration, continuity, and legitimatization for many decades for it and other socialist countries (Dixon & Scheurell 1992).

The basic concept can be outlined as follows (Ruzica 1985):

- Material compensation should be provided for all risks of disabilities (work accidents, illness, old age, maternity, childbirth).
- All employees should be covered (and their families).
- Benefits should be on the same level as prior earnings, and all costs should be covered by the state and employers.
- A uniform and united social security system should be established and entirely run by the insured workers.

The same conceptualization was implemented in Yugoslavia. Social security became the main social value and, on the other side, the objective of the whole program. The uniform social security system—invalid-retirement and health insurance, child care—were established in 1947 covering all employed people. But it should be emphasized that people employed in the nationalized sector of the economy represented just 10 percent of the total active population in 1948. Peasantry and self-employed were, however, excluded from these programs until the early 1970s when their social security programs were established as a separate and differently run program from those in the public sector. The idea of social equality has inspired all social policy programs devoted to the children, women, and the family. The best example is a child allowance in 1950 having paid more than the average wage of a low qualified worker for a three-child family.

The idea of "full employment policy" was announced in a quite optimistic way, and a great amount of energy was invested in order to carry this out through an intensive industrialization program. It was an undisturbed belief that everything should be radically changed; the pre-war humanitarian organizations (and religious) as well as private corporations were cancelled and new organizations were established. This was done in the form of a "re-registration" in the belief that these new organizations would be more successful and would themselves contribute to the "building of socialism." This implied that a separate public assistance program and unemployed insurance would not be necessary and thus should not exist. The poor and unemployed people were seen as a relict of the capitalist past.

Professions and vocations simply did not exist within the framework of autonomous agencies and associations. The almighty state regulated and oriented all forms of social life in an administrative and centralized manner, depriving institutions and citizens from any autonomy. As a result of this, routine logic within the welfare system was subsequently narrowed to an administrative and technical transfer of money and some services.

After the clash with the USSR in 1948 there began a process of liberalization in a slow way. There was an opening out toward Europe, as well as beginning of the self-management experiment. Further changes occurred within this framework, in terms of economy modernization and social welfare system design. The developed model of West European countries (technology, division of labor, economic cooperation, market forces) was accepted as appropriate. Within the social welfare domain, West European concepts, programs, as well as family and employment legislation, were adopted.

New institutions were founded, and new professions and vocations were born, which became a lasting inheritance. This refers first to the foundation of the new and main personal service: Social Work Centers (in 1956). The functions of these centers were to offer immediate and individualized services (advice, financial support, treatments) to the aged, handicapped, children, and the families. At the same time, research institutions were started, beginning researches, personnel training, technical aid, and supervision. Even schools for social workers and undergraduate programs for sociologists and psychologists were started. Some old socialist dogmas were gradually abandoned in regard to poverty and unemployment. The first public assistance program and unemployment insurance in all of communist Eastern Europe were established. Most of these innovations or re-emerging of professions were started in 1957 (approved and legitimated in the Constitution of 1963).

YUGOSLAV SOCIAL SECURITY SYSTEM REFORMED

Under the Constitution of 1974 the federal institutions lost their jurisdiction over social welfare. They were limited to recommending, coordinating, and keeping the whole system consistent. The regulation of the social welfare was taken over by the member-states. There was a redistribution of responsibilities between state departments and the new forms of self-management. The governments of the states were still the law-makers and retained the right to distribute public funds and even to control the choice of all officials, in an unofficial way.

The special characteristic of the Yugoslav welfare system was that every social service was organized as a separate self-managed and self-regulating sub-system (namely, invalid and pension insurance, health insurance, unemployment insurance, public assistance, and child care) were organized the same way. Regulation within each of them was taken over by the Self-managed Community of Interest (SCI), including their means of financing, the carrying out of welfare rights, the development of a professional network, the standards of services, and supervision. Every SCI was an elective and representative body in which the professionals who worked in a specific field as well as citizens, as possible users of services, were represented. It was constituted like an assembly and had its own executive and expert teams. For any social services (such as health, education, child care, social assistance, invalid and pension insurance, and so on) there existed a special SCI, which formally took over complete management of its own field within the member-state. As the political system was decentralized, similar logic was applied, even within the framework of communes: the local infrastructure of SCI's network regulated social welfare sectors at this level. There were no SCIs at the federal level.

Invalid and Old-Age Pension Insurance

There exists an invalid and old-age pension insurance system that covers employed people in the nationalized sector, whereas for farmers, private owners, and some professions there are separate insurance systems. The history of such retirement insurance for farmers is very interesting. Up to 1972 there was no insurance for them. Over the next 10 years some member-states (notably Slovenia) began various insurance programs, but only on a voluntary basis. In 1983 compulsory retirement insurance for agricultural producers was introduced for the whole country. Some member-states, however, have not yet started to implement this program.

Although every member-state takes over the formal regulation of retirement (invalidity and old-age) pension insurance programs, their logic remains similar, but they do differ in their benefit rights prescribed and especially in the benefit rates paid. The pension insurance programs for the employed in the socialized sector is taken as a model for all the other programs. For the other groups of the insured individuals (peasants, private owners, and some other professions) there exists a particular network.

The common condition for obtaining a full pension are: attaining the age of 60 for men (55 for women) and achieving 40 years of service.[1] In this case the pension is as high as 85 percent of the earnings over the ten-year period before retirement. The pension is decreased for every year below 40 years of service. If length of service is less than 15 years, there is no right to a pension, except for the so-called privileged jobs (where every year of employment earns a length of service entitlement of two or three years and, at the most, six months of work benefit). The highest pensions cannot be more than 3.5 times higher than the average salary in the member-state. There is no minimum pensions, but appraisals are made, as well as corrections, through the so-called right to protective allowance. In the course of 1987 some 23 percent of retired people were eligible for a retirement pension. The economic crisis has brought about the introduction of a minimum pension equal to about 80 percent of the guaranteed minimum (earnings) in the member-state.

There is also an early retirement option for men who are at least 55 years old and who have 35 years of service, and for women who are at least 50 years old, and who have 30 years of service. But, for every year under the early retirement age the pension maximum is decreased by 1.5 percent, and 0.5 for every year under the minimum years of service. Except Slovenia, all other member-states prescribe a compulsory retirement when one of the conditions for pension is fulfilled (40 years of employment or 60 years of age), so that at 65 years of age a worker is obliged to retire with few exceptions (university professors, and top experts in various fields can work to the age of 70 years).

Since 1980 the increase in the number of retired people (estimated to be 4.9 percent) highly surpasses the growth rate for employment.[2] The total number of retired people in 1985 amounted to 31.3 percent of the employed population (see Table 9.1). In Slovenia, the percentage of pensioners to the pension-insured population in 1987 had already reached 33 percent, but by 1991 it had fallen to 27.9 percent. Pensioners then were 14.9 percent of the total population.

The pension paid depends upon the amount of earnings and the length of service, which for the greater number of pensioners is less than 40 years of service. This is particularly obvious through the number of invalid pensioners, which in some of the member-states surpasses the number of retired pensioners. Only in developed Slovenia, with its longest industrial tradition, are there more retirement pensioners, almost twice the national average.

The classification of retired people in Table 9.1 reveals several problems about conditions at work, about the quality of life in the low income strata, and about disablement criteria. All this indicates that workers are being treated just as a technical and economic factor of production: the exploiting of labor or manpower was the main way to industrialization. This classification indicates that the system of care for the disabled has failed, for invalid pensioners make up some 80 percent of all invalids who have

Table 9.1
Classification of the Retired in Yugoslavia: 1985

All Retired Employees	Old-age Pensioners	Invalid Pensioners	Family Pensioners	All Pensioners
2,035,000	38%	34%	28%	6,500,000

Source: See note 2 for statistical sources.

worked. The remaining 20 percent continue working, of whom some 10 percent undertake half-time work. The number of those who join the vocational rehabilitation programs is negligibly small; in a 20–year period it makes up between 0.6 and 0.1 percent of the work invalids (Ruzica 1980).

The reduction of funding of the social welfare impacted upon the invalid and old-age pension insurances, particularly between 1983 and 1985. This trend was reversed the following year. Slovenia spent 8.4 percent of its gross national product on social welfare in 1986, increasing to 9.4 percent the following year.

Given the influence of the economic crisis in the 1980s, it must be concluded that pensioners (in particular survivers' pensioners) are the poorest part of the population. According to official evaluations, more than 50 percent of pensioners are situated below the poverty line. During the period from 1980 to 1985 the real value of pensions was decreased at a yearly rate of six percent. Due to inflation a revaluation of pensions is made every three months, but it has been suggested that it should be done monthly. The average amount of the pension in relation to the average earnings of the employed were about 50 percent for many years; in 1987 this increased to 68.4 percent (in Slovenia to 75.5 percent). This is, however, just a false improvement, because the level of earnings strongly decreased over this period, so the real economic impact was a worsening of the pensioners' material position.

Unemployment Insurance and Programs

The employment problem in Yugoslavia has long had a structural characteristic, originating with the industrialization of a farming-based and under-developed economy. In 1948 the employed made up just 10 percent of the active labor force. In the mid-1950s the "idea of full employment" was abandoned. Ten years later a series of unsuccessful economic reforms began which, together with a bad economic policy, led to a crisis and an enormous rate of unemployment.

The contemporary unemployment insurance program was introduced in 1965, although Yugoslavia was a signatory of the ILO's Convention 102 long before then. That year saw the first unsuccessful program started, when about 10 percent of those in employment were without jobs. The unemployment benefits provided were subject to a means-testing. This program was abandoned at the beginning of 1970s. Currently, the funding for these programs is obtained through wage-related employer contributions. The unemployment benefits paid are based on past earnings. The volume of these funds is very limited; in 1979 it was 0.22 percent of the GNP, by 1987 it was just 0.14 percent.

The basic entitlements for the unemployed are: monthly cash benefits, the vocational re-training, as well as subsidies to cover the costs of dwelling change.

The derived rights include: health insurance, a recognition as work in service, the time spent in waiting for a job, as well as child's allowance.

Other benefits include being given priority for (new) employment.

The amount of the monthly cash benefit depends on the applicants' average earnings over the last three months (subject to a minimum rate equal to the minimal salary in the member-state), which is payable for just three months after nine months of service, up to a maximum of 18 months (36 months in Serbia, respectively, for those whose work in service is at 20 to 25 years).

The number of people receiving unemployment benefits is between 2.5 and 3.5 percent of all unemployed and 10 percent of the unemployed who have previously been employed. The number of the recipients of the program has been small for two reasons. First, because first-time job seekers have no right to a benefit, and they constitute about 30 percent of all the unemployed in the late 1980s, of whom about 80 percent are young people. They may have been working from time to time, but their total length of service is typically under 12 months and typically involved uncovered seasonal employment. This means that the workers employed on a permanent basis are very much protected from losing their jobs, and thus hardly represented within the mass of unemployed. Second, because after three-to-18 months of unemployment the right to a benefit is lost, depending on length of previous employment.

Health Insurance

Health insurance is almost universal. However, there are various subsystems (for peasants, for self-employed professions, and for professional army members), but the most popular one, and the model for all others, is the health insurance for employed people in the nationalized economy. All these sub-systems cover 85 to 90 percent of the population. Those individuals excluded from health insurance for the longest period of time were the peasants who owned private land. They were finally included into the program in 1959, on a voluntary basis initially, but compulsory from 1969 to 1971. Their entitlements are essentially the same, except that the peasants have no rights to a paid sick leave.

Health services are not paid for by the users, but rather by insurance funds. The users pay a minimum participation fee, which discourages them requesting unnecessary and expensive medical services. In addition, there are also certain services that are paid for by the user (such as aesthetic surgery and eyeglass frames). All of these services, together with the user participation fee, account for two percent of the total health insurance fund.

There is also a sick leave benefit equal to 100 percent of average monthly earning in the preceding year for pregnancy and childbirth, work injury, and work-related diseases, otherwise 70 to 90 percent of earnings, at the discretion of the employer, subject to a minimum benefit equal to the minimum wage guaranteed by the member-state. Because benefits have not been linked to current monthly earnings, the conditions of enormous inflation have resulted in long-term sickness beneficiaries being completely impoverished.

The first 30 days of sick leave are paid by the employers, which is why the employers are required to decide whether the sick leave benefit would be 70, 80, or 90 percent of earnings.

On an average, every insured person takes 14 days' sick leave a year under the health insurance program, but it should be noted that nearly 10 percent of all sick leaves goes to the care of the family member (typically children), so that women use about 64 percent of all sick leave.

Maternity leave also formally belongs to health insurance. For childbirth and child's care the mother (or father, too) acquires the right to leave for six to 12 months on an allowance equal to 100 percent of the earnings in the previous year, and half-time until the child is one year old, although at the recommendation of the physician even until the child is three years old. Maternity benefits were denied to peasants for decades. From 1984, however, this benefit became the right of the child, which means it is independent of the parent's employment.

Public Assistance

For those who have neither means of their own (earnings, pensions, or savings) nor children to support them, and who are older than 65 or permanently disabled, there is a public assistance program. The major benefit is called "permanent money support." It is a regular monthly benefit given through a means-tested procedure. It is regulated by the member-state's laws, and usually fixed at not lower than 50 percent of minimum wage in that member-state. During 1987 in the whole country there were 138,000 elderly public assistance clients, who represented 0.59 percent of the total population, or about 5 percent of all old people (Milosavljevic & Ruzica 1989).

There exists in addition financial aid given occasionally in specific emergency or crisis situations (such as to help care for a sick or disabled family member). There is also limited welfare housing, the so called municipal housing stocks, which are below the usual housing standards and thus the smallest flats possible of the lowest quality. These flats are being distributed to public assistance clients after a means-tested procedure.

Child Welfare

The key item of child welfare is the children's allowance, which is a permanent monthly cash allowance paid per child. This program began, with enthusiasm, at the beginning of the post-war years, when every employee obtained such a right in the form of an allowance added to his salary. In the early 1950s these amounts were relatively high—the children's allowance for an unskilled worker with three children was even higher than his entire salary. These allowances have since been subsequently decreased substantially, so that in 1989 they were about 15 percent of the lowest salary for one child, and for average families between five and 10 percent. There is, however, an upper income limit after which the right to an allowance is lost. If a child or young person attends school, this allowance can be granted up to age 27.

The right to children's allowances was initially only enjoyed by those children whose parents were employed in the nationalized economy. The children of peasants and private land owners were excluded. Since 1984, however, children's allowances have become any child's right no matter where the parents of the child were working.

In the 1980s the criteria for obtaining any allowance became more discriminatory, and the number of families receiving this allowance began decreasing; in 1960 there were 2.96 million beneficiaries, by 1986 there were just 1.8 million. Therefore, in most member-states this program is used by those who are below the poverty line (Todorovic 1990).

ECONOMIC AND POLITICAL CRISES AS A
FRAMEWORK FOR TRANSITION

In the late 1970s a severe and long-lasting economic crisis began. In the period from 1965 to 1980 the average yearly economic growth was six percent. From 1980 to 1985 it was hardly 0.6 percent, but for 1987 and 1988 it was negative, –1.1 percent and –2 percent, respectively. The introduction of new and radical economic reform by the end of 1989 brought the economy to the edge of catastrophe. The economic growth declined by 10.8 percent in 1990, and by more than 20 percent in 1991 and 1992. Real annual income of employed people was increasing by 5.4 percent to 7.2 percent in the 1960s, by a mere 0.9 percent to 1.5 percent in the 1970s, thereafter decreasing at the rate of six-to-eight percent a year a decade later. Therefore, real earnings in 1985 were 28 percent lower than what they were in 1979, and in Macedonia they were even worse, 45 percent lower. It has been estimated that in the course of 1988 real earnings fell to the level of 1968. The most recent analysis, however, shows that the real earnings in the spring of 1991 are on the level of a remote 1960 (Horvat 1991). A galloping annual inflation rate was also achieved in the late 1980s: 1985, 70 percent; 1986, 9.6 percent; 1988, 250 percent, and 1989, 1,365 percent. Inflation was, however, greatly diminished during the first half of 1990 due to a new economic program since the beginning of that year: 41.5 percent in January (maximum) and less than one percent in June 1990 (Ruzica 1991). The economic policy changes that produced this were:

- the introduction of a labor and capital market;
- the liberalization of foreign trade (abolition of quantitative import restriction);
- the liberalization of control over foreign capital investments;
- the reform of enterprises, which become independent market-oriented units regardless of the type of ownership;
- the introduction of legal arrangements to stimulate private initiatives; and
- the functioning of a foreign currency market

However, due to a total disarray of the political system and civil war, a new spiral of galloping inflation began in the summer of 1991 and still continues unabated.

Apart from the general decrease of the living standard of the population, other symptoms of crisis appeared. Unemployment existed in the early 1960s (5.4 percent). At that time the problem was postponed by the departure of the labor force surplus to Western Europe, where 1,000,000

Yugoslavs migrated until the end of 1972. Up to 1975 the rate of unemployment was lower than 10 percent. In the late 1980s, however, the number of unemployed had begun to increase, 1,128 million workers or 14.1 percent of the labor force. Regional unemployment rate differences are enormous: Slovenia 1.8 percent, Macedonia 40 percent. It is estimated that the number of unemployed individuals in September of 1991 was about 1.6 million, and it is expected that this should increase by a further 1.3 million by the end of 1994 (Todorovic 1990).

The emerging issues of mass unemployment and the pauperization of the Yugoslav population were, however, beyond the limits of any economic strategy to address. The main resistance to economic reform came initially from Serbia, because of the structural and technological backwardness of its economy, and later from Slovenia and Croatia, because reform has implied a certain degree of re-centralization and the strengthening of the position of federal government.

In the shadow of the developments in Eastern Europe and in the former Soviet Union, a real drama has been happening inside and around Yugoslavia. The creation in 1918 of the "State of Slovenes, Croats and Serbs," the first official name of the country, seemed to be a defensive strategy of the Croats and Slovenes vis-à-vis the expressed expansionist aspirations of Italy and the potential renewal of the Austrian-Hungarian Empire, rather than a Pan-Slavic idea of a common state. The struggle over political supremacy, the unitary, federal concept of the state, and the diverse economic strategies have prevented Yugoslavia, from the very beginning, from achieving the stability and integrity of a unified country. It appears that all aspects of social, political, and economic life had been the subject of conflicts. After the first free elections in the member-states in 1990, the test was a new Constitution: will Yugoslavia be a federation or a loose confederation, or will it disintegrate? Formal secession of Slovenia and Croatia from Yugoslavia occurred in June 1991, which began a civil war, and ended Yugoslavia. How many new states will emerge? It is uncertain because of the "imperialistic" aspirations of Serbia (and Croatia), and the possible involvement of neighboring countries.

DISMANTLING OR MUTATING THE YUGOSLAV SOCIAL SECURITY SYSTEM

The radical economic reform from December 1989 announced Yugoslavia's drastic break with its "socialist welfare state legacy" and thus with its past approach to social welfare. There was a re-conceptualization of its almost universal social security schemes, its free medical services, and its subsidized public services, especially housing (Federal Committee 1990a).

Yugoslavia's transition to a market economy involved privatization, the market regulation of prices, market regulation, and its integration into Western economies, which involved, among other things, foreign investments, technology transfers, and transplantation of European institutions (banks, marketing, services). The same broad approach has been adopted in the welfare system, notably "welfare pluralism" (that is, the co-existence of public, voluntary, and private welfare sectors); a shift from universal social (health and pensions) insurance toward supplementary and parallel private insurance; the privatization of some social services (such as medical services, care for the elderly and children, and even education); the privatization and commercialization of public housing (selling the socially owned apartments, the creation of a housing market); the elimination of social program provision by business enterprises in favor of the state or public administration; the imposition of economic prices for all public services, which are funded by a combination of private fees, public funds, and private insurance schemes (Ruzica 1991; Juresko 1991).

The system of Self-managed Community of Interest (SCI) was abolished, and as a consequence a more centralistic way of funding at the member-state and local level has been introduced. All welfare programs are now financed directly from the budget of the member-state and local governments. The states have begun to develop a centralistic welfare system. But they are not strong enough to stimulate the development of non-government sectors (private, voluntary, informal). The member-states prefer to (and can easily) subordinate the non-government welfare sectors rather than trying to stimulate their autonomy.

Although it is too early to identify the main trends in implementation of the announced social policy programs, the most likely outcome is easy to predict: "the tyranny of status quo." This means that the major organized groups are still able to resist the radical reduction of the core of the "socialist welfare legacy" (such as universal social security programs, free medical and educational services). Many of the new political parties are focusing their core programs on this legacy and try to manipulate the transitional period and to put themselves up as the sole protector of the working class, even of the entire population. The deep and long-lasting economic crises seem to have given them the opportunity to play such a role. Thus the relative balance of power and weakness is producing a block to the introduction of any extreme options. This gives rise to a working hypothesis: the transition in the welfare area is going to be an organic and self-restructuring process,

the outcome of which is hard to predict. There are, however, some indications that the limitations placed on change could mean that transformation
process might produce a set of stable, durable, and politically acceptable
arrangements.

The first sign of transition was the breaking-up of the uniformity of the
state-run welfare network and the mobilization of new resources, which
has begun to revive entrepreneurship in social welfare, through the growth
of local autonomy and the development of the voluntary sectors. This shift
toward the "welfare mix" is a general trend. However, it is a result of the
shrinking of the public sector, not of the real expansion of private, voluntary, and private sectors. The new providers do not enlarge the supply of
services but only fill the gap created by the retreat of the state. Thus it has
a compensatory effect for the time being, but the nature of the sectoral
balance that will emerge remains to be seen.

Pauperization and Economic Dislocation

Poverty and pauperization of the people, a product of the economic
crisis, is now the main social policy concern. The response has been a
radical change in the public assistance system, the creation of a "safety net"
or "emergency welfare aid," although some cynics describe it as the "redistribution of poverty" programs. It has been funded by increasing the budget
deficit, through the permanent re-allocation of government expenditures,
which then either burdens the population and the commercial sector with
new taxes or results in the printing of new money, thus sky-rocketing the
inflation rate. The federal budget for 1991 promised that 25 percent of
federal expenditures would be devoted to supporting the member-states'
so-called social programs. The purpose of these programs is to provide
unemployment benefits, re-training, and re-employment for the workers
who are going to lose their jobs (Markovic 1991). The civil war that began
in the summer of 1991, however, ended the existence of a federal budget.
The new states that emerged had transformed their economies and re-
aligned their budgets to accommodate civil war.

Pauperization and Public Assistance

The conceptualization of public assistance has changed. It was based on
the premise that no one who worked could be on the welfare role, so only
the "surplus population" (old people, disabled, children without parents)
were eligible for public assistance. Now the application of a poverty line

has become the leading eligibility criteria, and a family income a major focus. The problem is, however, that a growing number of employees have become the dominant users. At the same time, the benefits provided are shrinking and thus not able to cover the basics of life.

An important intellectual activity is the conceptualization of a poverty line in the ever-changing environment. Instead of determining fixed and uniform levels of financial support, there are innovations taking place that have resulted in the emergence of some sort of guaranteed income approach. The innovator was Slovenia, and a new concept is going to be accepted all over Yugoslavia. In essence, financial support is given to the level of 43 percent of the average earnings in the community. The cash transfer is equal to the difference between existing family income and the level of 43 percent of average family earnings in Slovenia (Consortium 1989). When the family income equals that threshold, the cash transfer becomes zero. The question is, of course, whether the provided guaranteed income is high enough to cover the basic needs.

Cash Transfers, Average Wages, and Poverty

The expected fertilization of the options is not going to be conceptual, but rather pragmatic. Although there are the proponents of the liberal ideas of a minimum level of benefits and services in order to eliminate poverty and stigmatization, it is hard reality that shapes the practical responses. The Yugoslav response is very indicative: an average wage for a four-member family defines the minimum levels for all other social benefits (pensions, unemployment allowances, even the minimum wage levels), while their upper limits are very close to the average wages. For example, the guaranteed minimal wage is now 70 percent of the average wages, while pensions are 70 to 80 percent of the average wages. But the paradox is that both average wages and the highest social security benefits are situated on or often below the poverty line. It has been estimated that an average Yugoslav four-member family needed 7.218 dinars in August 1990 to cover the basic needs; yet the average wage was only 4.317 dinars. It has also been estimated that an average Yugoslav family had 1.6 employed members (Federal Committee 1990b). So, even a two-earner family was hardly able to cover the basics beyond the official poverty line.

Universal or Residual Social Security Programs

Formally the universal skeleton of major social security programs has survived. Many selective measures are, however, being built in, tightening the eligibility criteria, reducing some programs (all additional programs, para-medical services), or eliminating others (the state-owned housing sector).

There were announcements about the introduction of a two-tier (even three-tier) social security system. The first tier would provide a flat-rate and basic benefits for all (pensions, basic medical services); the second tier would be mandated by the government and provide supplementary benefits based on the contributions paid for social security benefits (pensions, additional health insurance); the third tier would provide further benefits funded by private occupational welfare schemes based on bargaining procedures (Bueml 1991; Working Group 1990).

Such a conceptualization of the new social security program implies differences in the nature of the tax system. The advocates of the two- and three-tier social security system suggest that the first tier should be financed through the general government budget, the second tier through the contributions of employers and employees, and the third tier through private schemes of private users. But others disagree, concerned about the implied inequalities in access to, and quality of, services and transfers (Federal Committee 1991).

The Shift toward Market Regulation

That is the general trend and the key idea of dominant reformers. However, the reduction and impoverishment of the major public programs has caused the business community to resist this trend and thus increase its efforts to reorient some programs (such as the public housing programs). This has occurred because the dismantling of the public housing has produced an incredible growth in private rents. The radical dismantling of enterprise-based social programs, moreover, may also be entirely counterproductive. The new and global trend in the developed world is emerging, led by new technology, which is emphasizing the importance of a supportive and friendly working environment and the social role of enterprises. It also acknowledges the need to reduce working time, to develop elastic work organization, to have flatter organizational structures, to give greater autonomy to working teams, and to give workers more leisure activities and benefits. These are the envisioned features of this new strategy. The decomposition of enterprise social programs is re-introducing nineteenth century industrial models, rather than the concept of a post-industrial society.

Does this perspective have anything to do with Yugoslav reality in the early 1990s? Enterprises are politiced: they are chaotic. Business is improvised: its leadership is neurotic, its workforce is demotivated, its employees are scared. Trade unions are devalued. Is the introduction of an extreme market and economic orientation the only shock therapy that will accelerate transition? The new work balance could be established through an organic development later.

Employment Policy

Employment policy is being re-focused on training and re-qualification program. New employment services are trying to mediate between employees and employers (by means of information and counselling). The government is trying to articulate its new role as a stimulator, regulator, or coordinator, as distinct from direct service provider. Through new laws, this new employment policy is introducing more flexible forms of employment: part-time jobs and job-sharing. There are now the financial compensations given to those who voluntarily give up their jobs, and the years of service required to obtain pensions have been reduced (at least in Macedonia). All employers are obliged to announce any planned reduction of employees, in order that community programs of re-employment, re-training, and re-qualification can be provided. The local employers are expected to hire their new workers from a prioritized list of people who had previously lost their jobs.

A POSTSCRIPT

The skeleton of the old Yugoslav social security system still survives. There are, however, many initiatives, new concepts, and formal proposals being considered, which imply a radical revision of the existing model. Due to the total disarray of the former Yugoslav political and economic systems, however, changes made to its social security programs have generally been postponed, although radical rhetoric abounds. What can be seen is only a pragmatic and minor adaptation to a hard politico-economic reality. All social security programs have became nothing more than emergency welfare aid to a scared and impoverished population. The main social actors are the now entirely independent republican governments. They are strictly anti-communist (except in Serbia) and entirely separatist-nationalist in orientation. The main visible trends are toward ethnic homogenization and authoritarian pragmatism. No one knows, of course, what civil war and its attendant social, economic, and political disintegration bring, whether a loose confederation is possible, and how it should be done. Only one thing is certain: Yugoslavia has ceased to exist.

NOTES

1. The description of basic social security entitlements is based on the Federal Committee for Labor, Health, Veterans' Questions, and Social Policy's document *A Proposition of a Law on the Basic Rights in Pension-Invalid Insurance* (February 1990) (Belgrade: Federal Committee for Labor, Health, Veterans' Questions, and Social Policy).

2. Most of the statistical data have been taken from the *Statistic Yearbook of Yugoslavia*, which is the official organ of the Federal Statistic Institute of Yugoslavia, Belgrade, 1987, 1988, and 1989. All other details from the rest of the chapter, if not stressed in some other way, came from this source.

REFERENCES

Bueml, V. 1991. "The Designers of Uncertain Old Age" *Danas* 10(465) (January 15): 24–26.

Consortium of Yugoslav Social Policy Institutes 1989. *Criteria for Defining the Poverty Line* (Belgrade: Federal Committee for Labor, Health, Veterans' Questions, and Social Policy).

Dixon, J. & Scheurell, R. P. (eds.). 1992. *Social Welfare under Socialism* (London: Routledge).

Federal Committee for Labor, Health, Veterans' Questions, and Social Policy 1990a. *Social Policy in the Conditions of Economic Reform* (Belgrade: Federal Committee for Labor, Health, Veterans' Questions, and Social Policy).

Federal Committee for Labor, Health, Veterans' Questions, and Social Policy 1990b. *A Proposition of a Law on the Basic Rights in Pension-Invalid Insurance* (Belgrade: Federal Committee for Labor, Health, Veterans' Questions, and Social Policy)

Federal Committee for Labor, Health, Veterans Questions, and Social Policy 1991. *The Framework for Implementation of Reform in the Areas of Labor, Health, and Social Policy* (Belgrade: Federal Committee for Labor, Health, Veterans' Questions, and Social Policy).

Horvat, B. 1991. *Danas* 10 (April 16).

Juresko, G. 1991. "When the Patients Choose" *Danas* 10 (465) (January 15): 69–71.

Markovic, A. 1991. *Vijesnik* April 20.

Milosavljevic, M. & Ruzica, M. 1989. "Yugoslavia–The Effects of Economic and Political Crisis" in Munday, B. (ed.) *The Crisis in Welfare–An Interna-*

tional Perspective on Social Services and Social Work (New York: Harvester-Wheatsheaf-St. Martin's Press).

Ruzica, M. 1980. *Sheltered Workshops and Invalid's Protection* (Belgrade: School for Social Work and Institute for Social Problem Research).

Ruzica, M. 1985. *Social Policy–A Critique of its Theoretical Bases* (Belgrade: School for Social Work).

Ruzica, M. 1991. "Post-Communist State, Transition, Social Policy–Theses and Conceptual Framework for the Future Research." Paper presented at Boston College's International Conference on the Welfare State: Transition from Central Planning to Market Approaches, June 3–6, Budapest.

Ruzica, M. 1992. "Yugoslavia" in Dixon, J. & Macarov, D. (eds.) *Social Welfare in Socialist Countries* (London: Routledge).

Ruzica, M., Hojnik-Zupanc, I. & Svetlik, I. (1991.) "Shifts in the Welfare Mix–Social Innovation in Welfare Policies–A Case for Care for the Elderly–Report on Yugoslavia" *Eurosocial Report* 40/1: 73–92.

Todorovic, L. 1990. *Child Poverty and Deprivation in Yugoslavia Related to Transition to Market Economy* (Unpublished manuscript).

Working Group, Federal Committee for Labor, Health, Veterans' Questions, and Social Policy. 1990. *Recommendations for the Development of Health Care in Yugoslavia* (Unpublished report).

IV.

PROGRAM ANALYSES

10

Income Programs for the Elderly in Malaysia: A Policy Process Analysis

Martin Booth Tracy

Malaysia is representative of other economically developing societies in Asia that are increasingly challenged by the social and economic consequences of a growing number of elderly persons. While the family remains the primary institution for social and economic security in these societies, there are clear indications that patterns of rural to urban migration and increased female labor force participation are weakening the ability of families to fully function as traditional care providers (Baginda 1987; Cheung 1988; Heisel 1985; Martin 1988 & 1989; Sushama 1985; Williamson & Pampel 1993). The potential impact of these social changes on the economic well-being of the elderly, especially older women, is compounded by protracted longevity, greater incidence of widowhood, and an increasing likelihood of prolonged impoverishment.

It is difficult for governments to respond to the economic needs that are generated by aging populations by expanding income benefits for the elderly. In the first place, improving income support systems is replete with administrative and cost-related difficulties, which are discussed below. Further, most economically developing nations have targeted their youth and unemployed as the major benefactors of government social and economic programs as a means of ensuring a supply of workers in the labor-intensive industries that dominate the employment structure (Cheung 1988). But perhaps the most important reason for caution in establishing new, or expanding old, government income maintenance programs for the elderly is the perception that state assistance discourages families from assuming responsibility for caring for their elderly members. This is reinforced by an impression that is held by many policy-makers and analysts in Third World nations that elaborate and generous income maintenance programs under social security systems in industrial societies have contributed to a decline in the family as the primary mode of economic support (Burgess & Stern 1991; Chawla 1988; Gibson & Coppard 1989; Martin 1989).

Income policy issues related to the growing number of elderly persons in economically developing countries are extensively discussed in the international literature on aging, yet there are few efforts to explain the reasons for policy and program choices using an analytical comparative framework. Most published policy studies on Third World social security systems are descriptive analyses that focus on the fundamental socioeconomic issues and the basic program features with an occasional explanation of the rationale for them (see on aging, for example, Ahmad, Dreze, Hills & Sen 1991; Benda-Beckmann 1988; Gibson 1985; Hui 1987; Sennott-Miller 1989; Tout 1989; Williamson & Pampel 1993; U.S. Department of Health and Human Services 1992; American Association of International Aging 1985; Findlay & Findlay 1987; Kendig 1987; Mesa-Lago 1986; Neysmith & Edwardh 1984; Treas & Logue 1986; UN 1983). While these, along with various studies of socioeconomic macro-theories, make an essential contribution to the literature on income systems for the elderly, they tend to neglect an exploration of the conventional reasons attributable to social security policy and program differences among Third World countries.

Understanding conventional factors in decision making may be less useful than knowledge of macro-determinants in terms of predicting future developments, but it can provide insight as to why the preferences for a specific policy, program, or provision among the policy-makers of one country are different from the preferences of another. That is why decision-makers in one nation opt for plan "A" while those in another choose plan "B." Without some comprehension of the conventional reasons for government choices of strategies and tactics, it is difficult to achieve one of the major purposes of cross-national policy analysis, the determining of the feasibility of transferring all or part of a specific program from one nation to another.

In order to be able to explain why a particular nation has adopted a certain income approach, it is suggested here that it is essential to determine the factors that have shaped that government's decisions in terms of what the policy is intended to accomplish and how. More specifically, this requires an examination of the government's policy goals and objectives and its strategies and procedures in the context of the policy decision making process.

This analysis, therefore, is not concerned with examining the veracity of socio-economic or political theories of social security development (for example, convergence, diffusion, structuralist) customarily discussed as determinants of government policy (Antal, Dierkes & Weiler 1987; Schmidt 1989). It is, rather, an effort to analyze those factors that may have played a distinctive role in decision making, as measured by both public pronouncements and reports regarding government policy intentions and by tangible activities in the form of existing program provisions.

This chapter utilizes an analytical framework for cross-national studies of policy processes that was developed by the author for an earlier study of income, health, and social service programs for the elderly in the People's Republic of China, Kerala (India), Mexico, Nigeria, and Turkey (Tracy 1991 & 1992). The analysis here, however, is limited to income systems, particularly old-age benefits. The framework offers a guideline for examining the reasons that a nation has chosen a particular program approach by analyzing eight aspects of policy development, as follows:

- the role of government (federal, regional, local) in terms of legal and constitutional authority;

- the governments' attitudes toward involvement in state-supported social welfare systems;

- the major social, economic, and political obstacles to government intervention;

- the major social, economic, and political catalysts for government intervention;

- the identified issue (how the issue addressed by the program is defined);

- the specified goals and objectives of the program;

- a description of what the program does and how; and

- a synthesis of the information, along with a discussion of the implications for policy and programs and suggestions for additional study.

The analytical model is a composite of a variety of analytical frameworks in political science, social science, and social work that focus on examining government processes used in solving problems that are shared by more than one nation. The use of the model for cross-national comparisons is based on the notion that "similar nations" (Teune 1978) are suitable for comparative analysis (for a more detailed discussion of the origin and the features of the model see Tracy 1991).

BACKGROUND

Concern for the income needs of older persons as a government policy issue in Malaysia has been generated by demographic and social changes. The number of elderly persons is growing. Life expectancy is increasing, fertility rates are declining. This fact has prompted the government to actively pursue efforts to increase the population to 70 million by the year 2100 (Government of Malaysia 1986). The present population is estimated to be 18 million, 82 percent of whom live on the mainland Peninsula and about 60 percent of whom live in rural areas.

By the United Nations' definition of an old population as a nation with at least 10 percent of its citizens age 60 and over, Malaysia is a young country with the proportion aged 60 and over an estimated 6.2 percent in 1990. Those age 65 and over comprise 4.0 percent of the population, and persons age 55 and over constitute 8.9 percent. From 1970 to 1990 there was an increase of 19.2 percent in persons age 60 and over, compared to a 16.2 percent rise in persons aged 15 to 59. Based on current declining fertility rates the percentage of the population age 60 and over will reach 7.4 percent by 2000 and 15.5 percent by the year 2030. However, under projections based on the 70 million population policy the severity of the situation would be reduced to having 7.3 percent of the population at age 60 and over in 2000 and only 11.8 percent in 2030 (Baginda 1987).

While the proportion of elderly under either scenario is relatively low, government concern over the implications of the aging population is intensified by the fact that the number of elderly persons in Peninsular Malaysia has nearly doubled from 472,368 in 1970 to 904,432 in 1990. Since 1957 there has been a three-fold increase. This has been accompanied by an increase in life expectancy from the date of birth for men from 56 in 1957 to 68 in 1980 and from 58 to 72 for women (Baginda 1987). Life expectancy for men from age 60 is 16.3 years and for women it is 18.4 years (Malaysia Department of Statistics 1989).

A related demographic trend that reduces the ability of families to provide for their elderly is the diminishing size of families, which places a greater burden on fewer children (Baginda 1987). This increase in smaller families is attributable to a reduction in crude birth rates, which in Peninsula Malaysia have dropped from 41.1 in 1947 to 36.4 in 1980 among ethnic Malays (Bumiputeras), from 44.0 to 26.7 for the Chinese, and from 49.1 to 32.0 for the East Indians. Projected rates for the year 2000 are 27.9, 19.2, and 20.8, respectively (Baginda 1987). These trends reflect a growing preference for smaller families among all three ethnic groups.

The compelling policy issue facing the government stemming from these demographic developments is how to address the income needs of the growing numbers of elderly without contributing to a decline in the traditional family obligations. Or, conversely, what program measures can the government institute to strengthen family income support capabilities without abdicating government responsibility for social welfare? Evidence of struggle with this policy issue and the current government coping strategies are discussed below.

GOVERNMENT AUTHORITY

The government of Malaysia has historically been reluctant to assume legislative jurisdiction for providing social welfare services, which are deemed to be the responsibility of communities, families, and individuals. The government does play a supportive role, however, by instituting policies that promote family integration and mutual support (Cheung 1988). The limitations to government social welfare legislation are a legacy of British colonialism, which ruled the Malay Peninsula for over 125 years, (1824–1957). Government intervention was certainly practiced under British administration, but intercession was largely dictated by efforts to promote national economic development. It was assumed that if the economy was healthy, social problems would not require government intervention. Indeed, government involvement in social welfare programs was viewed as distinctly economically non-productive (Sushama 1985), and social welfare programs were viewed as the jurisdiction of localities in a federated system.

The British heritage of a federated government approach is also reflected in Malaysia's continuation of a system that gives each of the 14 states a high degree of political and administrative autonomy (Chow 1978). While the two non-peninsula states of Sabah and Sarawak are most noted for their independence from the central government, the remaining states also are administratively independent, especially in the development of programs for the elderly.

The element of decentralization under colonial rule notwithstanding, the British also established a precedence for central authority regarding income maintenance programs for workers, including retirees. Income protection policies were a government response to the effects of the shift from a payment-in-kind and agricultural economy to a wage-based and industrial economy, which placed workers at a greater risk of poverty when their income-earning capacity ended because of such contingencies as work accidents, poor health, or old age. Recognition that workers, mostly male breadwinners, needed some provision of insurance against these risks led the British colonial government to introduce work injury benefits in 1929 and the Employees Provident Fund (EPF) in 1952.

The choice of a provident fund as the principal income support system for retired persons, as opposed to a social insurance system, is an excellent illustration of the British colonial legacy of carefully limited government intervention. This system of enforced compulsory savings for retirement income emphasizes the concept of self-reliance, in direct contrast to a system of transferring payroll tax revenue from workers to the unemployed under a system of shared risks that is characteristic of social insurance systems found in industrial nations.

In the post-colonial period Malaysia also adopted a program for protecting workers from loss of income due to disability (invalidity) under the Social Security Act of 1969. The term "social security" in Malaysia refers only to work injury and disability benefits that are administered by the Social Security Organization (SOCSO).

It is important to note that in recent years the government has adopted a broader view about the role of the social sector in economic development efforts. In particular, the New Economic Policy (NEP) initiated in the second Malaysia Plan of 1971–1976, which was primarily designed to redress economic imbalance among the three major ethnic groups (Esman 1986), also formally affirms the idea that a lasting economic development strategy cannot be achieved without also fully integrating social factors (Sushama 1985). This concept is bolstered by the recent United Nations emphasis on stressing the role of social welfare, in general, and families and women, in particular, as an integral facet of economic development (UN 1986, 1987 & 1991).

CATALYSTS FOR GOVERNMENT INTERVENTION

A clear incentive for government-sponsored income maintenance systems is the growth of the elderly population at a time when the ability of the family to provide economic assistance is being weakened by external factors. This is not to suggest that the family has forsaken its role as the principal provider. Rather, it does appear that there are indisputable indications that changing social conditions are having a discernible negative impact on the ability of a significant proportion of families to provide income support. One such social change is the increase of women in the labor force, especially rural young women who have migrated to urban areas to find employment (Baginda 1987; Sushama 1985). Although they have become wage earners, there is no clear evidence that their wages are high enough to allow them to financially support their elderly parents, who remain in rural areas.

The government must also weigh its options for increased state income support in view of the lower number of children in families, which has resulted from increased uses of contraception and from later marriages. Moreover, later marriages have compelled many elderly to prolong their work activities in order to assist their children in obtaining an education (Baginda 1987).

Another concern is that the traditional respect for and authority of the elderly is being eroded in many families, creating a situation where the elderly parents are at greater social and economic risk. This erosion has been attributed in Malaysia to differential educational levels between the aged and younger people (Baginda 1987). Apparently, the practical skills and knowledge of the rural elderly are perceived as having limited value to young people who wish to obtain employment in urban areas that require technical training. About 20 percent of elderly males aged 60 to 64 and 50 percent of those 80 and over have no formal education (Andrews, Esterman, Braunack-Mayer & Rungie 1986). Of women ages 60 to 64, 70 percent have no formal education, and for those ages 75 to 79 the rate is 95 percent.

The social issues that influence government decisions about national income maintenance programs, however, are insignificant compared to economic considerations. There are pivotal economic factors that motivate the government to maintain a viable and effective EPF. Most importantly, the EPF is instrumental in generating revenue for financing domestic projects at a low cost through government investments (Chow 1978; Gillam 1982; Khan 1989). Indeed, the provident fund systems of Malaysia and Singapore have been labeled as "pension fund socialism" because they provide the government with investment capital (Cheung 1988; also Dixon 1989b). At the end of 1986, the EPF in Malaysia had assets of M $35.43 billion, of which 97 percent were primarily invested, as required by law, in Malaysian government securities. To put this amount in perspective, the fund is contributing nearly 61 percent of the total government borrowing requirements during the Fifth Malaysia Plan (Employees Provident Fund 1989).

Another reason for continued support of a state-supported income maintenance program is that provident fund benefits and other types of public assistance for the elderly are a significant source of individual income. A study of the elderly in Malaysia in the mid 1980s by the World Health Organization (WHO), for example, showed that pensions comprised 23 percent of all income for elderly men (Andrews et al. 1986). The lower the age group, the more important the pension becomes, reaching 30 percent of total income for men aged 60 to 64 compared to only nine percent for men aged 80 and over. This differential in the percentage of income reflects increased EPF benefit amounts in recent years and the maturity of the system. Notably, only six percent of elderly women's income was derived from pensions, reflecting the low proportion of women covered by EPF as wage earners.

It should be mentioned that these data do not include income from occupational (private) pensions. Data on the number of workers covered by occupational pension plans are fragmentary, but there is some information to suggest that an appreciable number are enrolled and that those who are tend to receive higher benefits than those paid under the EPF. A survey of 120 companies with about 52,000 employees in 1982, for example, showed that 110 of them provided retirement benefits that exceeded those under the EPF (Spencer & Assoc. 1983).

IMPEDIMENTS TO INTERVENTION

The weight of social and economic concerns for government intervention in income maintenance programs is greatly modified by the fact that families continue to be the foremost source of income support for the elderly. It is generally accepted, although certainly questionable for impoverished families, that the elderly who live with their families have less need of state income assistance. The pressure for state involvement is reduced in view of studies that show that 72 percent of all Malaysians live in a family setting, and about 81 percent of the elderly in urban areas live with one of their children. Despite the relative inaccessibility of adequate housing space, the proportion of elderly living with families with seven or more children is 90 percent. Nor is the situation in rural areas viewed as critical, as 67 percent of the elderly reside with their children (Andrews et al. 1986), particularly when other demands for state resources are considered. Moreover, the lower proportion in rural areas is of little concern because it is known that there is more space in rural localities for children to live near but not necessarily with their elderly parents (Andrews et al. 1986).

Efforts to expand the government's involvement in retirement income systems is also impaired by an apparent satisfaction among the elderly with regards to their level of income. The WHO study in the mid 1980s revealed that only 11 percent of the rural and eight percent of the urban elderly felt that they did not have sufficient income to meet their basic needs. Surprisingly, there were no gender differences in the survey responses (Andrews et al. 1986). While the positive responses may be a reflection of an apparent high level of fatalism among rural elderly (Baginda 1987), the data do not support a crisis situation that would justify an extraordinary government policy response.

An additional factor that tends to restrain government intervention is related to cultural and ethnic diversity. There are three major ethnic groups in Malaysia: the indigenous Malay, or Bumiputeras, who constitute 54 percent of the population; the Chinese, who first arrived as laborers in the tin mines during the 1860s, who also came in the early 1900s to work on the rubber plantations, and who now comprise 33 percent of the total population; and the East Indians, who also immigrated as laborers on the rubber plantation and who now represent 10 percent of the population.

The Malays, as the politically dominant population (Esman 1986), have traditionally been the least motivated to initiate government income assistance for the elderly, as they have tended to live in rural areas where family support systems remain quite strong. Malays are still primarily engaged in agricultural work, although in 1985 about 41 percent of the urban population were Malay, compared with 47 percent who were Chinese and 11 percent who were East Indian (Baginda 1987). Nor is there great pressure from the Chinese community for retirement income assistance because they are generally the most economically prosperous (Esman 1986; Baginda 1987). The mean monthly household income of the Chinese population in 1987, for example, was M $1,430, compared to M $1,089 for East Indians and M $868 for Malays (Malaysia Department of Statistics 1989). The relatively small East Indian population is the least politically represented and the least influential with respect to pension policies.

Even if the government were persuaded that expanding the EPF to a larger proportion of the work force, especially agricultural workers, was a high priority, expansion of the EPF would be complicated by the difficulty of collecting revenue (payroll taxes) from rural, geographically isolated individuals with irregular work patterns (Dixon 1989a, 1989b) who make up 32 percent of the total work force (Malaysia Department of Statistics 1989). Moreover, the relatively weak economic position of rural communities and generally low educational levels make it difficult to extend pension coverage. Similarly, it is virtually impossible to effectively cover workers in the informal work sector or subsistence economy, thereby eliminating most of the needy from potential coverage.

There are also major problems due to the absence of an administrative infrastructure in rural sectors, the difficulty of educating rural populations as to the purpose and utility of a compulsory savings plan, the lack of a close employee–employer relationship, and the large number of self-employed agricultural workers who would have to make contributions as both an employee and employer (SOCSO 1986).

CURRENT GOVERNMENT STRATEGIES

At present the old-age benefit strategy of the central government is focused on a goal of improving EPF efficiency within the parameters of limited federal involvement by decentralizing selective aspects of administration of the fund (Committee on Provident Funds 1990). This approach is modeled after the independently operating systems of the off-peninsula states of Sabah and Sarawak. This initiative also includes an improved computerized system of record keeping and imposes heavier penalties for non-compliance of payment of contributions (Employees Provident Fund 1989). These tactics have apparently resulted in some measurable success in terms of improving efficiency as, since being introduced, the rate of default for the nearly 150,000 employers who pay contributions dropped from 41.8 percent in 1987 to 36.3 percent in 1989 (Kow 1990).

As in other former British colonies with provident fund retirement income systems, there has been considerable discussion of the merits and disadvantages of converting the EPF to a social insurance scheme (Dixon 1989a). In Malaysia this idea is obstructed by widespread support for the current system among employers, government policy-makers, and employees alike. This support is based on the view that the current system is a socially and culturally accepted mechanism because it reinforces Asian values of self-help, hard work, and independence (Cheung 1988). Employers also prefer the status quo because the EPF represents a known and stable expenditure that is actuarially sound and easy to administer. Employees prefer the EPF because they have a perception of ownership in the fund, which, as Dixon (1989a) notes, is an almost universally shared perception of provident fund members. In addition, the EPF provides employees with an opportunity for substantial housing loans, which is very important to Malaysian workers.

The government did make an effort to improve the EPF by raising the level of benefits in a 1985 proposal, which would have also increased contribution rates. The government had to abandon this proposal in the face of employer resistance. Private sector employers were instrumental in preventing the adoption of the proposal, suggesting instead that employees should have an option for occupational pension coverage outside the state scheme. The credibility of this argument, at least from one survey of employers, is that occupational plans were viewed as superior to the state scheme (Spencer & Assoc. 1983). Evidently, some employers, especially the multinational businesses, offer lump-sum benefits in addition to those of the EPF (Waddingham 1983).

The government has made some provision to encourage the development of occupational benefits by providing tax incentives, such as limited tax deductible company contributions and tax-free investment of pension fund income, as well as tax-free benefits. The Minister of Human Resources has also tried to persuade private sector trade unions to provide pension insurance for their members (Spencer & Assoc. 1990a). Despite such government actions, employers argue that the growth of occupational schemes has been stunted by the EPF's extensive coverage and high contribution rates (Stott 1987). There were, in fact, reductions in occupational retirement benefit arrangements in 1980 following an increase in contribution rates from six to seven percent for employees and from nine to 11 percent for employers (Gillam 1982).

There appears to be a renewed effort by the government to increase the role of the private sector in providing occupational pensions. In the early 1990s the Minister of Human Resources encouraged trade unions to follow the lead of the Transport Workers Union in establishing a multiple benefits pension scheme (Spencer & Assoc. 1990a) to help address the future income needs of the elderly.

The government has also operationalized its policy of encouraging filial piety by providing a tax relief for the support of elderly parents. This provision has been in force since 1979 but, because of its limited impact, consideration is being given to limiting tax exemption only to persons who provide financial support to their elderly parents (Baginda 1987). In the Malaysian budget for 1991 discussion is focusing on an additional tax deduction for an individual's support toward documented parents' medical expenses (Baginda, personal communication, January 28, 1991).

The relatively modest attention that government pays to income-maintenance systems for the elderly has also been criticized for giving preferential treatment to the elderly and the most vulnerable low-income groups. This, it is argued, has been to the exclusion of benefits for the middle class, which violates a fundamental tenant of government social service programs of providing basic benefits for all regardless of age or income (Sushama 1985).

PROVISIONS OF THE EMPLOYEES PROVIDENT
FUND (EPF)

The Employees Provident Fund of Malaysia was first implemented in 1952 during a politically volatile time of an attempted communist insurrection from 1948 to 1953 known as "The Emergency." Thus, the EPF was begun five years before the Federation of Malaya acquired its independence from Britain as one of various government measures to obstruct the threat of communist subversion by promising workers a sense of financial security (ISSA 1982). In 1963 two other former British colonies, Sabah, Sarawak and, for two years, Singapore joined the federation, which was renamed the Federation of Malaysia.

All employees age 16 and above are covered, except for members of existing equivalent occupational pension schemes, teachers, members of the Armed Forces (USDHSS 1992), and persons not covered under the government pension plan for civil servants. The government attempted to include civil servants, who are covered under the Government Pension Scheme in the EPF, in 1987 as a means of strengthening the financial condition of the latter, but union opposition forced a reversal of the decision (Spencer & Assoc. 1987a & 1987b). The self-employed are also eligible for coverage on a voluntary basis (SOCSO 1986). The payroll tax or contribution rate is nine percent of earnings, according to 24 wage classes, paid by employees and 11 percent of wages, according to wage class, paid by employers. Contributions are credited to a member's account, which accumulates interest (Khan 1989). For the last 12 years the average annual interest rate has been eight percent (Dasuki 1992). The level of interest has been questioned as being substantially lower than that paid by banks. The process of interest accumulation has also been charged as being unfair because interest is not paid for contributions made during the year (Consumers' Association of Penang 1985).

In 1988 more than 80 percent of all EPF savings amounted to less than M $10,000 each (Kow 1990). Given that the mean annual gross household income in urban areas is M $17,604 (Malaysia Department of Statistics 1989), the average lump-sum total savings is equivalent to less than two years' earnings. Under the national minimum poverty line of M $350 a month, this amounts to a monthly minimum income equivalent to a period of less than two and a half years after retirement, when life expectancy is 16 to 18 years.

In general, benefits are payable as a one-time lump-sum payment in the event of a worker's attaining the age of 55 years, dying, experiencing permanent disability, or permanently migrating from Malaysia and Singapore. Since 1968 workers have had the option of receiving one-third of their benefit at age 50, and since 1977 workers can receive the benefit as a monthly annuity in place of the lump-sum benefit. Credits to the fund can also be used to withdraw a loan for the purpose of purchasing a house or reducing a house mortgage up to the lesser of either 40 percent of the purchase price or 45 percent of the member's contributions (Spencer & Assoc. 1989).

The number of workers covered by EPF has increased from 0.50 million when the scheme started in 1952 to 5.27 million in 1988, at an annual growth rate of 6.68 percent (Kow 1990). In 1987 there were 5.04 million covered workers, which represent about 84 percent of the total active labor force of 5,983,900 and 37 percent of the total population of 13,653,061 (International Labor Organization 1990; Kow 1990).

SUMMARY

A growing elderly population that has been accompanied by the nuclearization of families and by the rural-to-urban migration of young people in Malaysia, has placed the income needs of the elderly on the policy agenda. The issue for the government is how to assist the traditional income support system of families without weakening that system. The government's programmatic response suggests an overall policy goal of maintaining a balance between the role of government and customary responsibilities of the family. In keeping with this goal the government has limited its intervention in the area of income maintenance to the Employees Provident Fund. Failing earlier efforts to improve this system by raising benefit and contribution levels, the most recent strategy has been to improve the efficiency of the Fund through administrative reforms. More specifically, this has involved the decentralization of some administrative functions from central to state governments and the computerization of record keeping to improve the process of collecting contributions.

Any attempts at a more ambitious reform of the income maintenance system, such as converting the provident fund to a social insurance system or expanding its coverage to agricultural workers, are restricted by employee and employer resistance to change and the difficulties of instituting a system among rural laborers. Moreover, the government itself is reluctant to alter its current reliance on the EPF as a major source of investment revenue for low-cost domestic projects that are a critical part of government economic initiatives. Finally, the political will for the government

to adopt a more assertive posture in promoting retirement income maintenance programs is weakened by limited financial resources, a preference
for allocating scarce resources to young people, and the absence of a clearly
documented need among the elderly, especially those of the Malay population who are politically dominant.

ACKNOWLEDGMENT

The preparation of this chapter was aided by a grant from the University
of Iowa's Center for International Rural and Environmental Health.

REFERENCES

Ahmad, E., Dreze, J., Hills, J. & Sen, A. (eds.). 1991. *Social Security in Developing
Countries* (Oxford: Clarendon Press).
American Association of International Aging. 1985. *Population Aging in Develop-
ing Nations: A Strategy for Development Support* (Washington, D.C.:
American Association of International Aging).
Andrews, G. A., Esterman, A. J., Braunack-Mayer, A. J. & Rungie, C. M. 1986.
Aging in the Western Pacific: A Four Country Study (Manila: World
Health Organization).
Antal, A. B., Dierkes, M. & Weiler, H. N. 1987. "Cross-national Policy Re-
search" in Dierkes, M., Weiler, H. N. & Antal, A. B. (eds.) *Comparative
Policy Research: Learning from Experience* (Brookfield, VT: Gower).
Baginda, A. M. 1987. "The Emerging Issues of the Aging of Population: Malaysia"
in *Population Aging: Review of Emerging Issues* (Asian Population Studies
Series No. 80) (Bangkok: Economic and Social Commission for Asia
and the Pacific).
Benda-Beckmann, F. von, Benda-Beckmann, K. von, Casino, G. R., Woodman,
E. & Zacher, H. (eds.). 1988. *Between Kinship and the State: Law and
Social Security in Developing Nations* (Dordrecht: Foris).
Burgess, R. & Stern, N. 1991. "Social Security in Developing Countries: What,
Why, Who, and How" in Ahmad, E., Dreze, J., Hills, J. & Sen, A. (eds.)
Social Security in Developing Countries (Oxford: Clarendon Press).
Chawla, S. 1988. "The Participation of the Elderly in Development." Paper
presented at the Expert Group Meeting on Policies and Strategies for the
Participation of the Elderly in Development, Valletta, Malta.
Cheung, P.P.L. 1988. "The Best of Times, the Worst of Times: Growing Old in
Asia." Paper presented at the Annual Meeting of the Gerontological
Association of America, San Francisco, CA.

Chow, N.W.S. 1978. *A Comparative Study of Social Security Systems in East and Southeast Asian Countries* (Geneva: International Social Security Association).

"Committee on Provident Funds 1990" *International Social Security Review* 43(1): 99–105.

Consumers' Association of Penang. 1985. *EPF's Missing Billions? Losses Suffered by Contributors due to EPF's Interest Policy* (Penang, Malaysia: Consumers' Association of Penang).

Dasuki, Z. 1992. "Adapting the Legal and Administrative Structures of Provident Funds to Achieve Optimum Efficiency: The National Experience of Malaysia." Paper presented at the XXIVth International Social Security Association General Assembly, Acapulco, Mexico.

Dixon, J. 1989a. *National Provident Funds: The Enfant Terrible of Social Security* (Canberra: International Fellowship for Social and Economic Development).

Dixon, J. 1989b. "A Comparative Perspective on Provident Funds: Their Present and Future Explored" *Journal of International and Comparative Social Welfare* 5(2):1–28.

Dixon, J. 1994. "National Provident Funds: The Challenge of Harmonizing Social Security, Social and Economic Objectives" *Policy Studies Review* 12 (1/2): 197–213.

Employees Provident Fund. 1989. "Decentralization, Collection of Contributions and Enforcement of the Scheme" *Asian News Sheet* 19(4): 15–17.

Employees Provident Fund. 1990. *1989 Annual Report* (Kuala Lumpur: Employees Provident Fund).

Esman, M. J. 1986. "Ethnic Politics and Economic Power" *Comparative Politics* 19(4): 394–418.

Findlay, A. & Findlay, A. 1987. *Population and Development in the Third World* (London: Routledge & Kegan Paul).

Gibson, M. J. 1985. *Older Women Around the World* (Washington, D.C.: International Federation on Ageing).

Gibson, M. J. & Coppard, L. C. 1989. "Family Support of the Elderly: Policy and Program Implications." Paper presented at the XIV International Congress of Gerontology, Acapulco, Mexico.

Gillam, A. 1982. "An Introduction to Employee Benefits in Malaysia," *Benefits International* 11(9): 11–15.

Government of Malaysia. 1986. *Fifth Malaysia Plan, 1986–1990* (Kuala Lumpur: Government of Malaysia).

Heisel, M. A. 1985. "Aging in the Context of Population Policies in Developing Countries" *Population Bulletin of the United Nations* 17: 49–63.

Hui, Y. F. 1987. "Nature and Adequacy of Formal and Informal Support Programs to Deal with the Problem of the Aged" in Economic and Social Commission for Asia and the Pacific (ed.) *Population Aging: Review of Emerging*

Issues (Asian Population Series No. 80) (Bangkok: Economic and Social Commission for Asia and the Pacific).

International Labor Organization (ILO) 1990. *Yearbook of Labor Statistics, 1989–90* (Geneva: ILO).

International Social Security Association (ISSA). 1982. "Malaysia: Historical Development of the Fund" in *Sixth Meeting for the Conversion of Provident Funds into More Comprehensive Social Security Schemes* (New Delhi: International Social Security Association, Regional Office for Asia and Oceania).

Kendig, H. L. 1987. "Roles of the Aged, Families and Communities in the Context of an Aging Society" in Economic and Social Commission for Asia and the Pacific (ed.) *Population Aging: Review of Emerging Issues* (Asian Population Series No. 80) (Bangkok: Economic and Social Commission for Asia and the Pacific).

Khan, M. (ed.). 1989. *Labor Administration: Profile on Malaysia* (Bangkok: International Labor Organization, Asian and Pacific Regional Centre for Labor Administration).

Kow, C. A. 1990. "Current Problems and Issues Encountered by Provident Fund Schemes in Asia and the Pacific: Malaysian experience" *Asian News Sheet* 20(3): 27–31.

Malaysia Department of Statistics. 1989. *Yearbook of Statistics, 1988* (Kuala Lumpur: Malaysia Department of Statistics).

Martin, L. G. 1988. "The Aging of Asia" *Journal of Gerontology: Social Sciences* 43(4): S99–S113.

Martin, L. G. 1989. "Living Arrangements of the Elderly in Fiji, Korea, Malaysia, and the Philippines" *Demography* 26(4): 627–43.

Mesa-Lago, C. 1986. "Comparative Study of the Development of Social Security in Latin America" *International Social Security Review* 39(2): 127–52.

Neysmith, S. M. & Edwardh, J. 1984. "Economic Dependency in the 1980s: Its Impact on the Elderly" *Ageing and Society* 4(1): 21–44.

Schmidt, M. G. 1989. "Social Policy in Rich and Poor Countries: Socio-economic Trends and Political-institutional Determinants" *European Journal of Political Research* 17(6): 641–59.

Sennott-Miller, L. 1989. *Midlife and Older Women in Latin America and Caribbean: A Status Report* (Washington, D.C.: American Association of Retired Persons and Pan American Health Organization).

Social Security Organization (SOCSO). 1986. *The National Experience of Malaysia in the Field of Social Security Protection for the Rural Population.* (Proceedings of the Asian Regional Round Table Meeting on Social Security Protection for the Rural Population, Jakarta). (Geneva: Regional Office for Asia and Oceania, International Social Security Association).

Spencer & Associates. 1983. "Malaysia" in *IBIS Briefing Service* (August 2) (Chicago: Spencer, C. D. & Associates, Inc.): 16–18.

Spencer & Associates. 1987a. "Malaysia" in *IBIS Briefing Service* (January 22). (Chicago: Spencer, C. D. & Associates, Inc.): 18.

Spencer & Associates. 1987b. "Malaysia" in *IBIS Briefing Service* (May 28) (Chicago: Spencer, C. D. & Associates, Inc.): 17.

Spencer & Associates. 1989. "Malaysia: Employees Provident Fund" in *IBIS Briefing Service* (September 14) (Chicago: Spencer, C. D. & Associates, Inc.): 38.

Spencer & Associates. 1990a. "Minister Calls for Private Pensions." *IBIS Review* (Chicago: Spencer, C. D. & Associates, Inc.) 5(4): 26–7.

Spencer & Associates. 1990b. "Malaysia: Occupational pensions" in *IBIS Briefing Service* (September 16) (Chicago: Spencer, C. D. & Associates, Inc.): 17.

Stott, G. 1987. "Investment Performance Measurement of Asian Pension Plans" *Benefits & Compensation International* 16(8): 2–10.

Sushama, P. C. 1985. "Malaysia" in Dixon, J. & Kim, H. S. (eds.) *Social Welfare in Asia* (London: Croom Helm).

Taueber, C. M. 1993. *Sixty-five Plus in America* (Valletta, Malta: International Institute on Aging).

Teune, H. 1978. "A Logic of Comparative Policy Analysis" in Ashford, D. F. (ed.) *Comparing Public Policies: New Concepts and Methods* (Beverly Hills, CA: Sage).

Thompson, K. 1980. *Outline of Selected Rural Social Security Schemes in Developing Countries Outside Asia* (Social Security Documentation: Asian Series, 6). (New Delhi: Regional Office for Asia and Oceania, International Social Security Association).

Tout, K. 1989. *Ageing in Developing Countries* (New York: Oxford University Press).

Tracy, M .B. 1991. *Social Policies for the Elderly in the Third World* (Westport, CT: Greenwood).

Tracy, M. B. 1992. "Cross-national Social Welfare Policy Analysis in the Graduate Curriculum: A Comparative Process Model" *Journal of Social Work Education* 28(3): 341–52.

Treas, J. & Logue, B. 1986. "Economic Development and the Older Population" *Population and Development Review* 12(4): 645–73.

United Nations (UN). 1983. *Vienna International Plan of Action on Aging* (New York: UN).

United Nations (UN). 1986. *Developmental Social Welfare: A Global Survey of Issues and Priorities since 1968* (New York: UN).

United Nations (UN). 1987. *Interregional Consultation on Developmental Social Welfare Policies and Programs* (Pt I, Vol. 1, No. 25) (Vienna: UN, Centre for Social Development and Humanitarian Affairs).

United Nations (UN). 1991. "Report of the Secretary-General on the Work of the Organization: 1991" *Social Development Newsletter* (Vienna: UN, Centre for Social Development and Humanitarian Affairs) 28(2).

United States, Department of Health and Social Services (USDHSS). 1992. *Social Security Programs Throughout the World, 1991* (Social Security Administration, Office of International Policy, Research Report No. 61–006) (Washington, DC: Government Printing Office).

Waddingham, A. 1983. "Retirement Benefits in Malaysia and Singapore," *Benefits International* 12(12): 21–7.

Williamson, J. B. & Pampel, F. C. 1993. *Old-age Security in Comparative Perspective* (New York: Oxford University Press).

11

Financial Support for Long-Term Institutional Care in Britain

Anne Corden

In common with other developed nations, Britain has an aging population. Reductions in mortality at all ages and trends toward lower birth rates have increased the proportion of elderly people in the population (OPCS 1984 & 1989; Family Policy Studies Centre 1988). People aged at least 65 represented approximately 15.8 percent of the population in 1991, compared with 4.7 percent in 1901 (Henwood 1990). By 1985, the United Kingdom had, among European countries, the highest proportion of population aged 60 and over (HMSO 1988b). While the overall proportion of elderly people is likely to remain relatively static up to the end of the century, the balance will change between the younger post-retirement component and the very old. The number of very old people will increase rapidly (CSO 1993), which makes this a significant group in terms of their special needs for services and care.

Most elderly people live in private households in community settings. This was true of 96.6 percent of those of pensionable age in England and Wales in 1981. Bosanquet, Laing & Propper (1990) estimated that only 1.2 percent of people aged 65 to 74 were in some form of long-term institutional care in 1989. This rose to 23 percent of people over 85 years. Nevertheless, compared with other developed countries, the overall level of long-term care in institutions remains low. In 1989, the United Kingdom had 5.5 places in long-term care per 100 people aged 65 and over, compared, for example, with eight per 100 in France (Bosanquet, Laing & Propper 1990).

Despite the relatively small proportion of elderly people living in institutions, arrangements for their financial support remains a controversial area of social security policy. There were major changes in the regulations governing payments of benefits to people in long-term care in 1983 and 1985, and further adjustments in 1986. Two joint central-local government working parties were established to consider financial support for long-term care (DHSS 1985 & 1987), and the Audit Commission, the watchdog on government spending, considered current arrangements in 1986 (Audit Commission 1986). The whole area was reviewed again in Griffiths' enquiry into community care policy (HMSO 1988a) and a White Paper (HMSO 1989) followed, laying the basis for a fundamental reorganization of financial support for long-term care. New legislation was enacted in 1990 (HMSO 1990), and reorganization is being phased in from April 1991, achieving implementation by April 1993.

This chapter traces post-war policy developments to explain the current pattern of institutional care for elderly people and the support available to residents through social security. It addresses the policy issues raised by the current mixed economy of private, voluntary, and public sector provision and finance, including the suitability of funding mechanisms, levels of reimbursement from the public purse, regulation of standards, and the overall pattern of provision. Some of these issues and problems that have arisen are seen in parallel in other countries. The proposals for the 1990s are presented, and the chapter concludes by looking at suggested methods of self-financing that might in the long-term reduce dependence on social security.

THE PATTERN OF PROVISION

Long stay care for elderly people is currently provided in National Health Service (NHS) hospital wards, local authority residential homes (called "Part III accommodation"), and the independent sector (which includes private for profit) and voluntary (non-profit foundation) residential care homes and nursing homes. There is also a handful of experimental NHS nursing homes (Bond et al. 1989). Figure 11.1 shows how the total number of places provided for elderly, chronically ill, and physically disabled people was distributed among the various sectors in 1988. Most of those places were occupied by elderly people.

The dominance of the independent sector shown in Figure 11.1 is relatively recent. Early post-war policy was based on commitment to NHS hospital geriatric facilities, together with public authority residential care,

Figure 11.1

Places Provided in Long-Term Care for Elderly, Chronically Ill and Physically Disabled People, United Kingdom, 1991

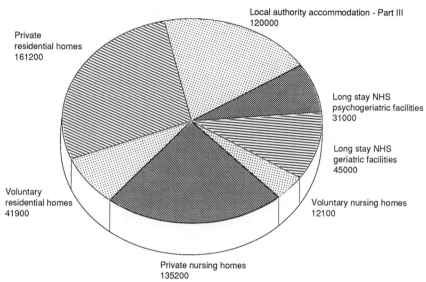

Source: Laing's *Review of Private Health Care 1992.* Laing and Buisson Publications Ltd., London.

which was, and has remained, the responsibility of local government. Part III of the 1948 National Assistance Act laid upon local authorities the duty of providing accommodation for "persons who by reason of age, infirmity or any other circumstances are in need of care and attention which is not otherwise available to them."

In discharging their responsibilities for residential provision, local authorities may also pay for places in independent homes. This became important during the 1970s, when local authorities found themselves unable to make their own provision for the growing numbers of elderly people needing care. While policy for elderly people had moved away from institutional care toward provision in the community (Means & Smith 1985) resources for community care followed more slowly. Demand for residential care continued, and local authorities increasingly paid for places in voluntary sector residential homes run by religious or charitable foundations. In the mid 1970s the pattern of institutional provision began to change. Hospital provision for the elderly was already falling as long stays in wards were curtailed under community care policies. Local authorities, implementing financial cutbacks following the oil crisis, stopped investing in Part III homes. The voluntary sector remained stable but the private sector began to expand. While in 1960 only about 10 percent of pensioners in residential care were in private homes (Townsend 1962) and these the wealthier members of society, by 1979 there were more places in for-profit residential homes than those run by voluntary foundations. Shortly afterwards, the private nursing home sector also started to grow.

The expansion of the private long-term care sector throughout the 1980s is well documented (Laing 1985; Laing & Buisson 1988; Bosanquet, Laing & Propper 1990). There are several likely contributory factors (Bradshaw 1988), including demographic pressures, cutbacks in local authority spending, community care policies, increases in financial resources available to some pensioners, the "enterprise culture" of the Thatcher government and, not least, changes in social security policy. The residents of the private sector are no longer only wealthy people. In 1990, about 56 percent of elderly people in independent homes were receiving income support, the main national non-contributory means-tested benefit (Bosanquet, Laing & Propper 1990).

FINANCIAL SUPPORT FOR THE INDEPENDENT SECTOR

The combined effects of the increase in the number of residents in independent homes, the increasing proportion dependent on income support, and increases in the amount of benefit that may be claimed has led to a remarkable increase in social security expenditure, as shown in Table 11.1.

The regulations governing payments of public assistance to people in long-term care have been changed several times during the 1980s as the government has struggled to bring the massive expenditures under control. The story is summarized here—fuller accounts can be read elsewhere (Bartlett 1987; Parker 1987; Land 1988).

Centrally funded public assistance has been available to people of limited means living in independent homes since 1948. Before 1980 the allowance was based on prevailing local charges for general board and lodging for an independent adult. Higher rates could only be paid on a discretionary basis. So elderly people did not go into homes in the expectation that supplementary benefit would meet fees, although there were cases where discretionary higher payments were made to elderly people whose private money had run out.

Table 11.1

Income Support (Previously Supplementary Benefits) for People in
Independent Residential Care and Nursing Homes

	Expenditure (million, current prices)	No. of Claimants (thousands)	Average Payment (per week, current prices)
Dec. 1979	10.0	12.0	16.0
Dec. 1980	18.0	13.0	26.6
Dec. 1981	23.0	13.0	34.0
Dec. 1982	39.0	16.0	46.9
Dec. 1983	104.0	26.0	76.9
Dec. 1984	200.0	42.0	91.6
Dec. 1985	348.0	70.0	95.6
Feb. 1986	459.0	90.0	98.1
May 1987	671.0	117.0	110.3
May 1988	878.0	147.0	115.0
May 1989	1,105.0	176.0	120.7

Source: House of Commons, Hansard, 19 December 1989:col. 172.

Revision of the supplementary benefit system in 1980 to place the public
assistance scheme on a regulated basis included apparently minor changes
to the board and lodging regulations. Allowances were now determined by
reference to charges in "equivalent establishments," taking into account
the needs of residents. This meant that "reasonable charges" were determined locally according to the local fees in independent homes.

Benefits paid at rates fixed at the discretion of adjudication officers were
made automatically to elderly people, for supplementary benefit officers
were reluctant to ask frail elderly people to move if fees rose. It became
clear that supplementary benefits now offered secure financing for poor
people in independent homes, on the basis only of financial need. This was
a major contributory factor in the expansion of the private sector, but
probably not by government intention. Between 1982 and 1983, as shown
in Table 11.1, there was a 64 percent rise in the number of claimants in
independent homes, and supplementary benefit expenditure rose from 39
to 104 million pounds.

There followed a series of attempts to control the rising expenditures.
In November 1983 a three-tier system of local limits was introduced,
distinguishing between ordinary board and lodging, residential, and nurs-

ing homes. Discretionary elements were abolished, but this was offset by the setting of limits based the highest reasonable charge in the area. The supplementary benefit bill went on rising, and there was some concern that the local limits system allowed unscrupulous proprietors to form cartels to inflate charges.

In April 1985 locally determined limits were abolished and replaced by a set of national limits based on the type of care received. This was determined by reference to the category of care for which a resident's care home was registered under the terms of the Registered Homes Act of 1984—there was still no assessment of need for care. Further minor amendments in July 1986 introduced an additional category for payment for very dependent elderly people in residential care, and a London weighting to acknowledge higher costs in the capital.

By April 1992 the national weekly limit for an elderly person in residential care was 175 pounds (205 pounds for the very dependent elderly with disabilities), and 270 pounds in nursing homes, with an additional entitlement to 12.20 pounds to cover personal expenses. The amount of benefits paid is based on the difference between the elderly person's personal income (for example, from state and occupational pensions, disability pensions, and investment income) and the appropriate limit of benefit available. Capital of up to 3,000 pounds is disregarded completely; capital of 8,000 pounds disqualifies completely; capital between 3,000 and 8,000 pounds is dealt with by assuming tariff income of 1 pound per week in every 250 pounds.

FINANCIAL SUPPORT FOR THE PUBLIC SECTOR

There are different structures of support for elderly people in the public sector as compared with the private sector. Care in NHSA hospitals is paid for from national tax revenue, and there are no direct charges to patients. Long-stay patients receiving contributory state pensions, such as retirement pensions, have these reduced by 40 percent after six weeks in the hospital, and further reduced to a personal allowance after a year's stay because living expenses are being met. Income support is reduced to a personal weekly allowance (13.55 pounds in 1992) after a stay of six weeks.

Financing Part III accommodation remains the responsibility of local authorities, who are required both to assess the need for entry and to make charges to residents. There is a standard rate, based on actual costs of accommodation and care. An elderly person's ability to pay is assessed on a financial means-test administered by the local authority (DH 1990a). A few people pay this full charge. All residents are liable for the minimum charge, set by the Secretary of State at about four-fifths of the state retirement pension. This leaves a small personal weekly allowance (10.85 pounds). Residents without resources to cover the minimum charge and the personal allowance are eligible for income support, but there are now few people in this situation. The local authority means test also incorporates a capital disregard, which at 1,200 pounds, is lower than the disregard limit for income support. Capital above 1,200 pounds is dealt with by assuming tariff income of 25 pence per week for every 50 pounds. The shortfall between the costs of care and charges to residents is met by the local authority and paid for by a mix of local tax revenue (community charge) and central fundings.

Some local authorities "sponsor" people in independent residential homes, and some health authorities have similar arrangements with independent nursing homes, the "contracting-out" of beds for elderly people discharged from the hospital (Wright 1985). Approximately four percent of elderly people in private and voluntary homes are supported in this way (Bosanquet, Laing & Propper 1990). The local authorities and health authorities pay agreed fees to the independent homes, and the elderly people undergo the normal benefit reductions for hospital care, or a local authority financial assessment.

DIVERSITY OF PROVISION AND FINANCE: THE CURRENT ISSUES

Until the major changes in arrangements in 1993, long-term institutional care in Britain was characterized by diversity in both provision and financial underpinning. Elderly people of similar dependency might pay for all their care, part of it, or none depending on the type of institution they live in and their personal circumstances. Those undergoing financial assessment were dealt with differently, according to central or local income tests. Some elderly people had their need for care assessed before public financial support was made available; others did not. Not surprisingly, this situation led to controversy and posed problems that were difficult to solve.

First, there was the issue of whether, and how far, public finance should be made available in ways that promote private profit, especially when public expenditures are restricted and other needs cannot be met. Those who supported the availability of central government funding to individual elderly people in independent homes emphasized the apparent advantages. The amount of choice available to elderly people was increased by the thriving and variable private sector that has grown under the current social security arrangements. Opportunities for self-determination were increased, it was argued, since elderly people could choose the kind of care that suits them, without bureaucratic intervention—official assessment procedures, controlled waiting lists, and local boundary issues. People of limited means gained access to the same homes that wealthier people were prepared to pay substantial fees to enter. And, it was argued, the private sector, run by energetic and committed entrepreneurs responding to market forces, could produce care of high quality, in some cases superior to that available in the public sector. These apparent advantages could be seen in a different light (Corden 1990). While the private sector provided a range of type and size of home, the choice of homes was constrained by the geography of the market (Corden 1991), the availability of vacancies, and the extent to which the income support limits matched the fees charged. Real choice includes choosing between entering a home or not, and, as shown later, availability of social security finance for institutional care could act toward limiting this choice. What appears to be opportunities for self-determination to some might be experienced by others as isolation and absence of help and advocacy. Access to homes was democratized, but two-tier arrangements of facilities and services still developed, distinguishing those who could pay privately and those who depended on income support, particularly in regard to room sharing and security of tenure (Corden 1992). Private enterprise can have negative connotations for long-term care caused by, for example, high levels of turnover of ownership.

Given that the for-profit sector is now firmly established and of major importance in the overall pattern of service provision, policy-makers were initially less concerned with whether social security should be available to generate private profit for proprietors than with how much money need be passed over. Independent proprietors were free to charge as much as they wished, and social security policy-makers found it difficult to know how much money to make available to elderly people who could not meet fees. Since there is no official routine monitoring of fees, the government had to commission new research every time it needed full information (Ernst & Whinney 1986; Darton et al. 1990), and the information rapidly went out of date. It was even more difficult to obtain information about costs in independent homes (Price Waterhouse 1990). Without good information about costs and charges, it was hard to determine "adequate" or "reasonable" levels of charge that social security payments might be expected to meet (Gibbs & Corden 1991). Proprietors and welfare agencies argued continuously throughout the last decade that the levels of income support available were inadequate, leaving a gap between the fees charged and elderly residents' benefit income (NACAB 1991). In August 1988 it was estimated that 42 percent of income support recipients were in homes where fees exceeded benefit income (HC 1990). Many claimants had to rely on contributions from relatives, or charities, or use their personal expense allowance to meet this difference. Homes that found the standard national income support limits particularly inappropriate included those in regional high-cost areas, newly established businesses with high business loans, and voluntary homes with high-running costs that are reluctant to borrow or take business risk. The problem of deciding what levels of charges to meet was made more difficult because responsibility for maintaining standards in homes lies outside the domain of the Department of Social Security (DSS), in the various district health authorities and social services departments. National regulatory legislation laid down minimum stand-ards, but many registering authorities and proprietors strove to raise stand-ards of care. The resultant variable quality of provision raised issues of value for money for the public purse.

Further anxiety about value for money, as the demand-led budget has soared, arose from the lack of assessment of need for care (Audit Commis-sion 1985). Local studies of dependency levels of elderly people in care homes in the early 1980s (reviewed in Bradshaw & Gibbs 1988) suggested that a considerable number might not need to be there. The current income-support scheme, it was suggested, was thus wasteful in paying high levels of benefits to people who did not need institutional care. Pilot studies commissioned by the DSS (Bradshaw & Gibbs 1988) suggested that the proportion of elderly claimants in private residential care who could have managed in their own homes was not as high as some had thought, given the level of services and facilities available to those elderly people before admission. While an assessment of need for entry might have improved the current scheme for income-support policy-makers, income-support officers were not themselves equipped to make such decisions.

These specific problems in designing rules for financial support of people in the independent sector raised issues of government efficiency, and equity between elderly people. The effects of the scheme in operation until 1993 had an even wider impact, however, where they impinge on policies of local authority social services departments and district health authorities, and the overall pattern of provision.

The current diversity of financing arrangements for the different sectors of long-term care had created financial incentives and disincentives, which the local authorities and health authorities had been quick to recognize and act on. There was a rapid withdrawal of local authority sponsorship of elderly people in voluntary homes as it became clear that financial responsibility could be transferred from local to central government. The number of people aged over 65 years supported by local authorities in voluntary homes dropped from 12,886 in 1979 to 2,205 in 1989 (DH 1990b). With the loss of this sponsorship went one channel of public accountability for elderly people in the independent sector. Health authorities, too, were able to save money by discharging elderly patients to independent homes, effectively transferring financial responsibility to centrally-funded social security.

As well as shifting the balance between different sectors of institutional care, a more "perverse incentive" encouraged moves into institutional care from community settings. While an elderly person remained at home, the cost of supporting services (such as home helps and meals-on-wheels) are the responsibility of local authority social services departments, which had been under increasing financial pressure. Should that person move to independent care financed through income support, the local authority had no further financial or supervisory responsibility. Such perverse incentives toward institutionalization and greater dependency might also have effects within the private care industry, since higher levels of income support were available for more dependent people. We do not know how far this is influencing the recent more rapid expansion of the nursing home sector compared with residential provision, or development of specialist private homes registered for people with severe disabilities and high dependency levels.

Similar Issues in Other Countries

These issues, of course, are not confined to the British experience, but find parallels in other Western countries with a mixed economy of long-term care. Australia, the U.S., and Canada all have a mix of public sector, voluntary, and for-profit long-term provision for elderly people, and all have experiences with different mixes of central (federal) and local (state) financing. The Australian and Canadian schemes are similar to the current British scheme in that benefits are paid to residents to meet charges in a market system.

In Australia, where the federal government paid nursing-home benefits to individual elderly people, there has been a similar debate as that in Britain about how to set benefit levels, what constitutes "costs necessarily incurred," and what is "a reasonable return" for proprietors (Parker 1987).

Certification of need for entry to a nursing home was introduced as part of the qualification for financial support as early as 1972. An experiment in "deficit funding" was introduced in 1974 in which the federal government undertook to meet the annual deficit incurred by voluntary agencies running nursing homes. Homes could choose funding under the deficit scheme or continue with nursing home benefits paid to individual patients. This scheme was criticized for poor value for money. Costs in deficit-funded nursing homes were found to be higher than in those whose individual patients claimed benefits. The scheme was also difficult to administer centrally, involving annual scrutiny of homes' accounts. Moreover, patients in the deficit funded homes were found not to be primarily people of limited means. This funding model has produced an expensive subsidy to middle class patients (Parker 1987).

Canadian schemes include some federal cost-sharing in selective provincial health programs, but control of long-term care arrangements and financial support to residents is mainly a provincial responsibility, with considerable variation between the provinces (Forbes, Jackson & Kraus 1987). A "steering effect" toward placement in institutions providing more intensive care has been a notable feature in some provinces, as a result of financial incentives in different sectors of care. For example, in Ontario in the mid 1980s, a resident paid the whole cost of the residential care but a smaller amount for extended care in nursing homes because of availability of an extended care benefit from the Ontario Health Insurance Plan. Residents with no private income were supported by the provincial government in a similar way to the British scheme of support in local authority accommodation. The elderly contributed a proportion of their old-age social security pension, leaving a small amount for personal expenses. This arrangement contributed to a similar "two-tier" system as developed in the private sector in Britain, since payments made by a resident with provincial support only met the cost of standard ward accommodation in residential care and nursing homes, and not double or single rooms.

In the U.S. there was greater movement toward cost-related reimbursement systems of payments to homes, with federal government funds available to states for nursing home services for people of limited means under "Medicaid." Methods of reimbursement to homes, while variable, were based on the homes' costs, including property costs, and involved complex administrative and accounting procedures (Halahan & Cohen 1987). In the U.S., debate has focused on cost containment, effects of reimbursement schemes on the structure of the industry, maintaining quality of care, and efficient use of resources (Malhotra et al. 1981).

A NEW STRUCTURE FOR FINANCIAL SUPPORT

The British government, in fundamentally reorganizing financial support for long-term care after the enactment of the National Health Service and Community Care Act in 1990, has chosen a version of the traditional client-based support scheme, but has transferred most of the financial responsibility from central to local government (HMSO 1990). Payments of special rates of income support for new entrants to independent care homes ended in 1993, when local authorities took responsibility for assessing elderly people's care needs, and for meeting the cost of institutional care for those of limited means who need this type of care.

Such elderly people are eligible for the national means-tested income support at the same level as paid to people living at home and a residential allowance to cover accommodation charges (45 pounds outside London in 1993). These benefits will be paid directly to the local authority, which now meets the additional full costs of care (HC 1990).

By making local authorities responsible for assessment of need for both community and institutional care as well as paying for the care, the government hoped to eliminate some of the perverse incentives toward expensive institutionalization and establish a more rational basis of provision. Alignment of the local authority rules for changes for Part III homes with the rules for treatment of income and capital under the income-support scheme is also expected to contribute to rationalization (House of Commons, *Hansard*, 26 October 1990: col. 321). New local authority inspection units to regulate both private and public residential care will, it is hoped, help the purse-holders maintain high standards of care and assess the value for money of services paid for.

The new arrangements have already introduced a new set of financial incentives. Since elderly people in Part III homes do not receive the residential allowance, the private sector appeared to be cheaper to local authorities than care in Part III homes. Many councils quickly arranging to transfer Part III homes to housing trusts sell them to housing associations or private buyers (Fielding 1990). The loss of a public residential sector could become problematic, for example, if local cartels of private proprietors push up prices, or some residents are hard to place in independent homes (Glennester, Falkingham & Evandrou 1990).

ALTERNATIVES TO SOCIAL SECURITY FINANCE?

While the government's new arrangements go some way toward rationalizing the basis for financing long-term care through social security, another recent development in this policy arena in Britain has been a growth of interest in the idea that elderly people might increasingly be able to fund their own long-term care, with corresponding reduction in public finance necessary. There is increasing interest in the concept of long-term care insurance schemes (which have been available in the U.S. since the 1970s). An example of a prototype model is that developed by Wittenburg (1988), for sale to people reaching retirement age, paying benefits for fees in care homes, or for domiciliary care. Wittenburg argues that long-term care insurance could act to increase market choice and promote competition and cost-effectiveness among providers, as well as to reduce public expenditure. Davies (1989) has applied ideas of the American Health Management Organizations to the British situation, suggesting an alternative to insurance by introducing third-party financing. Local Social Care Maintenance Organizations would manage packages of care services for subscribers and provide insurance mechanisms for financing the purchase of the services. However, research by Walker (1988) throws doubt on the extent to which those elderly people likely to need long-term care will be able to make substantial financial contributions in such schemes. In the light of this, Baldwin (1990) sees possible disadvantages in removing financial responsibility for paying for long-term care from the social security system.

This whole area of self-financing long-term care has recently been reviewed by Oldman (1990), who questions, again, whether elderly people in Britain will be able to finance their own care through surplus income. An alternative to using income might be to release equity from owner-occupied housing. Some models have already been developed to transfer home equity into revenue release to fund the cost of care, either in community settings or in care homes. A prototype model based on actuarial principles has been described by Benjamin (1989). Benjamin envisages a structure operating like a unit trust, with policy-holders, carriers, and shareholders.

As Oldman notes, a particular feature of both Benjamin's and Davies' models is their capacity to accommodate public finance as well as private investment. Local or central government could contribute as "shareholders" or "subscribers" on behalf of beneficiaries who cannot subscribe from private resources. A second notable feature is that the schemes are based on the concept of long-term care over a range of settings; both institutional and community based. In this they fit well into the general policy goal in Britain at present: to reduce the previously rigidly defined boundaries between institutions and community settings, in terms of both provision of facilities and financial underpinning, toward a more unified concept of care for elderly people, although experience from the U.S. suggests that problems in establishing such schemes should not be under-estimated.

CONCLUSION

This chapter has addressed current arrangements for financing long-term care in Britain, looking at the patterns of provision and changes in arrangements that led to a major reorganization in the early 1990s. What is missing is the consumer viewpoint. Given the number of places in the various sectors of care, and an annual combined market value (already some 3,900 million pounds in the mid 1980s [Laing & Buisson 1988]), it is perhaps surprising that we know so little about the expectations and preferences of elderly people in this matter. In considering the policy options, we really need to know more about elderly people's views and attitudes, and how people's behavior might be affected by different arrangements. We need to know the extent to which elderly people in care are able to want to manage their own finances, in order to work out the best ways of transferring benefit income. We need to have attitudinal data about inheritance and inter-generational property transfer, from elderly people and their younger relatives, in order to assess the possibilities of funding long-term care through equity release. We need to know whether elderly people in homes expect to be financially independent citizens with entitlements to national pensions and benefits, or elderly recipients of locally determined care packages and pocket money. Factors such as these may be of key importance in the implementation of policies, and their acceptance and support among the general population. As such, they represent an area for valuable new research initiatives.

REFERENCES

Audit Commission. 1985. *Managing Social Services for the Elderly More Effectively* (London: Her Majesty's Stationery Office [HMSO]).
Audit Commission. 1986. *Making a Reality of Community Care* (London: HMSO).
Baldwin, S. 1990. "Cash and Care in the Mixed Economy of Care for Frail Elderly People: The United Kingdom Experience" in *The Social Protection of the Frail Elderly* (Studies and Research, 28) (Geneva: International Social Security Association).
Bartlett, H. 1987. "Social Security Policy and Private Sector Care for the Elderly" in Brenton, M. & Ungerson, C. (eds.) *Yearbook of Social Policy 1986–87* (Harlow: Longman).

Benjamin, S. 1989. "Private Funding of Long Term Care: An Actuarial Perspective." Paper presented to conference on Care of Elderly People organized by Laing and Buisson/Health Care Information Service, sponsored by Peat Marwick and McLintock, London.

Bond, J., Bond, S., Donaldson, C., Gregson, B. & Atkinson, A. 1989. *Evaluation of Continuing Care Accommodation for Elderly People*, (Report No. 38) (Newcastle: University of Newcastle upon Tyne, Health Care Research Unit).

Bosanquet, N., Laing, W. & Propper, C. 1990. *Elderly Consumers in Britain: Europe's Poor Relations?* (London: Laing and Buisson Publications).

Bradshaw, J. 1988. "Financing Private Care for the Elderly" in Baldwin, S., Parker, G. & Walker, R. (eds.) *Social Security and Community Care* (Aldershot: Avebury).

Bradshaw, J. & Gibbs, I. 1988. *Public Support for Private Residential Care* (Aldershot: Avebury).

Central Statistical Office (CSO). 1993. *Annual Abstract of Statistics* (London: HMSO).

Corden, A. 1990. "Choice and Self Determination as Aspects of Quality of Life in Private Sector Homes" in Baldwin, S., Godfrey, C. & Propper, C. (eds.) *Quality of Life: Perspectives and Politics* (London: Routledge).

Corden, A. 1991. "Geographical Development of the Long Term Care Market for Elderly People" *Transactions: Institute of British Geographers* (New Series) 17: 80–94.

Corden, A. 1992. "Arrangements for Paying for Care in Independent Homes for Elderly People" *British Journal of Social Work* 22(6): 695–706.

Darton, R. A., Sutcliffe, E. M. & Wright, K. G. 1990. *Survey of Residential and Nursing Homes* (PSSRU Discussion Paper 6 54/2) (Canterbury: University of Kent at Canterbury, Personal Social Services Research Unit and University of York, Centre for Health Economics).

Davies, B. 1989. *Long Term Social Care: Challenges for the Nineties* (PSSRU Discussion Paper 5 67) (Canterbury: University of Kent at Canterbury, Personal Social Services Research Unit).

Department of Health (DH). 1990a. *National Assistance (Charges for Accommodation) Amendment Regulations* (SI, 498) (London: HMSO).

Department of Health (DH) 1990b. *Personal Social Services Local Authority Statistics* (RA/89/1) (London: Department of Health).

Department of Health and Social Services (DHSS) 1985. *Supplementary Benefit and Residential Care. Report of a Joint Central and Local Government Working Party* (Chair: Scott Whyte) (London: DHSS).

Department of Health and Social Services (DHSS) 1987. *Public Support for Residential Care. Report of a Joint Central and Local Government Working Party* (Chair: Fifth) (London: DHSS).

Ernst & Whinney. 1986. *Survey of Private and Voluntary Residential and Nursing Homes for the Department of Health and Social Security* (London: Ernst and Whinney).

Family Policy Studies Centre. 1988. *An Ageing Population Fact Sheet 2* (London: Family Policy Studies Centre).

Fielding, N. 1990. "Grey Power" *New Statesman and Society* (23 March): 26.

Forbes, W. F., Jackson, J. A. & Kraus, A. S. 1987. *Institutionalization of the Elderly in Canada* (Butterworths: Toronto and Vancouver).

Gibbs, I. & Corden, C. 1991. "The Concept of Reasonableness in Relation to Residential Care and Nursing Homes" *Policy and Politics* 19(2): 119–29.

Glennester, H., Falkingham, J. & Evandrou, M. 1990. *How Much do we Care? A Comment on the Government's Community Care Proposals* (Discussion Paper WSP/46) (London: London School of Economics).

Halahan, J. & Cohen, J. 1987. "Nursing Home Reimbursement: Implications for Cost Containment, Access and Quality" *The Milbank Quarterly* 65(1): 27–42.

Henwood, M. 1990. *Community Care and Elderly People. Policy, Practice and Research Review* (London: Family Policy Studies Centre).

Her Majesty's Stationery Office (HMSO). 1988a. *Community Care: Agenda for Action* (Griffiths Report) (London: HMSO).

Her Majesty's Stationery Office (HMSO). 1988b. *Social Trends 18* (London: HMSO).

Her Majesty's Stationery Office (HMSO). 1989. *Caring for People. Cmnd 849* (London: HMSO).

Her Majesty's Stationery Office (HMSO). 1990. *National Health Service and Community Care Act* (London: HMSO).

House of Commons (HC). 1990. *Social Services Committee Second Report. Community Care: Future Funding of Private and Voluntary Residential Care.* (House of Commons, 257) (London: HMSO).

Laing, W. 1985. *Private Health Care* (London: Office of Health Economics).

Laing & Buisson. 1988. *Laing's Review of Private Health Care 1988/89 Volume 2. Long Term Health and Social Care* (London: Laing & Buisson Publications).

Land, H. 1988. "Social Security and Community Care: Creating Perverse Incentives" in Baldwin, S., Parker, G. & Walker, R. (eds.) *Social Security and Community Care* (Aldershot: Avebury).

Malhotra, S., Wills, J. M. & Morrisey, M. A. 1981. *Profits, Growth and Reimbursement Systems in the Nursing Home Industry* (Washington, D.C.: Department of Health and Human Services).

Means, R. & Smith, R. 1985. *The Development of Welfare Services for Elderly People* (London: Croom Helm).

National Association of Citizens Advice Bureaux (NACAB). 1991. *Beyond the Limit. Income Support for Elderly People in Residential Care and Nursing Homes* (London: National Association of Citizens Advice Bureaux).

Office of Population Censuses and Surveys (OPCS). 1984. *Britain's Elderly Population, Census Guide 1* (London: HMSO).

Office of Population Censuses and Surveys (OPCS). 1989. *1989 Population Projections 1987–2027* (London: HMSO).

Oldman, C. 1990. *Paying for Care* (Report to the Joseph Rowntree Foundation) (York: University of York, Department of Social Policy and Social Work).

Parker, R. A. 1987. *The Elderly and Residential Care: Australian Lessons for Britain* (Aldershot: Gower).

Price Waterhouse. 1990. *A Survey of Residential Care Homes* (Report to the Department of Social Security) (London: Price Waterhouse).

Townsend, P. 1962. *The Last Refuge* (London: Routledge).

Walker, R. 1988. "The Financial Resources of the Elderly, or Paying Your Way in Old Age" in Baldwin, S., Parker, G. & Walker, R. (eds.) *Social Security and Community Care* (Aldershot: Avebury).

Wittenburg, R. 1988. *Prototype Long Term Care Insurance Policy* (London: Department of Health, Health Economists' Study Group).

Wright, K. 1985. *Contractual Arrangements for Geriatric Care in Private Nursing Homes* (Discussion Paper, 4) (York: University of York: Centre for Health Economics).

12

The Right to Medical Health Care for the Disabled in Sweden

Lotta Westerhall

The purpose of this chapter is to illustrate in the Swedish setting one aspect of the legal rights of disabled people: the right to obtain quality health care. The Swedish health care system is known for its high quality and level of technical and social development. Its characteristic features are: universal coverage; strong state intervention, even though administration is largely the responsibility of non-government organs; a well-organized hospital system providing inpatient care for both acute and long-care patients; a profession of physicians that is well educated and highly specialized; the highest number of hospital beds per capita in the world; a public medical health care insurance system that achieves universal coverage but at extremely high costs.

How well do the physically and mentally disabled manage to obtain quality medical health services in Sweden? Is the provision of health services based on the legal principles of equality and justice, so that disabled people, who generally have more difficulties in exercising their rights than others, have equal access to the health care services?

Before trying to answer these questions the concept "disabled person" needs explanation. A disabled person, as defined by Swedish pensions legislation, is one who has his or her work capacity reduced by at least 50 percent for a period of two or more years. There are of course many other ways of determining disability, but this definition is suitable for the purpose of investigating the Welfare State's attitude toward individuals with a long-term illness and disability that results in a more or less permanent incapacity to work.

The following questions are pertinent to the issue of legal rights of the disabled:

- If everyone has a right to become a patient, is there a difference in access to the health care system between the disabled and the non-disabled?
- What happens once an individual has received the status of a patient?
- Does she or he have any legal rights as a patient?
- If the individual has legal rights, are there any differences between the rights of the disabled and the non-disabled?

BACKGROUND

Almost all health care in Sweden is publicly provided and is part of a compulsory health care insurance system with heavily subsidized fees. Traditionally, fees for public medical and hospital care have been very low. In 1969, a uniform fee was introduced for the entire outpatient health care system. Later, a uniform fee included the majority of private practitioners as well, which allowed universal access to medical care. Health and medical care services in Sweden are therefore responsibilities of the public sector. Health and medical care services are provided mainly by 26 regional authorities, comprising 23 county councils and three municipalities outside the county council system.

The Swedish Constitution protects certain legal rights of the individual. The most relevant legislation pertaining to medical services is the Swedish Social Law, which includes health and medical care legislation, which is also part of the Special Administrative Law. The field of health care services contains few legal rules as far as the rights of the patient are concerned.

The Health and Medical Services Act ("Halso-och sjukvardslagen" [HSL]) defines the terms "health" and "medical care" and the targets for all health and medical care including private care. The Supervision of Health and Medical Personnel Act ("Tillsynslagen") contains general provisions concerning the duties of health and medical personnel, the authorization of medical practitioners, and the special disciplinary measures affecting health and medical personnel. In addition, there are a number of statutory provisions and regulations regarding the qualifications and education of various personnel. Finally, the HSL requires county councils to set up advisory boards to promote contact between patients and health and medical personnel and to provide patients with assistance.

An institution of importance in Sweden is the Liability Board of Health and Medical Care (HSAN-Board). The HSAN-Board is an independent authority under the National Board of Health and Welfare, which handles patient complaints in cases of malpractice (HSL 19). In addition, the patient has the right to appeal to the Administrative Courts of Appeal and the Administrative Supreme Court. The Board takes cases of disciplinary responsibilities among the health care personnel. However, the possibility of registering a complaint with the HSAN-Board is restricted, since the individual cannot receive a second treatment or obtain a second opinion. The complaint reviewed is for a specific treatment and does not enforce the right to secure other treatment. The HSAN-Board is not a way to enforce the legal right of the individual to medical health care.

THE PROBABILITIES OF DISABLED PERSONS RECEIVING PATIENT STATUS

In the HSL a general goal of health care is articulated: "good health and care on the same conditions for the whole population" (HSL 2). This goal is an overall aim, not demanding that it be fulfilled in every instance. The signification of the concept of "health" is not self-evident, and a universal definition of this term does not exist. In the classic definition taken from the World Health Organization's regulations, health is "a state of complete physical, mental and social well-being and not merely lack of illness or weakness."

The legislative explanatory statement on the HSL states that "good health" is one of the qualities of life and points out that such indicators as meaningful free time, absence of stress in the work place, and overall physical and mental well-being ought to receive more attention than they normally do. A second goal for the health care system expressed in the HSL is care on the same condition for everyone (HSL 2). This involves, according to the legislative explanatory statement, the possibilities of everyone—irrespective of place of residence—being able to access the services offered by the health care system when needed and under uniform conditions. The possibility of receiving care should not be dependent on such circumstances as age, sex, ability to take initiative, education, financial means, nationality, or cultural differences. Waiting lists for health care, if they exist, should be influenced by the above circumstances. Even for less acute or serious illness, treatment must be available, within limits of available resources and scientific knowledge, to offer care for everyone in need of care. Therefore, according to the legislative explanatory statement, it is very important that society take care of high risk groups, such as the elderly and disabled. If the state obligations described are legal rights, then the individual should be able to argue in court that she or he had been bypassed on a waiting list for treatment and has had to step aside for a younger and healthier person, therefore not receiving treatment. On the other hand, if it is not a question of legal rights, the above-described circumstances for health care are not more than general outlines that sometimes may be ignored.

The right to equal treatment signifies the ethical stand that all people, disabled and non-disabled, should be treated equally. This belief is very strong in Sweden, which has tried to turn this philosophy into reality. However, for this to be a true "right," the individual should be able to go to court and argue that, for instance, she or he, as a disabled person with rheumatism, has had to wait in the medical health care line, while the famous football player received treatment, that she or he had not received as costly treatment as the neighbor, that she or he had a much longer distance to travel for treatment, and so forth. If this is not possible, then the principle of equality is not enforceable by an individual through the law. The conclusion in such circumstances would have to be that no legal right to equality exists. This is also what the legislature admits in the legislative explanatory statement, which concludes that the question of equality is a goal-oriented, service-related issue, not a legal right that the patient can claim.

Even if the legislative explanatory statement says that the disabled person shall be cared for with special attention, there is no doubt that the construction of the legislative regulation can influence a disabled person's ability to gain patient status. Since there are only scanty resources, different values will formalize a structure for accessing health care. In principle, these values advocate that everybody who needs health care should receive patient status. But, in some situations, access priorities bring legal questions to light. The legal duty to supply "good health care" is not a duty to offer all the health care needed to fulfill this duty. If there are several ways of providing health care in a special situation of treatment, it is legally sufficient that the provider is placing one of them at the patient's disposal.

The above situation shows there is legal and ethical flexibility in terms of the distribution of medical health care resources. Life-threatening and other serious illnesses are usually given priority over other illnesses. It is not, however, self-evident that the individual who has the greatest probability of recovery will be treated before the individual with less probability of recovery. Chronic invalids, old persons, and persons needing care who have relatively low probability of recovery should all have a chance to gain health care. The level of access is, however, in favor of those patients with the greatest probability of recovery. Questions like which wards are going to be built away from the hospital, possibly closed in times of vacations, will determine the probability of an individual becoming a patient. Other questions raised are: are health care resources concentrated on providing many small operations, or on few large operations, such as heart transplants? Does medical research and teaching influence the decisions on who should have the right to be a patient, such as when a researcher needs a certain number of specific category patients, or when a professor needs a patient with a certain disease in order to give students the best possible education? Are a person's social status, age, tax-paying capacity, and nationality criteria for determining who has priority access to health care? Is it therefore possible, using the example from above, that a disabled person (for instance, a rheumatic person with years of handicapping injuries) has to step aside for a famous football player, who has been injured during a game and another important game is waiting?

The only answer to all these questions is that there is no legal protection built into the Swedish health care system that prohibits these practices. Therefore, in reality they happen. As the goal-oriented HSL is currently operated and given the still adequate availability of resources in the health care system, the author has not found any cases in administrative law at the HSAN-Board that show these kind of inequalities. This does not mean, of course, that inequality of access to health care services does not happen now and then without legal implications.

THE DISABLED PERSON'S RIGHTS AS PATIENT

When a person has received patient status, she or he has some legitimate claim on the care and the treatment. According to HSL, health care must be implemented so that it meets the standards of "good care," irrespective of whether it is private or public care (HSL 2). The standards of "good care" are four-fold: meeting the patient's need for a sense of security about the care and treatment provided; providing easy assessibility; respecting the autonomy and the personal integrity of the patient; and promoting adequate and professional contact between the patient and the medical personnel.

Quality of the Health Care

Even if HSL itself does not define treatment in accordance with scientific knowledge and professional experience, the physician has a duty to have a high level of competency and skill (HSL 2). Skill is a special competence that is the result of aptitude developed by special training and with experience. Failure to display this skill and care, so causing the wrong treatment to be given or proper treatment to have failed, constitutes negligence. The implementation of treatment can be *contra legem artis* if it is done without the proper and reasonable standard of skill, care, and competence of the medical profession. The omission of some treatment may be *contra legem artis*. The treatment ought to be provided according to the proper and reasonable standards of the profession. One can distinguish between active medical treatment on one hand, and the omission of such treatment on the other. Both practices can be *contra legem artis*. What about disabled people and this matter? Is the quality of the care they receive as good as that received by other people?

A review of all disciplinary cases reported during the 1980s does not show explicitly that the quality of the care received by the disabled is as good as that received by other people. However, in the public debates that opinion is voiced. Individuals with cataracts may have to wait up to two years before they can obtain an operation, due to scanty resources. Treatment provided in the meantime must, of course, be in accordance with scientific knowledge and professional experience. Here the disabled person may be in the situation that other people, who have more acute problems and perhaps from the physician's point of view are more "interesting" as patients, will have preference before a physically or mentally disabled person.

Accessibility of the Health Care

Medical care must be easily accessible. According to the statements in the government bill (Propositioner 1981/82: 97), geographical conditions should be considered in the distribution of health care facility. All people may not have the same geographic accessibility to a health care institution. However, through a decentralization of the health system it is possible to place health care institutions within reasonable proximity to most people. Studies have found a link between the geographical distance from a medical institution and the frequency of the use of health care service. Geographical proximity of health services thus increases the demand for health care. According to the government bill, however, geographical proximity is not the only issue of accessibility. Others include the opening hours of the clinics, the number of acute-care facilities versus long-term care facilities, and the occurrence of waiting lists for certain types of patient care. Since an expansion of health care facilities naturally demands increased resources, it is important to balance the need for easily accessible care with the available economic and personnel-related resources. For geographical reasons, people in the north of Sweden do not have the same access to medical health care as people in the middle and southern regions. But because more money has been spent on acute-care than on the long-term care facilities in the northern regions of Sweden , the disabled have been treated more unequally than other medical patients when it comes to geographical accessibility.

Respect for the Autonomy and the Personal Integrity of the Patient

Another form of professional responsibility is that of respecting the autonomy and the integrity of the patient. When a disabled person comes in contact with a health service institution, she or he confronts a system with rules and routines, which can result in the patient feeling that she or he is being treated merely as an object, not as a human being. The patient should thus be kindly received; should be well informed about her or his state of health and the purpose of the treatment; should be given the right to see her or his case sheet; and should be protected from receiving treatment without her or his consent. All of the rights ensure the autonomy and personal integrity of the patient.

Many cases at the HSAN-Board relate to the question of whether rights have been infringed upon by medical personnel. Studies show that among those cases involving a lack of information, conclusion cannot be drawn that the disabled people are considered differently from other people. A special category is the mentally retarded. It is very important that the mentally retarded have all the information they need and that no treatment is given to them without their consent. There are special regulations guaranteeing this. There is, however, legislation under which compulsory treatment can be ordered against the individual's will or without having any informed consent. This regulation is very strict and legally shows a high respect for the legal rights of the individual.

When it comes to questions of information and informed consent, it is difficult to decide what will be the legal content of the concepts, when the physicians are exercising their professional judgment, and when patients are making judgments from their, unprofessional, point of view. This could be a very important legal question, especially for varied groups of disabled individuals, although it is of common interest to all patients. The judicial material concerning informed consent is limited and not very well developed, when it comes to the right to compensation for damages (tort law liability and patient insurance liability) and disciplinary responsibility. A recent verdict in the Supreme Court ruled that Swedish tort law does not acknowledge the doctrine of informed consent. Therefore, in the patient insurance system, the number of cases put to the HSAN-Board on this issue is very small.

Adequate and Professional Contact

When it comes to cases concerning the medical personnel's reception of the patient, there is no evidence that the disabled receive poor reception or poor professional contact. In most of these cases involving the disabled, there is not sufficient proof of poor reception or poor professional contact, and the physician (nurse) did not receive a disciplinary sanction.

CONCLUSION

The Swedish health services have expanded rapidly in terms of medical technology, staff, and cost. Public authorities invested a large amount of money and resources in the 1970s for both inpatient and outpatient care. Services specifically for the elderly, disabled, and mentally ill have increased correspondingly. The disabled are, however, a high risk group when it comes to the question of their legal right to become a patient. It is possible that they may be placed in situations where they have to wait longer for medical care than people who are acutely ill. For example, in the case of rheumatic care, long-term care and psychiatric or mental care, due to scanty resources, there is a waiting list in Sweden for access to health care. Even if the legislative explanatory statement states that a special consideration will be given to the disabled, the reality can be the opposite. Other parts of the health care system obtain the resources, and other categories of patients receive greater medical attention. When it comes to the question of having received patient status, it is more difficult to conclude that there are any differences between the terminally ill, disabled person, and the acutely ill person. It has been difficult to derive any conclusions from the relevant legal sources. Even if they do not show any treatment and care differences between disabled persons and other ill persons, the judicial material points out several situations where the question concerning patients' rights in general has arisen. It is important to have guidelines on these rights from the disabled person's point of view, because the statistics generally show that disabled individuals have more difficulties than others in enforcing their rights. Legally, the disabled (like other sick people) do not have any legal rights, for in most situations, they cannot go to court and have their case examined. In principle, there is an enforceable right in the tort law system, but in practice it cannot be used. Instead, one has to go to the patient insurance system to obtain compensation, but these claims are not enforceable in court. Disciplinary sanctions are handled by an administrative board with the possibility of appealing to the Administrative Superior Court and the Administrative Supreme Court. But one cannot claim their "rights" as a patient, only generally improve the minimum demands of the society to offer good care. Patient rights, in the strict legal meaning, are not very well developed in Sweden. In practice, the health care system has managed satisfactorily up until now, but there is no guarantee as a patient that this situation will continue. The legal rights of patients should be clearly articulated.

13

Industrial Accidents: Why Should They Have Special Preferential Conditions?

Celso Barroso Leite

Industrial accidents should be covered by social security without unnecessary, inconvenient, and anachronistic special treatment. This is a polemical chapter that addresses the treatment of industrial accidents in social security. It has been influenced by Brazilian reality, but it recognizes that the issues canvassed have a broader currency.

ORIGIN AND EVOLUTION OF INDUSTRIAL ACCIDENTS AS A BRANCH OF SOCIAL SECURITY

The indemnity to the victims of industrial accidents under tort liability started long before the existence of modern social security (Higuchi 1970: 110; Dixon 1986: 11–15). The workers had to go to court to claim the indemnity of the damage suffered. However, the situation of these claimants was quite precarious, especially due to the slowness and complexity of the judicial machinery. In this connection the indemnity for an industrial accident may be compared with a legal lottery. Even those who succeeded in overcoming such barriers sometimes had unpleasant surprises, since some employers ordered to indemnity the victims did not have the means to pay for it. In other words, the victims may have won in court but did not receive the indemnity. In other cases, the indemnity was so small that it probably did not cover the lawyer's fees and other judicial expenses.

In any event, before the existence of social security the payment of an indemnity to the victims made sense. Today, however, the indemnity under tort liability has largely been replaced, in Brazil and most other countries, by social security benefits, which makes the separate social security treatment of industrial accidents anachronistic, unnecessary, and harmful.

INTEGRATION INTO SOCIAL SECURITY

The integration of industrial accidents into social security constitutes a long-standing aspiration. While 91 countries now provide employment injury benefits as a branch of their social insurance system, a further 39 countries have adopted the occupational risk principle that requires employers, individually, to finance and provide industrial accident benefits, mostly without compulsory public or private insurance, irrespective of the ultimate cause of the employment injury (Dixon 1986: 32 & 12–13; ILO 1936: 26–28). In Brazil the coverage of industrial accidents is already incorporated as a branch of its social security system, which means that while it is no longer exploited by private insurance companies, it is still subject to special conditions as regards benefits, medical care, and other services, as well as financing.

What is recommended here is the integration of industrial accident benefits with other social security benefits by simply making industrial accidents one of the various causes of disability or death. As much as possible, the special, more favorable conditions applying industrial accidents should be generalized. This is an old campaign in which a few battles, but not the war, have been won.

The modern trend in social security is toward the coordination if not integration of coverage. In fact, discreet but clear statements favoring greater coordination have become more and more frequent, even in reports and other publications of specialized international agencies. It would seem that the concept of coordination does not cause the same reaction of protest or surprise as it did in the past. Sometimes it would even seem to be accepted. This is certainly a promising development.

WHY DO INDUSTRIAL ACCIDENTS STILL RECEIVE SPECIAL TREATMENT?

Interest of Private Insurance

The isolated claims of indemnity for industrial accidents have been replaced, in most countries, by either social insurance or compulsory insurance for the coverage of this risk. This is certainly a step ahead, since it has solved the problem of the economic inability of the employers to pay the indemnities, but only in part, since in some 12 countries there still are judicial actions needed before the employment injury benefit can be paid, this time between the victims and the private insurance carriers, which means that the lottery of justice still exists.

In countries like Brazil, for instance, which had a mixed public-private approach to industrial accidents benefits for many years, the private insurance industry, naturally, fought with all its might to keep the bonanza of a compulsory form of insurance. Even where employment injury has already been transferred completely to social security, the private insurance carriers try mightily to bring it back to their domain. This is certainly the case in Brazil. There are good reasons to believe that the integration of industrial accidents completely into social security will help eliminate such attempts.

Other Reasons

Industrial accident benefits are considered by many as a sacrosanct right of the workers, forgetting that such a right, long surpassed by social security, is today a kind of a sad privilege, to the detriment of the workers and their dependents who may be entitled only to the regular benefits. The author disagrees with this and similar positions, but respects those who hold them; and advocates the full integration of both programs.

In the case of the trade unions, the workers may accept the theory of this sacred right, forgetting that it applies only to a small minority, in contrast with the enormous majority, but even some workers have already voiced their discontent as regards such unequal criteria. However, it is more difficult to understand the apparent indifference of the employers and their institutions to this question, which could be easily solved and thus remove an unnecessary complexity from, for them, an already complex social security system.

The members of the legal profession who operate legitimately in the area of industrial accidents have strong professional reasons to oppose the integration of employment injury into social security. It would be unrealistic to expect from them a disinterested attitude.

There still remains, on the short list of the more powerful opponents, the mafia that operates in the underworld of the so-called industry of industrial accidents. This mafia includes—besides the amorphous mass of the recruiters of victims—dishonest middlemen, people presumed honest, such as other lawyers, and even magistrates. Obviously, the connivance of social security officials should not be overlooked.

In connection with this more somber aspect of the question, it is important not to forget that the industry of industrial accidents surrounds both benefits and financing. In the latter cases, the frauds consist chiefly of manipulating risk tariffs.

These special interests form a heterogeneous whole in some countries, which has become so powerful that it has not yet been possible to overcome resistance to the integration of industrial accidents into social security systems.

IDEOLOGICAL EVOLUTION

Civil Responsibility

Industrial accident indemnity involving judicial claims by the victims against their employers created a situation in which employers, when ordered to pay the indemnities, did not have the means, or otherwise succeeded in finding a way to avoid payment (thus robbing the victims), and led to the emergence of compulsory insurance with private (sometime public) carriers. This marriage created a paradox: the existence of a legal obligation in the private sector where free initiative should prevail. Directly or indirectly, this involved civil accountability.

The assignment of subjective responsibility, the apportioning of actual fault, and the inversion of the obligation to offer evidence are all theories that have been replacing each other in the course of the doctrinal evolution of industrial accident liability. Then came the doctrine that has lasted longest, the theory of occupational risk, which still underlines workman's compensation legislation, including that in Brazil. It can be summed up more or less thus: since the accident results from the performance of a occupational activity in the interest of the employer, the coverage of the resulting risk is the responsibility of the employer. Although this liability-without-fault legal principle is still in force, it does not make sense when we consider that the consequences of an industrial accident—a disability of some degree or duration, or death—which, when not related to an employment injury, constitute a contingency covered by social security.

Social Responsibility

The idea of social risks or contingencies covered by social security surpasses the legal principle of occupational risk and leads naturally to the theory of social responsibility for such risks, which is broader and more in keeping with the role of social security in the contemporary socioeconomic order. It is the responsibility of the state to guarantee protection to its citizens in the face of social risks. Legislation such as exists in Brazil has already inserted the coverage of industrial accidents within social security, although still with special conditions. The inclusion may have been inspired by the theory of occupational risk, but in realty it was recognizing a social responsibility. This new evolutionary step has a solid doctrinal foundation in the notion that it is no longer the indemnity of the damage that is at stake, as in the judicial claims of the past, but the concept is to alleviate the consequences of a social risk or contingency: the loss of income and therefore of the means of subsistence for the victims and their dependents.

Compensation and Prevention

As regards social contingencies in general and occupational risk in particular, the most advanced doctrine, already reflected in the legislation of several countries—again Brazil is among them—attributes to social security direct responsibility for the compensation of the consequences of damaging events and connects prevention more directly with working conditions, since in reality industrial accidents are related to working conditions, specifically hygiene and safety measures. Accident prevention is essential, and the compensation of their consequences is not less important, but they are two separate components. Compensation is a social responsibility, covered by social security, whereas prevention is a private responsibility, forced on the employers by the labor legislation.

ADMINISTRATIVE RESPONSIBILITY

We have a social responsibility for employment accident compensation and a private responsibility involving employers' obligation to observe the norms of labor hygiene and safety. It is important to underscore the significance of these dual but distinctive administrative responsibilities, since some specialists fear that, when coverage of industrial accidents is really integrated into social security, for which there is an undifferentiated employer contribution, the employers will have no motivation to adopt prevention measures. The issues cannot be analyzed in such simplistic terms, since the employers' incentive to avoid accidents is not to do only with the prospect of reduced social security contributions, for there are indirect costs of industrial accidents to be considered, which can be much more significant. In any event, the prevention of accidents does not depend on the employers' will or interest; it is a legal obligation that creates for them a legal responsibility.

Residual Civil Responsibility

The evolution of industrial accident coverage has moved responsibility from the employer, who was required to indemnify the victims of industrial accidents, to the state, which has now accepted social responsibility for the compensation of industrial accident victims. However, the employer's responsibility has not altogether disappeared. If the victims of accidents or their dependents prove in court that the accident resulted from the employer's negligence, such as the open non-observance of a safety norm, the former may, in some jurisdictions, sue the latter for indemnity, irrespective of their social security rights. In Brazil the Constitution expressly guarantees this residual civil responsibility.

In practice, the employer's negligence or fault is usually too difficult to prove, which makes the guarantee of the residual civil responsibility quite relative. Therefore, what is essential in such cases is to impose on the employers heavy economic penalties when they fail to observe safety norms, even if no accidents occur.

It has also been suggested that private carriers, instead of fighting, hopefully in vain, for the return to the compulsory and separate industrial accidents insurance, could offer the employers voluntary plans for additional coverage, similar to those of the pension funds. The voluntary character of these plans would be more compatible with private initiative.

THEORETICAL INCONSISTENCY

The special treatment of industrial accidents clashes with some principles and tenets of social security. Three of these conflicts are: the coverage of consequences, not causes; the character of social responsibility; and the character of the accident.

Coverage of Consequences, Not Causes

Social security coverage focuses on the consequences of the social risks or contingencies, not their causes. For instance, old age is a chronological situation, and disability is a physical, psychic, or psychosomatic condition, but the former implies, and the latter leads to, incapacity for work. In spite of their completely different causes, these facts have an equivalent effect, and it is the effect of either of the two risks that social security addresses by the means of a pension. Similarly, social security addresses the consequences of other risks. This relationship between causes and consequences becomes clearer when what is involved is, instead of equivalent consequences, the same consequence (disability or death) of the same cause (accident), only in different circumstances (at work or out of work). Social security must take care of consequences, to compensate for them. The causes are of interest, but largely in connection with prevention.

General Character of Social Responsibility

Social security relates to the state's responsibility for the protection of people in situations in which such protection becomes necessary. The state's social responsibilities should be as wide, as encompassing, and as uniform as possible, in view of the general, not specific, character of its responsibility. What is necessary, then, are common denominators that provide global and homogeneous solutions, instead of anachronistic distinctions that complicate and sometimes deteriorate the performance of the public agencies to the detriment of the quality of their services. The special treatment of industrial accidents is contrary to the general character of the social responsibility of the state.

Character of the Accident

Some opponents of the idea of coordinating or integrating industrial accidents with social security sometimes invoke the dramatic character of the accidents as a justification for its special treatment. That there may be some extremely painful aspects of many industrial accidents is undeniable, but we should not forget that this is also true of the non-industrial accidents. Thus, to the extent to which such aspects might justify special treatment, it should not be restricted to industrial accidents. In this connection, and having in mind the uniform treatment that social responsibility requires, it would be advisable, for instance, to eliminate the waiting period for entitlement to the benefits following an accident, industrial or otherwise.

PRACTICAL DISADVANTAGES

The special treatment of industrial accidents is an anachronistic situation.

Unjustifiable Complications

The special treatment of industrial accidents creates additional administrative difficulties and affects negatively the performance of the regular tasks, to the detriment of everybody, in this case, the victims, their dependents, and their employers. The uniformity of treatment is not just an imperative of social justice, it is also a factor of administrative effectiveness and efficiency. In Brazil's social security system, this is urgently imperative.

Accident *in itinere* and Occupational Diseases

The difficulties created by separation of industrial from other accidents begin with the very concept of industrial accidents, which also embraces both the so-called accident *in itinere* (on the way to or from the workplace) and occupational diseases.

To consider an accident *in itinere* as an industrial accident is an impropriety, as has been generally accepted.

Occupational diseases involve a complication that lies in the difficulty of precisely assessing to what extent the disease really results from the work situation or from other factors, such as individual characteristics or socio-economic conditions. Something similar occurs when a special pension is provided to workers in hazardous occupations, of which there is in Brazil a list. The obvious solution is to eliminate the negative factors that make the work activity hazardous and the same applies to occupational diseases.

Individual Employer Insurance Premiums

It may be well to remember the time, quite recently, when the employers in many countries, including Brazil, paid the industrial accident insurance premium according to their own risk conditions. Such individual employer insurance premiums lent themselves to a variety of administrative and financial manipulations and irregularities, highly profitable to the employer as well as to those involved with them. Brazil has already succeeded in alleviating this problem, but many countries still face it.

The Litigation Industry

Here is another long story, if not a tragedy. The litigation industry that feeds on industrial accidents has not been carefully studied anywhere, certainly not in Brazil. It must be considered very likely that the legal profession's litigation record would not have reached its well-known dimension without workman's compensation and the special treatment of industrial accidents. The author's conviction on this situation results especially from the fact that, although the other social security benefits are much more numerous, only recently in Brazil, where inflation has led to legal claims of benefit rate revision, can the number of litigations related to social security compare with those related to industrial accidents, a situation some considered to be only transient.

A Tragic Privilege

The special treatment of industrial accidents has created a tragic privilege, a kind of a prize to whoever is injured at work, in contrast to whoever suffers a comparable or more serious injury outside work. That is certainly why in Brazil well-documented records contain dramatic cases of workers who have injured or even mutilated themselves to receive an indemnity. With the replacement of the indemnities by periodical benefits, it is very unlikely that a person would go to such extremes.

THE JUSTIFIABLE IDEOLOGY AND INTERNATIONAL EXPERIENCE

The list of world specialists in social security and related programs that advocate the coordination of industrial accidents and social security programs advocated here is rather lengthy and includes Sir William Beveridge, Sir Owen Woodhouse, a justice of New Zealand's Supreme Court, and authors such as Brazil's A. F. Cesarino, Jr., Argentina's J. J. Etala, and Spain's J. M. Almansa Pastor. Naturally, the views of these top specialists have been heard in technical meetings, and thus the ideology advocated in this chapter has become ever more popular. Even the international meetings refer to this trend toward the integration of the two programs in their official documents. In this connection, it seems sufficient to mention the report of the International Social Security Association's Secretary General, on the occasion of its general assembly held in Madrid in 1977. The concept of the integration of these two programs is clearly an old preoccupation, which eliminates the perception of an idea of recent origin, or of a theory not yet reviewed and discussed by social policy specialists. On the contrary, the concept of integration is a rational position, whose solid premises have been repeated and repeated. We can also see that these ideas are not restricted to this or that country, but are discussed and exert an influence on various geographic areas.

Some concrete examples of countries that have changed their policies may be helpful. Holland and New Zealand no longer distinguish, for social protection purposes, industrial accidents from any other cause of disability or death (Uttley 1993). Guatemala only distinguishes for statistical purposes; industrial accidents are recorded for the purpose of prevention, but the benefits and services are the same as those of social security proper. Several countries, including Sweden, Norway, Denmark, Japan, and Spain, have already equalized the so-called short-term benefits, such as health allowance.

CONCLUSION: THE IMPERATIVE OF FULL INTEGRATION

It is an urgent imperative that there be a complete integration of industrial accidents into social security. The following steps need to be taken.

Abandonment of the Idea of a Separate Insurance. As an important preliminary, we should do away completely with the idea of industrial accident insurance. Brazil's present Constitution uses this old-fashioned terminology awkwardly, and such anachronistic language may delay the desired solution. It would have been better to forget entirely about industrial accidents, which would place these events as simply one of many causes of disability or death.

Special Coverage of Any Accident. If the frequently dramatic character of accidents really distinguishes them often from similar social security contingencies, which might otherwise justify a special social security benefit; whether the accident is industrial or not is irrelevant. Therefore, the special treatment of such accidents under social security may make sense, provided that the present preference, for the industrial accidents, not to mention the accidents *in itinere* and industrial diseases, is eliminated.

Equal Treatment of Accident Victims. The elimination of the waiting period in relation to any type of accident, and not only in relation to the industrial one, is also an imperative, especially in Brazil. It would also be advisable to generalize the additional payment made to the victim of an industrial accident who needs constant attendance. It seems possible to generalize two other benefits offered in Brazil for partial disability due to an industrial accident: namely, the accident-allowances (in the event of an incapacity that prohibits the return to previous work activities but not to other work activities) and the supplementary-allowance (to compensate for greater financial need resulting from the previous work activities). Finally, the provision of full medical care to industrial accident victims (which is not provided to other accident victims) does not make sense.

Need for Additional Financing. The elimination of the special treatment of industrial accidents would not permit in Brazil any reduction in the employers' social security contributions, for unfortunately, industrial accidents will keep occurring and therefore benefits will continue to be paid.

Aggravation of the Error. Finally, it might be remembered that an error is aggravated to the extent to which, being in a condition to correct it, we fail to do so.

Many social policy experts and politicians have already accepted the idea of an integration of social security and industrial accident programs. Therefore, it is time for action. To further delay is to persist with an error from the past.

REFERENCES

Dixon, J. 1986. *Social Security Traditions and Their Global Applications* (Canberra: International Fellowship for Social and Economic Development).

Higuchi, T. 1970. "The Special Treatment of Employment Injury in Social Security" *International Labor Review* 102(2): 109–26.

International Labor Organization (ILO). 1936. *Studies and Reports* (Series M, 16) (Geneva: ILO).

Uttley, S. 1993. "Adapting to Radical Innovation: Accident Compensation in New Zealand" *Policy Studies Review* 12(1/2) (Spring/Summer): 144–158.

Index

Contributors

FRANZ VON BENDA-BECKMANN is Professor of Non-Western Agricultural Law at the Agrarian University in the Netherlands.

KEEBET VON BENDA-BECKMANN is a Senior Lecturer in the Department of Social Sciences of Law in the Faculty of Law at the Erasmus University in the Netherlands.

NELSON W. S. CHOW is Professor of Social Work and Social Administration at the University of Hong Kong.

ANNE CORDEN is a Research Fellow in the Social Policy Research Unit at the University of York in the United Kingdom.

JOHN DIXON is Head of the Department of Social Sciences at Lingnan College in Hong Kong.

FRANZ HIRTZ is an Assistant Professor in the Department of Sociology at the University of California at Davis in the United States.

MITSUYA ICHIEN is Professor of Social Policy in the Faculty of Economics at the Kansai University in Japan.

EDWIN KASEKE is the Principal of the School of Social Work in Zimbabwe.

CELSO BARROSO LEITE is a Professor in the Centro de Estudos de Provindencia Social in Brazil.

M RAMESH is a Senior Lecturer in Political Science at the Unviersity of New England in Australia.

MIROSLAV RUZICA is Director of the East European Initiative, a joint program of the Center of Philanthropy at Indiana University and the School of Social Work at Purdue University in the United States.

ROBERT P. SCHEURELL is an Associate Professor of Social Welfare at the University of Wisconsin at Milwaukee .

MAX J. SKIDMORE is Professor of Political Science in the College of Arts and Sciences at the University of Missouri-Kansas City in the United States.

MARTIN BOOTH TRACY is Director and Associate Professor in the School of Social Work at the University of Iowa in the United States.

LOTTA WESTERHALL is Professor of Social Law at the University of Lund in Sweden.

ISBN 0-313-29654-5

90000>

EAN

9 780313 296543

HARDCOVER BAR CODE